HUMAN RIGHTS OF ACCUSED AND JUVENILES
Delinquent / in Conflict with Law

HUMAN RIGHTS OF ACCUSED AND JUVENILES

Delinquent / in Conflict with Law

JAISHREE JAISWAL

PUBLICATIONS

KALPAZ PUBLICATIONS

DELHI - 110052

HUMAN RIGHTS OF ACCUSED AND JUVENILES
Delinquent / in Conflict with Law
[*Human Rights*]

Rs. 790

ISBN: 81-7835-145-5

Published in 2005 in India by
Kalpaz Publications
C-30, Satyawati Nagar
Delhi-110052
e-mail: kalpaz@hotmail.com

Laser Typeset at: Alphabet, Delhi
Printed at: Salasar Imaging System, Delhi

Contents

Foreword

In the course of human history, various means were adopted to ensure the observance of rules in the interest of well-being of the community, nation or the State. However, the contradictions between individual interest and social interest as well as incompatibilities between the interests of an individual and group have created troubles in the path of smooth social order. On the other hand, the growing aspiration of an individual to seek an environment where one is treated with equity, equality and justice gave birth to the Human Rights Jurisprudence. "Without liberty, law loses its nature and its name becomes licentiousness." When a need was felt by the community of parting with a portion of individual freedom in exchange for peace and harmony in society, it developed an elaborate system of administration of criminal justice. However, there have been continuing debates at national and international level regarding the means and methods of preserving the human dignity against any kind of discrimination so that people have a sense of living with dignity and freedom of life and liberty. Specific rights of persons involved in criminal activities commonly known as "accused" are recognized at international level as well as national level and, as such rights are fundamental in nature, they cannot be taken away by the State. Such rights have been protected as Fundamental Rights of an accused under Articles 20 and 21 of the Constitution of India and they cannot be suspended even on the proclamation of emergency and may be termed as "human rights of accused". However, the concept of human rights is a dynamic and living concept; it has to be treated with sensitivity and its meaning should be interpreted and understood in the context of the developments in social, cultural, economic, civil and political spheres. Due to ever changing developments in the above mentioned spheres, further aspirations of the people continue to be developed and thus new human rights pertaining to equality, dignity and justice in finer respects are added to the existing core rights. The Constitutional mandate in India relating to criminal jurisprudence is that no one should be deprived of his fundamental (human) rights of life and liberty without just cause and except according to procedure established by law. Therefore, a person has a right to be treated with equality and human dignity even in the situation when he is arrested, detained or exposed to trial for offences. In addition to detailed provisions in various conventions, treaties and U.N. Charter, as well as the guarantees laying stress on dignity of an individual contained in the Indian Constitution, the Supreme Court of India and various High Courts, by way of interpreting and expanding the ambit and scope of the fundamental rights enshrined in the Constitution, have also issued detailed directives regarding the rights of an accused to humane treatment and not to be subjected to torture or degrading punishment during police or judicial custody. In spite of various detailed mandates protecting the life and dignity of an accused at national and international levels, it is a matter of concern that inhuman treatment, brutality and torture even sometimes leading to death in police lock-ups or prisons have increased over the years. Further, the traditional criminal law applicable to adult accused is not expected to be applicable in case of children and throughout the world, special treatment is pleaded to be given; special laws have been made dealing with the child accused in the past and recently a new legislation, namely, the Juvenile Justice (Care and Protection of Children) Act, 2000, had been enacted. However, despite the special legislation, even the child accused are also, in practice, subjected to undesirable and objectionable treatment and denied the basic protections; the provisions meant for providing special protection to child accused are frequently violated or neglected by the different agencies involved in the administration of criminal justice.

In such an environment, the efforts made by Km. Jaishree Jaiswal, Lecturer, Newada Law College, Newada (Bihar) to present a critical review of various rights of an accused recognised or granted by the Constitution of India and other important criminal legislations, along with the special study related to the child accused commonly known as 'Delinquent juvenile' and named in India as 'Juvenile in conflict with law' by the latest legislation of 2000 relating to juveniles, in the present book — *Human Rights of Accused and Juveniles*, are praiseworthy because the subject, to the best of my knowledge, has not so far been considered seriously by the law academics in India particularly from the point of view of the accused – adult and juveniles. As the term 'accused' is used for persons in various different circumstances, the authoress has very rightly first tried to explain the meaning of the term 'accused' and thereafter has discussed the concepts of natural justice and personal liberty as the basis of the recognition of the various human rights of the accused. Thereafter, while tracing the evolution of the human rights of the accused has been traced by examining the status of human rights during Hindu Legal System in ancient India, Muslim Legal System and British period, and also by discussing the various rights of an accused recognized and guaranteed at International and National level. For the purposes of the detailed discussion of the various human rights of an accused the authoress has divided the rights into three parts: rights related to arrest, rights available at every stage and rights available during trial. The main rights of an accused which have been critically examined by the authoress are, *inter alia*, the Right to know the ground of arrest and the powers of arresting authority, the Right to be produced before the concerned Magistrate within the stipulated period, i.e., twenty-four hours; Rights to engage counsel of his own choice, Right to apply for free legal aid, Right to be released on bail; Right to Speedy Trial or accelerated hearing including speedy investigation, right to be presumed innocent, right to seek protection against self incrimination and also right to seek immunity against double jeopardy. As the 'child accused' commonly known as 'delinquent juvenile' are given special treatment different from the treatment given to adult accused, the authoress has very rightly devoted a special to the critical examination of the human rights of 'child accused'– (delinquent juvenile/juvenile in conflict with law–the term used in India) and juvenile justice in India. In this special study, after discussing in detail the special rules made for the protection of the human rights of the child accused at International level, the authoress has critically examined the statutory framework in India regarding juvenile justice (pertaining to Delinquent juvenile) viz., the Juvenile Justice Act, 1986 and also the Juvenile Justice (Care and Protection of Children) Act, 2000. In this endeavour, after explaining the meaning of the expressions "Delinquency", "Juvenile" and "Juvenile in Conflict with Law", various rights available to Delinquent juvenile (Juvenile in conflict with law) at the time of arrest, after arrest, during inquiry (trial in case of adults) and thereafter regarding reformation have been examined. The special study with regard to the child accused has been concluded with the discussion of the judicial response towards juvenile justice in general and, in particular, regarding the applicability of the Juvenile Justice Act or jurisdictional dilemma, award of jail sentence to juvenile or his detention in jail, grant of bail to him and his age determination. In the concluding chapter of the book, besides enumerating the various rights of an accused before arrest, after arrest during police custody and during judicial custody (pre-trial, during trial and post trial) and also during the period when the conviction is made but stayed, i.e., after conviction but when the conviction is stayed), rights of the accused during the detention in jail (as under trial prisoners) based on Jail Manual of U.P., the authoress has offered detailed recommendations and suggestions dividing them into three parts, viz., general recommendations and suggestions, specific recommendations and suggestions regarding an accused during detention and specific recommendations and suggestions with regard to juvenile accused (delinquent juvenile/juvenile in conflict with law). The detailed bibliography consisting of International instruments, Reports, Books, Articles, Statutes, Journals, Magazines and Newspapers given by the authoress in the end has definitely enhanced and enriched the standard and quality of the book.

It should be kept in mind by the jurists, academics, human rights activists and all other agencies involved in the administration of criminal justice that, while considering the human rights of an accused, a realistic approach should be adopted and in this context a proper balance is required to be maintained between the rights, liberties and privileges of a single individual (the accused) on the one hand and his duties, obligations and responsibilities towards the individuals collectively (society) on the other hand. It is a matter of serious consideration that in case of conflict of interest between the two who should be given priority- the accused or the society, the law violator or the law abider. I am happy that in the present book Km. Jaishree Jaiswal has tried to include all the related and relevant aspects of the rights of the accused and as the materials presented by her are quite comprehensive on the subject, I am sure that it will not only receive attention of the policy makers, law enforcement agencies and personnel particularly involved in the administration of criminal justice, human rights activists, students of law, academic institutions, general public and , of course, the accused, but would also prove to be of immense utility to them and the book will prove to be a valuable contribution to the world of human rights law. The efforts made by the authoress in collecting and presenting the relevant materials on the subject in readable manner, making the critical analysis of the same and offering useful suggestions for solving the various problems related to the human rights of accused in general and the child accused, i.e., delinquent juvenile/juvenile in conflict with law, in particular. Being the first of its kind, this book will go a long way in assisting the delivery of justice to the accused in reality and also help in maintaining a proper balance between the law violator and the law abider in the context of ensuring human rights to accused. I extend my good wishes to her and this academic child of her for all the best and success in the times to come.

(Prof. Surendra Nath)
Director, S.W. Law College, Varanasi,
Honorary Director, Newada Law College, Newada and
Chairman, A.C., Asian School of Cyber Laws, Pune.

Preface

A well established principle of criminal jurisprudence is that a person should not be deprived of his fundamental rights of life and liberty without just cause and except according to the procedure established by law. Every person has also the right to be treated with human dignity in all situations including those which involve arrest, detention and trial for offences. Such a process is also essential for improving the criminal justice system and making it more vibrant and more dynamic for the protection of human rights of such persons who are accused of committing offences. In order to maintain order and peace in society and to prevent, detect and control crime, the State provides its law enforcement machinery, particularly police, with wide ranging powers. If used arbitrarily, these powers impinge on the dignity and liberty of an individual. Concern for Human Rights of citizens in the modern criminal justice administration is of comparatively recent origin. After World War II , natural rights of people came to be fine tuned into Human Rights and various Declarations and Conventions at the International Law were announced which safeguarded the human rights of an accused in general from the date a formal accusation was made against him although he might not have been arrested till he was finally acquitted or convicted, and in particular, more intensively during the period when they were detained either in police or judicial custody. Besides the International Conventions and Declarations which were also adopted by India, Part III of the Constitution of India, adopted in the year 1950, guaranteed certain human freedoms and fundamental rights to an accused some of which were already available to him under statutory law governing the criminal justice administration (i.e., Code of Criminal Procedure and Evidence

Act). Further, during the last three decades, the Supreme Court as well as various High Courts have paid serious concern with regard to the protection of the right to life and liberty of a person in general and of an accused being arrested and/ or detained for a criminal proceedings, in particular. In this context, various directions have been issued by the judiciary for decent and humane treatment, care and custody of such persons, particularly under trial prisoners. The Supreme Court has in number of cases voiced of human rights of an accused during and after arrest and tried to restore to an accused some of the basic human rights by way of interpreting and expanding the ambit and scope of the constitutional mandates enshrined in Part III of the Constitution. Thus, the horizon of human rights has been expanding. However, at the same time, the crime rate is also increasing. Further, courts in India have also been receiving increasing complaints about violation of human rights because of indiscriminate arrests and inhumane treatment by police and other agencies towards the accused and detained persons. Experience shows that worst kind of violations of human dignity take place during the course of investigation when the police with a view to secure evidence often resorts to third degree methods; reports of dehumanizing torture, rape and death in custody of police or other governmental agencies often published in newspapers is indeed disheartening. In this context, the most important issue to be deliberated upon at the present day is : How are we going to strike a balance between the two – human rights of an accused on the one hand and the interest of the society, on the other? It is generally argued that a realistic approach should be adopted in the context of human rights of an accused. The law of arrest is one of the method of — balancing individual rights, liberties and privileges on the one hand, and individual duties, obligations and responsibilities, on the other hand; of weighing and balancing the rights, liberties and privileges of the single individual and those of individuals collectively; of simply deciding what is wanted and where to put the weight and the emphasis; and of deciding which comes first the criminal or society, the law violator or the abider.

Against the above stated background, the present book

entitled **"Human Rights of Accused and Juveniles"** has been prepared in which an humble attempt has been made to present a critical review of various rights of an accused recognized or granted by the Constitution of India and important criminal legislations. It also points out the extent to which national laws are in harmony with those set forth in the relevant international law human rights instruments. Further, as the traditional law applicable to accused who are adults are not applicable in cases of children and special treatment is given throughout the world including India in case they are involved in committing any offence, a separate chapter has been devoted to the special study with reference to the rights of 'Child Accused' commonly known as 'Delinquent Juvenile' and in India known as 'Juvenile in Conflict with Law' with regard to criminal justice administration after the enactment of the new legislation namely the Juvenile Justice (Care and Protection of Children) Act, 2000. Besides the last chapter containing conclusions and suggestions, the subject matter of the present book is divided into **six** more chapters, as under:

Ch. One	Meaning of the "accused" and basis of the recognition of the human rights of accused;
Ch. Two	Evolution of the human rights of accused;
Ch. Three	Human rights of "accused" related to arrest;
Ch. Four	Human rights of "accused" available at every stage;
Ch. Five	Human rights of "accused" available during trial; and
Ch. Six	Human rights of "child accused" (delinquent juveniles/juvenile in conflict with law) and juvenile justice in India (Rights available on and after arrest, during inquiry and thereafter regarding reformation)

In the First Chapter, the meaning of the term "accused" and the basis of the recognition of the human rights of accused, i.e., natural justice and the concept of personal liberty have been discussed. After discussing the meaning of the term accused and the basis of the recognition of the human rights of accused, efforts are made, in the Second Chapter, to examine the evolution of the

Human rights of accused - recognized under Hindu legal system in ancient India, recognized in Muslim legal system, recognized during British period, recognised at international level through various international instruments like - (i) Universal Declaration of Human Rights, 1948, (ii) International Covenant on Civil and Political Rights, 1966, (iii) United Nations Standard Minimum Rules for the Treatment of Prisoners, 1955, and (iv) International instruments with regard to the special rights of juvenile accused (known as delinquent juvenile) viz., (a) United Nations Standard Minimum Rules for the Administration of Juvenile Justice (The Beijing Rules), 1985 and (b) United Nations Rules for the Protection of Juveniles Deprived of Their Liberty, 1990. Thereafter, while examining the evolution of Human Rights of accused recognized and guaranteed at national level the various rights briefly discussed, inter alia, are: (i) Right of equality and equal protection of laws, (ii) Right against ex-post facto operation of criminal laws, (iii) Right to seek protection against double jeopardy, (iv) Right to seek protection against self-incrimination, (v) Right to have freedom from unwanted arrest and matters incidental thereto like - (a) the right to be informed of grounds of arrest, (b) Right to be produced before a Magistrate, and (c) No detention beyond 24 hours except by the order of the Magistrate, (vi) Right to seek legal services and legal defence, (vii) Right to have a public and speedy trial (viii) Rights relating to pre-trial detention and matters incidental thereto, and (ix) Right to approach higher judicial authorities by way of filing appeal, etc.

The subject matter of Chapter Three consists of the discussion with regard to the Human Rights of Accused during Arrest and includes, inter alia, the detailed examination of the Right to know the ground of arrest, Right to know the powers of arresting authority and Right to be produced before the magistrate within stipulated time, has been made. Further, the guidelines issued by the Supreme Court to be followed in all cases of arrest or detention have also been discussed. Chapter Four is devoted to the discussion on Human Rights of Accused available at Every Stage in general and, in particular, the Right to engage counsel, Right to apply for free legal aid and Right to be released on bail. Further, special discussion has been made with regard to the Rights of a juvenile accused to be released on bail and also regarding Judicial interpretation of the right of an accused to be released on bail. In Chapter Five, Human Rights of Accused available to him during trial have been discussed and in this context, the detailed examination has been made with regard to the Rights to speedy trial or accelerated hearing including speedy investigation, Right to be presumed innocent, Right to seek protection against self-incrimination and also Right to seek protection / immunity against double jeopardy. The subject matter of Sixth Chapter is devoted to the Special Study of Human Rights of "Child Accused" (Delinquent Juveniles / Juvenile in Conflict with Law) and juvenile justice in India (Rights available on and after arrest, during inquiry and thereafter regarding reformation). In this context, detailed discussions made in the Chapter include, inter alia, Special rules for the protection of the human rights of juveniles made at international level; Statutory framework in India regarding juvenile justice (particularly in reference to delinquent juveniles), viz. – (i) The Juvenile Justice Act, 1986, and (ii) The Juvenile Justice (Care and Protection of Children) Act, 2000; Meaning and definition of the expressions "delinquency", "juvenile" and "juvenile in conflict with law"; Rights of juvenile in conflict with law (delinquent juvenile) at the time of arrest, viz.- (i) Right of the juvenile in conflict with law to be released on bail and (ii) Duty of the arresting police officer to inform specified persons regarding the arrest of delinquent juvenile; Rights of delinquent juvenile after arrest and during inquiry including procedure to be followed by the 'Juvenile Justice Board' while conducting an inquiry and by the higher Courts during appeal and revision proceedings, and Powers of the 'Juvenile Justice Board' regarding delinquent juveniles. While discussing the special rights enjoyed by juvenile accused, efforts are also made to compare the provisions of the Code of Criminal Procedure,1973 with the provisions of the special enactment applicable to delinquent juveniles, i.e., The Juvenile Justice (Care and Protection of Children) Act, 2000/The Juvenile Justice Act, 1986. The present book closes with Chapter Seven which embodies in summarized form the various rights available to an accused under statutory laws, the Constitution, Jail Manual and also those which have been declared from time to time by the judiciary. In the end, concluding observations and suggestions have been given. It is hoped that the present book would be useful to the students of law, human rights activists, personnel involved in the administration of criminal justice, general public and of course the "accused".

Jaishree Jaiswal

Acknowledgements

I feel it my duty to acknowledge my deep sense of gratitude and sincere thanks to Prof. Surendra Nath, Director, Sudhakar Women's Law College, Pandeypur, Varanasi, Honorary Director , Newada Law College, Newada, Chairman, Academic Council, Asian School of Cyber Laws, Pune and formerly Head & Dean, Law School, Banaras Hindu University, Varanasi, who has been the ideal of my life, guardian and guide throughout my law studies and without whose continuous and untiring help, moral support and academic guidance it would not have been possible for me to complete my studies. I am also thankful to him that, in spite of his ill health, he had taken pains in going through the various chapters of the present book, made constructive suggestions for improvement and written the Foreword of the same.

I also wish to express my thanks to my learned teacher Dr. Sri Pal Singh Som, Head of the Department of Law, M.B.S.P.G. College, Gangapur, District Varanasi, who had supervised my LL.M. dissertation (which forms to basis of this book) and also had given guidance in the formative stages of this book. His suggestions had been very useful in the preparation of the final draft. I am thankful to him for all kind of assistance, constant encouragement and affectionate co-operation extended to me throughout my studies at LL.M. level. I am also thankful to Dr. Devi Prasad Singh, Principal of M.B.S.P.G. College, Gangapur, District Varanasi, and my all other teachers of the Department of Law where I have completed my Post-Graduate studies, particularly Mr. Girish Chandra Trivedi, Dr. Ram Nath Pandey, Mr. Vijay Narain Sharma and Dr. Dharmendra Kumar Mishra, for guiding me from time to time during the entire period of my studies.

I am also thankful to Dr. D.N. Mishra, Principal, Newada Vidhi Mahavidhyalaya, Newada and Dean, Faculty of Law, Magadh University, Bodhgaya, for extending encouragement and assistance due to which the task of writing this book has been possible. My thanks are also extended to Dr. Pankaj Kumar, Dr.Vinod Kumar and other colleagues of the Newada Vidhi Mahavidyalaya and Dr. Mamta Chaturvedi, Lecturer, A.N.College, Gaya.

My thanks are also acknowledged to Shri Ved Prakash Rai, student of LL.M. Final, and the staff members of M.B.S.P.G. College, Gangapur, Varanasi, and Mrs. Som Prabha Tripathi, Judicial Magistrate, Ghaziabad, for the necessary help extended to me. I am also thankful to my family members, in particular, Mr. Gopal Kanthale, for giving me moral support for continuing my higher studies.

In the end, I wish to express my deep gratitude to all those whose writings have been consulted and used by me in order to accomplish this work.

Jaishree Jaiswal

List of Cases

Amrita Ahluwalia v. Union of India, 1992 Cri. L. J. 1906 (Delhi).
Antaryami Patra v. State of Orissa, (1993) 2 Cri. LJ 1908 (Orissa).
A. Nallasivan v. State of Tamil Nadu, 1995 Cri. L.J. 2754.
A.K. Gopalan v. State of Madras, A I R 1950 S.C. 27.
A.V. Nachane v. Union of India, A I R 1982 S.C. 1126.
Abdul Ghani v. State, A I R 1955 J. & K 38 : Cr. L.J. 1953 (F.B.).
Abdul Rehman Antuley v. R.S. Nayak, A I R 1992 S.C. 1701.
Abhinandan Jha v. Dinesh Mishra, A I R 1968 SC 117.
Abraham Vergies v. State of Kerala, A I R 1965 Ker. 175.
Afjal Hussain v. State, A I R 1962 Raj., 216 : 1962 (2) Cri. L.J. 496.
Ajaib Singh v. State of Punjab, 1952 Cri. L. J. 1313 (Punjab): A I R Punj. 309 (F.B.)
Alamgir v. State of Bihar, A I R 1959 S.C. 436.
Amit v. State of U.P., (1999) 2 Cri. L. J. 1878.
Andhra Pradesh v. I B S Prasad Rao, (1970) Cri L.J. 733 (S.C.).
Aquil Alvi v. State of U.P., (1996) Cri. L. J. 103 (All).
Arjun Ram v. State of Rajasthan, (1998) 4 Cri. L. J. 4375 (Raj.).
Arnit Das v. State of Bihar, (2000) Cri. L. J. 2971 (SC): AIR 2000 SC 2264; (2000) 5 SCC 488.

Babu Ram v. State, (1961) 2 Cri L.J. 55 (All).
Balbir Singh v. State of Rajasthan, 1994 Cri. L.J. 2750 (Raj.).
Bandela Ailaiah v. State of A.P., (1995) Cri. L.J. 1083 (AP).
Bhim Singh v. State of J.K., (1985) 4 SCC 677.
Bhola Bhagat v. State of Bihar, A I R 1998 SC 23: (1998) 1 Cri. L.J 390 (SC).
Bhudha Singh v. State of Punjab, 1979 Chandigarh L R (Cri)114.
Bhupinder Singh v. State of Himachal Pradesh, (1997) 1 Cri. L. J. 339 (H.P.).

Bijoy Singh v. State, 1986 Cri. LJ 2016(Cal.).
Bimal Krishna Kundu v. State of Andhra Pradesh, A I R 1997 S.C. 3589.
Bir Bhadra Pratap Singh v. D.M.Azamgarh, A I R 1959 All 384.
Burhanuddin Tahavali v. Union of India, 1994 SCC 63.

C.I. Emden v. State of U.P., A I R 1960 S.C. 585.
Chajju Ram v. Radhe Shyam,1971 (Suppl.) SCR172 : A I R 1972 S.C. 1367.
Chandabai v. State of M.P., 1997 Cri. L.J. 3844.
Chandra Swami v. Central Bureau of Investigation, A I R 1997 S.C. 2575.
Christie v. Laachinsky, (1947) 1 All E.R.567.
Collector of Madras v. Erimonal Ebrahim Hazee, A I R 1957 S.C. 688.
Collector of Madras v. Erimonal Ebrahim Hazee, A I R 1957 S.C. 91.
Common Cause v. Union of India, (1996) 4 SCC 33.
Common Cause v. Union of India, (1996) 6SCC 775(Clarified).

D.A. Kelsikar v. State of Bombay, A I R 1966 Bom. 225.
D.K. Basu v. State of West Bengal, A I R 1997 S.C. 610.
D.T.C. v. D.T.C. Mazdoor Congress, A I R 1991 S.C. 101.
Dalbir Kaur v. State of Punjab, A I R 1977 S.C. 472 : 1977 Cr.L.J. 273.
Daljit Singh v. State of Punjab, (1992) Cri. L. J. 1051 (P&H).
Dayachand v. Sahib Singh, (1991) 2 SCC 379.
Deodat Rai v. State, A I R 1951 All. 718.
Deonandan v. State of Bihar, (1955) Cri. L.J. 1647 (S.C.).
Devi Prasad v. H.N. Vora, 1978 Cri. L.J. 79 (Cal.).
Dharambir v. State of Uttar Pradesh, (1979) 3 S CC 645.
Dilip Saha v. State of West Bengal,
Diwan Naubat Rai v. State through Delhi Administration, (1989) 1 SCC 297 : A I R 1989 SC 542.

Emperor v. Nga Tun Hlaing, A I R 1924 Rangoon 115 (F.B.).

Fanu *v.* State of U.P., (1997)1 Cri.L J 275 (All.).
Francus Coralie v. Union Territory of Delhi, 1981 Cri. L. J.306 (S.C.):A I R 1981 S.C. 738.

Gabinding Pao Kabui v. U.T. Manipur, A I R, 1963 Manipur 12.
Ganesh Prasad v. State, A I R 1954 All. 116 : 1954 Cri L.J. 216.
Gaurav Jain v. Union of India, (1997) 8 SCC 114.
Ghanshyam v. State of U.P., (1982) 2 SCC 400: 1982 SCC (Cri) 449: 1982 Cri. L.J. 138 (All.).
Gopi Nath Ghosh v. State of West Bengal, A I R 1984 S.C. 237.
Guddu v. State of U.P., 1996 ALJ 390: 1960 Cri. L. J. 470.
Gunpati Keshavran Reddy v. Nafisul Hasan, A I R 1954 S.C. 638 : 1954 Cri. L.J. 1704.
Gurpurb Singh v. Autar Singh, A I R 1960 J & K 55: 1960 Cri. L.J. 470.
Gurucharan v. State, 1957 Cri. L.J. 918: A I R 1957 All. 557.

Hadu Sahu v. State, A I R 1967 Orissa 37 : 1967 (1) Cri. L.J. 394.
Hallai v. B.M. Desai, A I R 1956 S.C. 20.
Hansraj v. State, A I R 1956 All 641 : 1956 Cri. L.J. 1267.
Hariharanand v. The Jailor I/C Dist. Jail, Banaras, A I R 1954 All 601.
Harold Hamre & Elin Aasland Hamre, Norwegian National, A I R 1999 Bom. 325.
Harpal Singh v. State, A I R 1950 All. 562.
Hathi Singh Manufacturing Co. v. Union of India, A I R 1960 S.C. 923.
Hussainara Khatoon (I) v. Home Secretary, Bihar, A I R 1979 S.C.1360: 1980 SCC 81: 1979 Cri. L. J. 1036 (S.C.).
Hussainara Khatoon (II) v. Home Secretary, State of Bihar, (1980) SCC 99.
Hussainara Khatoon (III) v. Home Secretary, State of Bihar, (1979) 3 S.C.R. 393 : A I R 1979 S.C. 1377.

In re Appaswami Mudaly, A I R 1924 Madras 555.
In re Madhu Limaye, A I R 1969 S.C. 1014.
In re Madhu Limaye, A I R 1982 S.C. 53.

In re Palani Moogan, A I R 1955 Mad 495 : 1955 Cri.L.J. 1197 (Mad.).

In re Sant Ram, A I R 1960 S.C. 932.

In re Sessions Judge Kalpetta, (1995) Cri. LJ330 (Ker.).

Joginder Kumar v. State of U.P., (1994) 2 SCJ 230 : (1994) 2 SCALE Vol. II No. 7. 662.

Janardan Reddy v. State of Hyderabad, A I R 1951 S.C. 217.

Jagdish Bhuyan Shri v. State of Assam, (1992) 3 Cri. L. J. 3194 (Gau.).

Jyoti Shankar Tripathy v. State of Orissa, (1995) Cri. L. J. 3048 (Orissa).

K.B. Ghose v. State of West Bengal, A I R 1960 S.C. 239.

Kadra Pahadiya v. State of Bihar,(1983) 2 S.C.R.384 : A I R 1983 S.C. 361.

Kali Ram v. State of H.P., (1973) 2 SCC 808.

Kali Charan v. State, A I R 1955 All 462.

Karuppayee v. State, (1997) 2 Cri. L. J. 1627 (Mad.).

Kashmira Singh v. State of Punjab, 1977 Cri. L.J. 1746 : A I R 1977 S.C. 2147.

Keshav Singh v. Speaker, Legislative Assembly, A I R 1965 All. 349.

Khatri & Others v. State of Bihar, A I R 1981 S.C. 928 : (1981) 1 SCC 627.

Kishore Singh v. State of Rajasthan, A I R 1981 S.C. 625.

Km. Anita v. Atal Bihari, (1993) Cri. L. J. 549 (M.P.).

Kochumminno Chettiar v. State of Kerala, 1977 Cri.L.J. 1872.

Krishan Keshvan v. State, 1957 Cr.L.J. 755 (Ker.).

Krishna Bhagwan v. State of Bihar, A I R 1989 Pat. 217.

Lakshmi v. Sub Inspector, N.P. Police Station, 1991 Cri. L. J. 226.

Lal Diwan v. State of U.P., 1995 Cr. L. J. 389 (All.).

M.G. Agarwal v. State of Maharashtra, (1963) 2 S.C.R. 405.

M.H. Hoskot v. State of Maharashtra, A I R 1978 S.C. 527.

M.P. Sharma v. Satish Chandra, A I R 1954 S.C. 300 : 1954 Cri L.J. 65 (S.C.): 1954 SCR 1077.

Machander v. State of Hyderabad, 1955 SCR 524 : A I R 1955 S.C. 792.
Maneka Gandhi v. Union of India. A I R 1978 S.C. 597.
Manipur Administration v. Bira Singh, A I R 1965 S.C. 87 : 1965 Cri. L.J. 120.
Maqbool Hussain v. State of Bombay, A I R 1953 S.C. 324.
Mata v. State of Rajasthan, (1996) Cri.L.J. 743 (Raj.- Jaipur Bench).
Mayank Rajput v. State of U.P., (1998) 3 Cri. L. J. 2797 (All.).
Mayor of Lyons v. East India Co., (1836) I Moore, Ind. App. 175.
Milap Singh v. State of U.P., (2000) Cri. L. J. 3059 (All.).
Mohamed Dastagir v. State of Madras, A I R 1960 S.C. 756 : 1965 Cr, L.J. 120.
Mohammad Hussain v. Provident Funds Inspector, A I R 1957 M.B. 58:
1957 Cri. L. J. 195 (M.B.).
Mohd. Salim Khan v. State of U.P., 1982 Cr.L.J. 1242 :
A I R 1982 S.C.1096.
Moinuddin v. State of Maharashtra, (1971) 3 S.C.C. 338.
Moti Bai v. State, 1954 Cr. L.J. 1951 (Raj.).
Moti Ram v. State of M.P., 1978 Cr. L. J. 1703(S.C.): (1978) 3 SCC 47: 1978 SCC (Cri.) 185.
Mst. Bhagwan v. State, A I R 1973 Pepsu 33.
Mukhwinder Singh v State of Punjab, 1992 Cri. L. J. 1897.
Munna v. State of U.P., (1982) 1 SCC 545 :. A I R 1986 S.C. 1778.

Nandini Satapathy v. P.L. Dani, 1978 Cr. L.J. 968.
Narayan Singh v. State of Punjab, A I R 1952 S.C. 106.
Nazir Hossain Haldar v. State, (1998) 2 Cri. L. J. 1720 (Cal.).
Nilebati Behera v. State of Orissa, (1993) 2 SCC 746.
Nimoon Sangma v. Government of Meghalaya, A I R 1979 S.C.1518: 1979 Cri L.J. 941.

Olga Tellis v. Bombay Municipal Corporation, A I R 1986 S.C. 180.
Om Prakash Sharma v. State of U.P., (1997) 3 Cri. L. J. 2710 (All.).
Om Prakash v. State of Rajasthan, 2001 Cri. L. J. 230.
Onkar Tiwari v. State of U.P., 2000 Cri. L. J. 4723 (All.).

Palvinder Kaur v. State of Punjab, 1953 Cr. L.J. 154 (S.C.).
Peoples's Union for Democratic Rights v. Police Commissioner, Delhi Police Headquarter, (1989) 4 SCC 730.
Pershadilal v. State of U.P., A I R 1957 S.C. 211.
Prabhakar Nath v. Distt. Magistrate, A I R 1960 All. 467: 1969 Cr. L.J. 1049.
Pradeep Kumar v. State of U.P., A I R 1994 S.C. 104.
Praveen Malhotra v. State (Delhi Admin.), 1990 (2) CCC 321 (Delhi).
Prem Dutta v. Suptt. Central Prison, 1996 Cr. L. J. 685 (All.).
Prem Nath v. Union of India, A I R 1958 Punj. 56.
Prem Shanker v. Delhi Administration, A I R 1980 S.C.1535.
Pritam Singh v. State of Punjab, A I R 1956 S.C. 451.
Public Prosecutor, A.P. v. Shaik Valli, (1971) Cr.L.J. 1229.
Pulin Krishna v. Shishupati, 1953 Cri L.J. 294 (Cal.).

R. v. Sarne (1887) CCC. Sess. Pap. C. VII 418.
R.C.Gupta v. State, A I R 1954 All. 219.
R.K. Ashere v. Tempton Jahangir, A I R 1961 Guj. 137 : 1961 (2) Cri L.J. 338.
R. M. Malkani v. State of Maharashtra, A I R 1973 S.C. 157 : 1973 Cri L.J. 228.
Raghubir Singh v. State, A I R 1952 All. 589.
Ragubir v. State of Haryana, A I R 1981 S.C. 2037.
Rahman Kunhappu v. Ali Ahmad, A I R 1957 Ker. 80.
Rahul Mishra v. State of M.P., 2001 Cri. L. J. 214 (M.P.).
Raj Bahadur v. Legal Remembrancer, A I R 1953 Cal 522: 1953 Cr. L.J. 1187.
Raj Singh v. State of Haryana, (2000) 6 SCC 759.
Raja Singh v. State of Bihar , (2000) Cri. L. J. 3388 (Pat.) .
Ram Lakhan v. State of U.P., A I R 1977 S.C. 1936 : 1977 Cri. L.J. 1566.
Ram Swarup v. State, A I R 1958 All. 191 : 1958 Cri L.J. 134.
Rama Kant v. State of U.P., (2000) Cri. L. J. 4682 (All.).
Rama Murthy v. State of Karnataka, 1997 SCC (Cri) 386.
Rameshwar Dayal v. State of Bihar, A I R 1968 S.C. 1303.
Ramlal Bhagilal v. D.D. Gupta, A I R 1973 S.C. 1196.
Ratilal Bhanji v. Asstt. Customs Collector, Bombay, A I R 1967 S.C. 1639.

Ratilal Bhopi Lal v. State of Gujarat, A I R 1966 Gujarat. 244.
Reg. v. Miles, (1890), 24 QBD. 423.
Rinkoo Khatri v. State of M.P., (1998) 1 Cri. L. J. 775 (Madhya Pradesh, Gwalior Bench).
Rohtas v. State of Haryana, A I R 1979 S.C. 1839.
Rudal Shah v. State of Bihar, (1983) 4 SCC 141.

S.A. Venkataraman v. Union of India, A I R 1954 SC 375.
S.L. Goswami v. State of M.P., 1972 SCC(Cri.) 258 : (1972) 3 SCC 22.
Sahib Singh v. State, 1991 Cri. L. J. 687 (Del.).
Sambashivam v. Public Prosecutor, Federation of Malaya, 1950 A.C. 458.
Sangeeta R. Jain v. S.A Dwivedi, (1996) Cri. L.J. 24. (Bom.).
Sanjay Suri v. Delhi Administration, A I R 1988 SC 414.
Santenu Mitra v. State of W.B., A I R 1999 SC 1587.
Sarita Nayak Sawant v. State, 1990 Cri. L.J. 351 (Bom.).
Sat Kumar v. State of Haryana, A I R 1974 S.C. 294: 1974 Cr.L.J. 345.
Shabra Babade v. State of Maharashtra, (1973) 2 SCC 793
Shanti Behal v. State (Delhi Administration), D.B.(1994) 1C.C. 618.
Sharifbai v. Abdul Razak, A I R 1961 Bom. 42.
Sharvan Kumar v. Supdt. District Jail, A I R 1957 All. 189.
Sheela Barse v. Secretary Children Aid Society, A I R 1987 S.C. 656.
Sheela Barse v. State of Maharashtra, A I R 1983 378: (1983) 2 SCC 96.
Sheela Barse v. Union of India, A I R 1986 S.C. 1773.
Sheo Mangal Singh v. State of U.P., 1990 Cri. L. J. 1698 (All.).
Shibban Lal Saxena v. State of U.P., A I R 1954 S.C. 179: 1954 Cr. L. J. 456.
Shivaji Sahabra Babade v. State of Maharashtra, (1973) 2 SCC 793.
Shokat Ali v. State of Rajasthan, 1992 Cri. L. J. 1335 (Raj.).
Shrawan Hanji Undirwada v. State of Madhya Pradesh, 1976 MLJ 654.
Shri N.Sri Rama Reddy v. Sri V.V. Giri, A I R 1971 S.C. 1162.
Shyam Narayan Singh v. State of Bihar (1993) 1 Cri. LJ 772 (Pat.).
Sitaram Kishore v. State, A I R 1956 Pat. 1; 1956 Cri. L.J. 86.

Smt. Kalawati v. State of Himachal Pradesh, A I R 1953 S.C. 131.
Srinivas Pal v. Union Territory, 1988 Supl (1) SCR 477 : A I R 1988 SC 1729.
State of Andhra Pradesh v. P.V. Pavithran, 1990 2 SCC 340: A I R 1990 SC 1126.
State of Bihar v. Uma Shankar Ketriwal, (1981) 1 SCC 75: 1981 SCC (Cri) 108 : 1981 S.C.R. 402.
State of Bombay v. Atma Ram, A I R 1951 S.C. 164.
State of Bombay v. Kathi Kalu Oghad, 1961 (2) Cri. L.J. 856 (SC) .
State of Gujarat v. Shyamlal, A I R 1965 S.C. 1215 : 1965(2) Cri L.J. 256.
State of Haryana v. Balwant Singh, (1993) 1 SCC 409.
State of M.P. v. Ashok Kumar (1995) 4 Cri. LJ 3955 (MP).
State of M.P. v. Shobharam, A I R 1966 S.C. 1910 : 1966 Cri. L.J. 1521.
State of M.P. v. Shyamsunder Trivedi, (1995) 4 SCC 262.
State of Maharashtra v. Ravikant S. Patil, (1991) SCC 373.
State of Punjab v. Ajaib Singh, A I R 1953 S.C. 10 : 1953 Cr. L.J. 18.
State of U.P. v. Abdul Sanad, A I R 1962 S.C. 1506.
State of U.P. v. Deoman, A I R 1960 S.C. 1105.
State of U.P. v. Kapil Deo Shukla, (1972) 3 SCC 504 : A I R 1973 S.C. 494.
State v. Gundan Lakhanmal, A I R 1960 Bom. 377.
State v. Mohd. Mirza, A I R 1964 Mys. 245 : 1964(2) Cri. L.J. 561.
State v. Prabhu Singh, A I R 1964 Punj. 325 : 1964(2) Cri. L.J. 199 (Punj.).
Suk Das v. Union of India, (1986) 2 SCC 401 : A I R 1986 S.C. 991.
Sultan Singh v. State of M.P. (1997) 1 Cri. LJ 657 (M.P., Gwalior Bench),
Sunil Batra v. Delhi Adminstration, A I R 1980 S.C. 1579: 1980 Cr.L.J. 1099.
Sunil Gupta v. State of M.P., (1990) 3 SCC 119.
Sunil Kumar v. State of U.P., 2000 Cr.LJ (All.).
Sunil Kumar v. State, (1983) Cr.L.J. 99.
Sunil v. State of M.P., 2001 Cri. L. J. 1862 (M.P.).
Sunita v. State (U.T. Chandigarh), (1998) 4 Cri. L. J. 4249.
Supreme Court Legal Aid Committee v. Union of India, 1989 Cri. L. J. 1126 : A I R 1989 SC 1278.

Suresh Prasad v. State of Bihar, 2001 Cri. L. J. 1088 (Pat.).

T.V. Vatheeswaran v. State of Tamil Nadu, (1983) 3 S.C.R. 562 : A I R 1986 SC 1773.

Tajuddin s/o Mohd. Yunus v. State of U.P., 2001 Cri. L. J. 350(All.).

Talab Haji Hussain v. Madhukar Purshottam Mandlar, A I R 1958 S.C. 376: (1958) 60 Bom. L.R. 465.

Tara Singh v. State, A I R 1951 S.C. 441: 52 Cri. L.J. 1491.

Thomas Leon Harris v. State of Oklahoma, (1977) 53 L. Ed. 2d. 1054.

Tolaram Relumal v. State of Bombay, A I R 1954 S.C. 496.

Uma Shanker v. State of M.P., 1982 Cri. L.J. 1186.

Upendra Chandra v. State, 1954 Cri L.J. 851 (Assam).

Usufalli v. State of Maharashtra, A I R 1968 S.C. 1479 : 1968 Cri L.J. 103.

Vaskaran v. State of Kerala, 1987 Cri. L.J. 1588 (Kerala).

Veera Ibrahim v. State of Maharashtra, A I R 1976 S.C. 1169.

Veerbhadra v. Ramaswami Niackar, 1959 SCR 1211: A I R 1958 SC 1032.

Venkataraman v. Union of India, 1954 Cri L.J. 993 : A I R 1953 S.C. 375.

Vimal Kishore v. State of U.P., A I R 1956 All 56 : 1957 Cri. L.J. 13.

Waghela v. Sheik, 1887, 14 I.A. 89.

One

Meaning of the "Accused" and Basis of the Recognition of the Human Rights of Accused

A. MEANING OF THE TERM "ACCUSED"

In any dispute in which justice is to be administered, two parties are involved which are named as plaintiff and defendant in a civil proceedings and the prosecutor or complainant and the accused in criminal proceedings and the court pronounces its judgement in favour of one or the other. Administration of criminal justice is concerned with a crime, which means an act deemed by law to be harmful to society in general even though its immediate victim happens to be an individual. Those who commit such acts (crime) are prosecuted by the State so that if found guilty and convicted by the court, they may be punished according to law of the State. As in every administration of criminal justice a trial is conducted which revolves around the accused, an important question may be asked as to who can be called an "accused". The word 'accused' has not been defined in the Code of Criminal Procedure which contains the procedure to be adopted in a trial. Simultaneously, this term has not been even used in the *International Covenant on Civil and Political Rights, 1966*. For this, the terms 'prisoners awaiting for trial', 'under trial prisoners', and also 'untried prisoners' have been used so far. The Supreme Court of India in the leading case of ***D.K. Basu v. State of West Bengal***[1], the expression ***'arrestee'*** has been used. Thus, the use of various expressions compels a person to think about the proper meaning of the word "Accused".

In the Earl Jowitt's, *The Dictionary of English Law*, the term accused has been defined as "a person charged with a crime commonly called "the prisoner" if the crime is felony and the 'defendant' if it is a misdemeanour."[2] In the *Law Lexicon's Dictionary*, the word 'Accused' has been defined as: "A person against whom an allegation has been made that he has committed an offence, or who is charged with an offence."[3] On the basis of these two definitions, it may be said that as soon as a person is alleged formally to commit a crime, he comes in the category of accused.

The word accused is a verb connoting to charge with a fault, offence or crime. As an adjective, the expression "accused" would amount to the person charged with an offence or crime and when the expression is used in terms of a noun, it connotes the defendant in a trial. The expression "accused" as is found in the Criminal Procedure Code, connotes "Accused Person" or "Person accused of any offence." "Accused of an offence" covers "accused of an offence at the trial."[4] In this context it would be apt to quote the views of the Supreme Court expressed in the ***State of U.P. v. Deoman***[5]:

> "The expression, 'accused person' in Section 24 of the Evidence Act and the expression 'a person accused of any offence' have the same connotations and describe the person against whom evidence, is sought to be held in a criminal proceeding . . . The adjectival clause "accused of any offence" is, therefore, descriptive of the person against whom a confessional statement made by him is declared not provable, and does not predicate a condition of that person at the time of a making the statement for the applicability of the ban".

According to the *Law Lexicon*, "Accused of an offence" means where evidence whether oral or circumstantial points to the guilt of a person and he is taken in the custody and interrogated on that basis, he becomes a person accused of an offence. The mere fact that his name was not mentioned as an accused in the First Information Report will not take him out of the category of persons accused of an offence.[6] It may be treated as a well settled principle that with the lodging of an F.I.R., a person is deemed to be an accused of an offence within the meaning of Article 20(3) of the Constitution of India. A person against whom a formal accusation of the commission of an offence has been made can be a person accused of an offence.[7] However, the expression "accused" as referred to in Section 202(1) of the Criminal Procedure Code,1973, has been used in the context of Section 200 of the same Code in relation to a complaint even before the issue of process. Section 200 of the Criminal Procedure Code also expresses similar view of the "accusation" even before issuing the process. This section contemplates that Magistrate shall have to issue process at first instance only when there is sufficient ground for proceeding against the accused for attendance.

It is clear from the above discussion that as soon as any person is alleged formally to commit an offence, i.e., afterwards an accusation is made against him for commission of an offence, he falls in the category of accused at the same moment and he continues to be accused till he is convicted or acquitted by the court. It is immaterial whether such person has been arrested or, after arrest, has been kept in the police custody or has been recommended to judicial custody or has been released on bail. So long as the trial continues and a judgment is not pronounced he continues to be an accused. After the pronouncement of the judgment against him, he becomes a convicted person. In case the conviction order is stayed by the appellate court and an appeal remains pending, it is debatable whether such person would remain to be an accused or not. For the purposes of the present study, the expression "accused" has been used to cover a person from the date when a formal accusation or allegation is made till he is finally convicted and punished by the highest judicial authority.

B. BASIS OF THE RECOGNITION OF THE HUMAN RIGHTS OF ACCUSED

In accordance with the changing societal needs and demands, concepts of legal norms have also changed from time to time. Historically speaking, at one time, a person, accused of a crime, was considered as an evil and was condemned with all possible brutalities. In early days, the accused was kept in total confinement, more or less secret, till his trial and he could not prepare for his defence for want of the advance notice of evidence against him and lack of legal assistance. It seems that there were no rules of evidence at all and if there were any, these were scantily observed at the trial. The prisoner was neither allowed to call defence witness nor was he necessarily confronted with prosecution witnesses. Confessional statements or accomplices were not only freely admitted against each other but were regarded as especially cogent evidence. This attitude has, however, since a long time changed. The person who is charged with an offence now gets certain protections in the absence of which many persons accused of an offence might not have been able to establish their innocence.

In the modern times, every matured legal system of the world accords certain basic protections to accused persons - who may be deprived of their personal liberty by way of imprisonment for the commission of offences. The principles on which such protections have been granted are : natural justice (protection of basic/ natural / human / fundamental rights) and of safeguarding of personal liberty.

1. Natural Justice and Human Rights of Accused

The concept that a human being "has the right to be respected.. .."[8] is basically derived from the natural law. In Europe, the maxim *"nulla poena sine lege"*, in England, the principles of *'natural justice'*, couched in the maxim *"audi alterm partem"*, and in the United States, the procedural rule of *"due process of law"*, provide focal points in natural law with regard to the protection of rights of an accused. The maxim *'nulla poena sine lege'* is based on the elementary principles of justice that the criminal law should be pre-determined, fixed and be as much certain as possible so that men may know in advance as to what conduct is prescribed so as to be visited with penal sanctions and , thus, envisages the following four cardinal principles of criminal justice:

(a) The area of the criminal law should be pre-determined by general rules;
(b) A person should not be punished unless his acts are in breach of these rules;
(c) The penal statutes should be strictly construed; and
(d) The penal laws should not have retrospective operations.[9]

An accused person, being a human being, cannot be denied to enjoy the 'right to life' and 'personal liberty'. *The Universal Declaration of Human Rights, 1948*, vividly declares that all human beings are born free and equal in dignity and right.[10] The Declaration contains: (a) The Right of equality before the law,[11]

(b) Right against cruelty and inhuman punishment,[12] (c) Presumption of innocence,[13] and (d) Right against ex-post facto laws.[14] On the other hand, *the International Covenant on Civil and Political Rights, 1966,* deals with the Rights of Prisoners - awaiting for trials or under trial - including the rights of delinquent juveniles.

In the society, economic situation and status have not been proportionately distributed by nature; one is handful and abundant whereas the other is just able to eke-out his livelihood. This economic imbalance sometimes make a person to be not good in any manner and is one contributory in making such person aberrating from natural course of life. In modern penology such aberrated persons are termed as men of bad character or accused of crime.[15] Whereas all things are governed by eternal law of God, such persons alone choose to differ from eternal (Natural) law (Obey or not to Obey). By nature, natural law and natural rights are innate qualities, character possessed by every individual, of which the latter (natural rights) signifies simply "absence of external impediments" which equate to liberty - "a product of Natural Law". That is why all human beings have equal rights according to natural law and no one is above the law, for the natural law devises means for making a good life or a secured life.[16] Hence, a "man as a physical being" comes to this state of nature along with free movement - "Liberty" - which is a burning topic of modern times of this century, specially with reference to the accused. Thus, the concept of personal liberty becomes another important basis for the conferment of various rights to accused persons which includes prisoners.

2. The Concept of Personal Liberty and Human Rights of Accused

Generally, in the ordinary sense, "Liberty" means freedom from bondage or physical restraint, but under law the expression is not confined to only "freedom from bodily restraint", it also extends to the conduct which an individual is free to pursue. In the Constitution of India, the word "liberty" has been qualified by the word "personal" and, therefore, the expression "personal liberty" can be given restricted interpretation. Whatever it may be, either restricted or liberal interpretation, "personal liberty" is too precious a thing to be taken lightly by any one much less the

State and its functionaries and nothing could be more precious and sacrosanct than the liberty of an individual.[17] Hence, liberty of an individual is a matter of great constitutional importance in the system of governance [18] in India.

It may be worthwhile to quote some provisions of the *Universal Declaration of Human Rights, 1948.*[19] Article 3 of the Declaration provides that "Every one has the right to life, liberty and security of person". Article 5 of the Declaration prohibiting torture and inhuman punishment or treatment provides that : "No one shall be subjected to torture or to cruel, inhuman or degrading treatment or punishment". Article 7 of the Declaration provides for the 'Right of equality before the law and Protection against any discrimination.'

With regard to the rights of accused, Articles 14, 19 and 21 are the most important provisions in the Constitution of India. 'All citizens are equal' is the reflection in Article14, wherein it provides that "State shall not deny to any person equality before the law or the equal protection of the laws within the territory of India." In other words, each individual has equal right to the consideration by the state or no man is above the law. Therefore, the underlying object of Article 14 is, undoubtedly, to secure to all persons, citizens or non-citizens, equality before law or the equal protection of the laws. In view of Article 14, right to equality before law or the equal protection of the laws will be extended to the non-citizens if the circumstances prevailing arise within the territory of India less it would amount to violation of Article 21; hence personal liberty, howsoever precious, could be taken away only through laid down procedure. In view of foregoing discussion- "Personal Liberty" means "Personal Rights" not to be subjected to imprisonment, arrest or other physical coercion in any manner that does not admit of legal justification.[20]

The expression 'equality before the law' has its basis in English common law[21] which according to Dicey means "equal subjection of all persons to the ordinary law of the land administered by the ordinary law courts"[22]. 'Rights' and 'interests' are things which are to a man's advantage, yet they are not identical[23]. Laski defines that 'rights', in fact, are those conditions of social life without which no man can seek, in general, to be himself at his best. It is an interest recognized and protected by rules of rights and justice which are for the interest of citizens, yet they are against citizens for all interests are not protected, but restricted.

The following rights have been guaranteed under Article 19 in the form of Fundamental Rights by the Constitution of India :

(a) Right to have freedom of speech and expression;
(b) Right to assemble peacefully without arms;
(c) Right to form association or union;
(d) Right to move freely throughout territory of India;
(e) Right to reside or settle in any part of the territory of India;
(f) Right to practice any profession or to carry on any occupation, trade and business.

Article 19 protects not only the above rights but also acts as the most cogent attributive to Article 21 (Personal liberty). It is a great and basic right which is recognised as natural and inherent in the status of a citizen. Hence the Article protects some of the most important attributes of personal liberty as an independent right, and the expression "Personal liberty" has been used in Article 21 as compendious term including within its meaning all the varieties of rights which go to make up the personal liberties of men.[23] The protection of life and liberty has been guaranteed to every person by Article 21. While the scope of liberty had been discussed in a number of cases either by Supreme Court or various High Courts in reference to persons and since liberty can be secured and attributed to either living or non-living like corporation, or company etc., the scope of discussion on life or right to life with reference to Article 19 has been adjudged less.

The term 'life' is "the general or universal conditions of human being for a specific period of animate existence".[24] The definition would be supported by the known expression "dead" which means deprived of life or permanent and total cessation of all the vital functions of an individual ; it means that life is the period before death of a person (a human being).

It may be mentioned here that no Article referred to above speaks with regard to 'right of life' explicitly. Article 21 simply says that "no person shall be deprived of his life or personal liberty except according to procedure established by law". Therefore, the right to life and personal liberty, in its content, is not an absolute right but is a limited right having its ambit circumscribed by the risk of its being taken away by adopting the procedure established by law made by appropriate authority.[25] Therefore, the truth is that the right to life and various freedoms of a person are primary rights attached to a person[26] and they are usually termed as personal liberties. These liberties or freedoms are briefly listed in the Indian Constitution as substantial rights with restrictions imposed thereon; hence they are regulated freedoms. While both the Articles 19 and 21 are found in Part III of the Constitution of India, each one has its circle differently. While Article 19 gives list of individual liberties which can be restricted or restrained by law, Article 21 gives the right to safety of one's life and limbs which are inherent birth right. Thus, it may be said that Article 19 declares the substantive rights of "personal liberty" while Article 21 provides procedural safeguards against their deprivation.[27] What would be the result if there had been no Criminal Procedure Code despite the existence of Indian Penal Code. If Article 21 is to be understood as providing only procedural safeguards, where is the substantive right to "personal liberty" – a question has been raised.[28]

Earlier, the Supreme Court in ***In re Sant Ram Case*** [29] declared that the word 'life' in Article 21 did not include 'livelihood'. The Supreme Court, however, later on, over-ruling its earlier view, confirmed in ***A.V. Nachane Case***[30] and ***Olga Tellis Case*** [31] that since the word "life" has widest meaning, the "right to livelihood" would come within the four corners of Article 21, and the right to life includes the right to livelihood. Income is the foundation of many Fundamental Rights and when work is sole source of income, the right to work becomes very much fundamental.[32] It may, thus, be said that life and liberty of a person are co-related by and large with those of practice, profession, business, trade and commerce through which a life (a human being) earns its livelihood. Right to work is the most precious liberty that a man possesses. The non-supply of nourishment to organism fails to sustain life. When there is no life, procedural safeguarding of the deprivation of life enshrined in Article 21 is useless unless they are supported by substantive Article as enumerated in sub-articles (d), (e) and (g) of Article 19 and Article 301 despite the restrictions imposed on the respective fields by the authority concerned. Hence, life and liberty enshrined in Article 21 is co-related with those of Article 19 and 301 for there is always nexus between life and means of livelihood. It is useless to have procedural safeguards when there is no substantive right to personal liberty.[33]

The combination of Articles 19 (1) (d), 19 (1)(g) and 301 also can be seen from the fact that "the Right to life" includes the "right to live with human dignity" and that goes with it; namely, the bare necessities of life such as adequate nutrition, clothing and shelter over head and facilities for reading, writing and expressing oneself in diverse forms, freely moving about and mixing and communicating with fellow human beings".[34] It has been observed by the Supreme Court of India that fundamental rights are not distinct and mutually exclusive rights. Each freedom has different dimensions and merely because the limits of interference with one freedom are satisfied, the law is not free from the necessity to meet the challenge of another guaranteed freedom. Hence, law affecting personal liberty under Article 21 will also have to satisfy the tests of Articles 19 and 14.[35]

In short "personal liberty" is a right of doing whatever one pleases. The words "whatever one pleases" amount to unlimited liberty, and in such cases some times one may do harm to the other. Hence, "one can do only that which law permits". Therefore, it is "a right of doing whatever law permits". A person also shall not be compelled to do things which law does not permit. In short, the person has to balance himself and the society. In the modern state of nature, such act of doing whatever one pleases comes from the Constitution.[36] They are sometimes bound by manner and customs that received incorporation in the Articles of the Constitution. It is to stop abuse of liberty and at the same time to give him a secured life in the nature by way of free movement.[37] After the ***Maneka Gandhi's Case,***[38] Article 21 of the Indian Constitution has got a wider expression or meaning. Inherent in personal liberty is the right to be communicated and to communicate, right to privacy, right against hand cuffing and speedy trial also. Within this wider meaning personal liberty has covered the area of criminal justice administration involving an accused.

It may, thus, be said that while granting or recognizing the various rights of an accused, the principles of natural justice and personal liberty form the main basis at both national and international levels. Being based on the principles of natural justice the human rights of an accused have been in existence from time immemorial. Before examining these various rights in detail, firstly it is proposed to discuss, in the chapter to follow, the evolution of the human rights of an accused.

REFERENCES

1. AIR 1997 S.C. 610.
2. Earl Jowitt, 'The Dictionary of English Law', London Sweet & Maxwell, Second impression, 1965, p. 34.
3. Law Lexicon, (Govt. Publication), T.P. Mukherjee & K.K. Singh 1977 Vol. 1, Allahabad Printing Press, University Road.
4. Ramlal Bhagilal v. D.D. Gupta A I R 1973 S.C. 1196.
5. A I R 1960 S.C. 1105: see also Abraham Vergies v. State of Kerala, A I R 1965 Ker. 175 at 176.
6. Law Lexicon, (Govt. Publication), T.P. Mukherjee & K.K. Singh 1977 Vol. 1, Allahabad Printing Press, University Road. p. 25.
7. Veera Ibrahim v. State of Maharashtra, A I R 1976 S.C. 1167.
8. Jacques Martitain, 'The Right of Man', London, 1944, p. 37.
9. Chaturvedi, A.N., 'Rights of Accused under Indian Constitution', 1984, Deep & Deep Publications, New Delhi, p. 9.
10. Universal Declaration of Human Rights, 1948, Article 1.
11. *Ibid.*, Article 7.
12. *Ibid.*, Article 5.
13. *Ibid.*, Article 11 clause (1).
14. *Ibid.*, Clause (2).
15. I.B.S. Thokchom, 'Rights of an Accused', 1996, First Edn., Kamal Publishers, Delhi, p. 9.
16. *Ibid.*, at p. 10.
17. Burhanuddin Tahavali v. Union of India, 1994 S.C.C. 63.
18. Rameshwar Dayal v. State of Bihar, A I R 1968 S.C. 1303.
19. Sinha, Manoj Kumar, 'Basic Documents on International Human Rights and Refugee Laws', Manak Publications, New Delhi,2000, pp. 107-111.
20. Diecy A.V., 'Law of the Constitution', London, 1964 pp. 207-208.
21. The doctrine of equality is the outcome of the bitter reaction to tyrannical treatments meted out in the hands of Baron landlords of

Anglo-Saxon period in England. This compelled the king John who conceded this right in the Great Magna Carta (1215). Clause 39 of Magna Carta reads: "No free man shall be taken or imprisoned .... except by the legal judgement of his peers or by the law of the land."

22. Dicey, A.V., 'Law of the Constitution', London, 1964, p. 202.
23. A.K. Gopalan v. State of Madras, A I R 1950 S.C. 27 at p. 111.
24. Random House Dictionary of English Language.
25. A.K. Gopalan v. State of Madras A I R 1950 S.C. 27 at 118.
26. *Ibid.*, at p. 108.
27. A.K.Gopalan v. State of Madras A I R 1950 S.C. 27.
28. *Ibid.*, at pp. 71, 95.
29. In re Sant Ram, A I R 1960 S.C. 932.
30. A.V.Nachane v. Union of India, A I R 1982 S.C. 1126.
31. Olga Tellis v. Bombay Municipal Corporation, A I R 1986 S.C. 180.
32. DTC v. DTC Mazdoor Congress, A I R 1991 S.C. 101.
33. A.K. Gopalan v. State of Madras. A I R 1950 S.C. 27 at p. 71.
34. IBS Thokchom, 'Rights of an accused', 1996, First Edn., Kamal Publishers, New Delhi, p. 15.
35. Maneka Gandhi v. Union of India, A I R 1978 S.C. 597.
36. IBS Thokchom, 'Rights of an accused', 1996, First Edn., Kamal Publishers, New Delhi, p. 15.
37. Maneka Gandhi v. Union of India, A I R 1978 S.C. 597.
38. *Ibid.*

Two

Evolution of the Human Rights of Accused

In the previous chapter, meaning of the term "accused" and the basis of the recognition of various human rights to an accused have been discussed. It has been observed that the concept of the rights of an accused person is mainly based on principles of natural justice and thus is time immemorial but it had assumed much importance at the international level from 1948 onwards due to *Universal Declaration of Human Rights*,1948 , *International Covenant on Civil and Political Rights*, 1966 and many other international documents and at the national level due to the various fundamental rights guaranteed under the *Constitution of India*. Thus , before examining the various human rights of an accused in detail, it would be useful to discuss in brief evolution of such rights. Which is proposed to be subject matter of this Chapter. The discussion of the evolution of the rights of accused may be made in five parts: (1) Rights of Accused recognised under Hindu Legal System in Ancient India; (2) Rights of Accused granted under Muslim Legal System; (3) Rights of Accused recognised during British period; (4) Rights of Accused recognised at International level and (5) Rights of Accused recognised and guaranteed at National level by the Constitution of India.

A. HUMAN RIGHTS OF ACCUSED RECOGNISED UNDER HINDU LEGAL SYSTEM IN ANCIENT INDIA

"The Human person possesses rights because of the very fact that it is a person" and accordingly he "has the right to be respected."[1] In India this concept dates back to the Vedic period or Sutra period dating back to at least about the Seventh or Sixth century B.C. Scriptural literature reveals that the concept of human rights in India has consistently and gradually developed in various stages. According to the observations of *Vardachariar:*

> No unbiased student of the *Smriti* literature can assert that the system whose beginning and developments are traceable from stage to stage was wholly imaginary. The rules laid down are so detailed and practical and their development is so natural that they must have been the result of actual experience in the daily administration of Justice.[2]

Under Hindu legal system more importance was attached to duty in comparison to right. Every deviation from Dharma (law), if brought to the notice of the King, was to be appropriately dealt with by him for which appropriate sanctions were prescribed, including the *Vagdanda* (Admonition), *Dhigdanada* (Rebuke), *Arthadanda* (Fine), and *Vadhadanda* (Corporal punishment). The latter two punishments could be inflicted only by the king alone, subject to certain limitations. The king also had an appellate authority. He had, thus, a threefold responsibility: Firstly, he had to look into the matter himself and give redress to the aggrieved party. Secondly, he had to punish the officers and *Sabhayas* responsible for the miscarriage of justice; and lastly, if a suitor made an unfounded allegation that justice had not been done to him, the king had to punish him. The *Juri* system was well recognised to settle the complicated questions of fact.[3] The Hindu legal system took every possible precaution consistently with the conditions of knowledge of the time to discover the truth. Circumstantial evidence was recognised to be used but with great caution as appearances might be deceptive. As *Yajnavalkya* said: "an injury to the body of the complainant might sometimes be self-inflicted". The expedient disposal of disputes appears to have been well recognised by the Ancient Hindu Jurists. This has found place in *Arthasastra* which recognised penalty for a judge who threatened, brow-beat, or unjustly silenced one of the parties or abused or defamed or asked questions which ought not to be asked or made unnecessary delay.[4]

The following three major rights of accused are found to be recognised in ancient Hindu legal system:

(1) Right to Engage Counsel,
(2) Right to File Appeal, and
(3) Right to Examine Witnesses.

1. Right to Engage Counsel

Although no institution of lawyers as understood in the present sense existed in ancient India, persons well versed in the law of *Smritis* were appointed and could be engaged by party for the representation of his case before the court. In the commentary of *Asahaya*, as edited by *Kalyan Bhatta* on *Narada*, it is found that well versed persons in *Smritis* helped the parties for monetary considerations. Similarly it is also found in *Sukra Nity* which provides punishment to a representative who allowed the dispute to fail owing to his greed; and such a representative was punished by the king[5]. Similar to the provision as to the fees of the agents propounded in the *Sukra Nity*, the fees for the agents who represented a party to a dispute before a court of law were provided in *Bengal Regulation VII* of 1793, *Bombay Regulation II* of 1827 and *Bombay Pleaders Act XVII* of 1920.

2. Right to File Appeal

Brihaspati and *Katyayana* said that where a party is not satisfied with the decision given by an inferior court, *'Kula'* etc., the King would look in it and if it had been found wrongly done he would set it right.[6] From the *Kula* there was a provision for an appeal to the *Sreni*, form thence a second appeal to *Puja*, thence again a third appeal to the *pradvivaka's court* and, finally an appeal to the King. A text of *Narada* repeated by *Katyayana* says that when another ruler had in his ignorance done something inconsistent with Justice, it should also be set right as is clear from the following verse:[7]

न्यायपेतम यदन्यन्य राज्ञाज्ञानाकतम भवेत्
तदप्य न्यायविहितमं् पुनारन्येय निवेसयत्।।

It means that a decision by subordinate court was liable to be set aside by the King but a decision arrived at by the King himself in a matter could not be set aside even if it had been wrongly done.[8]

3. Right to Examine Witnesses

The practice of the examination of the witnesses appears to have been well recognised by the ancient Hindu legal system as the judges had the opportunity of seeing the witness and to decide upon their reliability. *Katyayana* also recognises the examination of witnesses on commission, but *Medhatithi's* commentary on *Manu* has a reference to such procedure but does not recognise it.[9]

It may thus be summed up that the Administration of Criminal Justice under the ancient Hindu legal system was based on socio-religious concept emanating from Vedic revelation, *Srutis, Smritis, Puranas* and *Nibandha Granthas* prescribed by ancient Hindu sages. The present rule of 'presumption of innocence' of the accused appears to have been well recognised by the ancient King of Hindu period. No mention of the condemnation of the accused is found without providing him an opportunity of being heard and examination of his witnesses and the opportunity of cross-examination of the complainant and his witnesses. Except of King's court, no other inferior tribunal could award the punishment to the accused. Every inferior tribunal in order of its precedence on the finding of the guilt of the accused used to refer the matter to the next superior tribunal until the matter reached the King's Court or in his absence the *Pradvivaka's* Court.

B. HUMAN RIGHTS OF ACCUSED RECOGNISED UNDER MUSLIM LEGAL SYSTEM

The Muslim concept of the administration of justice is based on the tenets and injunctions of the *Holy Quran* which may, thus, be described as the supreme legislative code of Islam laying down the basic rules of justice.The Muslim Jurists had classified the Muslim law under two broad heads - *Tashriyi* (religious) and *Ghair Tashriyi* (Secular); the purely religious portion of law applied to Muslims only whereas the secular portion applied to Muslims and non-Muslims alike. The Muslim Criminal Law was also divided into two parts: (i) One part dealt with religious infringement such as drinking liquor, marrying within the prohibited degree, apostasy, etc and was applied to Muslim only — for such offences non-Muslims were not held liable to punishment; and (ii) The second part dealt with the punishment for the acts which constituted crimes in the estimation of all nations and was applied to Muslim and non-Muslim alike, e.g., adultery, murder, theft, robbery, assault, etc.[10]

The main rights of an accused which existed under the

Muslim Criminal Jurisprudence with a view to ensure a fair trial of a person - accused of crime - may be outlined thus:

(1) Right to be released on Bail;
(2) Right to engage Counsel;
(3) Right to have Speedy Trial;
(4) Right to get Benefit of Doubt;
(5) Right to file Appeal;
(6) Right to enjoy the Limitations on the power of arrest and custody;
(7) Right to get the offences Compounded; and
(8) Other Rights in the form of Procedural Safeguards.

1. Right to be Released on Bail

The right of an accused to be released on bail did exist during Mughal rule in India. Mohammad Amin Khan, the Governor of Lahore, put Manucci in prison on a false case of theft, but the Governor designate, Fidai Khan, granted bail for his release by issuing the order of release. In spite of his release order he was required by the Kotwal to furnish surety.[11] When Manrique (traveller) was arrested in Midnapur in Bengal his release was secured by a Muslim merchant on furnishing bail.[12]

2. Right to Engage Counsel

The institution of lawyers was found under Muslim legal system and an accused charged with an offence, if he so desired, had a right to be represented through a lawyer. Expert knowledge of law was required both for practice of law and for acting as *Qazi*.[13] Contemporary authorities have referred to the institution of lawyers (Vakil).[14] Every person who could afford could engage a *Vakil*; especially *Zamindars, Mansubdars, Kotwals* and *Fauzdars* were represented by *Vakils*. The Royal Princess had also their *Vakils*.

3. Right to have Speedy Trial

During Muslim rule in India, quick disposal of the criminal trial as a right of an accused was well recognized. In the 28th Illahi year (A.D.1585), *Akbar* constituted a Standing Judicial Committee for the purpose of expediting Justice and saving the people from the distress caused by delay as also for general improvement in tone and practice of justice.[15] Efforts were made to dispose of the criminal cases on the spot so that the evidence of the witness to be adduced in the case might remain authentic and the sequence of events might not be obliviated by lapse of time.

4. Right to Get Benefit of Doubt

The Right to get Benefit of Doubt was known in the Administration of Criminal Justice under Muslim Jurisprudence. as the doctrine of *Shubaha* (doubt) which entitled an accused to be acquitted. In the case of ***Madari Edd Faqir,*** [16] the accused was acquitted of the offence of theft as his merely running out of the house at night did not warrant conclusive proof of his guilt, so the benefit of doubt was given to him.

5. Right to File Appeal

It was permissible to file Appeals against orders of the trial court. The appellate court had powers either to confirm or reverse the order or remand for fresh trial or refer the point of law to *Quaziul Quzat* (the Chief Justice's Bench) or cause an additional evidence to be recorded. The appellate court could also try witness for perjury and the accused in such cases could run the risk of sentence of death.[17] Appeals could abate on the death of the appellant.[18] This rule is still in practice in criminal cases. Revision and Review were also made.

6. Right to Enjoy the Limitations on the Power of Arrest and Custody

In *Hadd and Tzir* (cognizable) cases, on the production of *prima facie* evidence, arrest (*Hirasat*) of the accused was made. The *Kotwal* in charge of arrest had to report the arrest to the *Quazi* and had to obtain his order whether the arrested person was to be released or prosecuted. Emphasis on *prima facie* evidence before arrest was laid down by *Aurangzeb* and courts were warned against keeping a man under trial for a term longer than was strictly necessary. Example of conviction of a *Shiqahdar* (Police officer) was for the offence of wrongful confinement and imposition of fine is found.[19] *Quazi* and police officer (*Shiqahdar)* both were authorized to make search and had the power to investigate on reasonable grounds. Wrongful obstruction in search led to punishment, unless justified.

7. Right to Get the Offences Compounded

While compounding of a private criminal complaint was generally allowed,[20] in other cases, permission of the court was necessary. According to the *Fiqhe-Phiroz Shahi*, the parties to a criminal case could compromise only if the accused was in the custody of the court lest a compromise could be exacted from him under pressure. For this reason, no weight was attached to the confession made to the police.[21]

8. Other Rights in the Form of Procedural Safeguards

The following rights in the form of procedural safeguards were available to an accused under Muslim Legal System:

(i) An accused could get his case transferred from one court to another – the power to transfer appears to have been vested in the King and the Governor only. Nothing is found as to the transfer by a Quazi of Sarkar (District) within his Jurisdiction.

(ii) A complainant could withdraw a case from one court and could take the same to the highest court on the same ground on which one can move a transfer application at present.[22]

(iii) The complaint was to be presented to court in person or through representative. Government prosecutions were instituted by *Mohtasibs* or *Kotwals*.[23]

(iv) The Court was empowered to summon the accused either at once or after hearing first the complainant's evidence.

(v) Evidence could be heard in the absence of an absconding accused, but the prosecution witnesses were to be recalled when he was arrested and his trial commenced.

(vi) In the absence of the complainant, the accused was to be released.[24]

(vii) A judgement of the Court was required to be pronounced by the presiding officer in the open court and in the presence of the parties and the same was also required to be recorded in a book mentioned for it.

(viii) No Judgment could be pronounced in the absence of both the parties or their counsel.[25]

It may be summed up from the above discussion that the Hindu and Muslim legal system - both - have put reliance on the *Veda* and the *Quran*-"The Book of Revelation, as the word of God which is meant for all times to give law to the people". The former derived law from *Manusmriti* and also from some of the important commentaries like *Yagyavalkya, Narada, Brihaspati*, etc. and the latter found amplification in well-known commentaries like *Sahih Mullim, Kitabus Sunnan by Abu Dawood Sijistani, Muwatta*, etc. Both laid emphasis on the trial of cases by the ruler himself and a duty to select learned men to act as judges. As both the systems had been founded on divine revelations, after the Hindu system, it was not a difficult task for the Turkish Sultans to change over to Islamic concept of rule of law in India.

C. HUMAN RIGHTS OF ACCUSED RECOGNISED DURING BRITISH PERIOD

In India although the Common Law principles of England were gradually transplanted in the Indian Subcontinent in accordance with the conditions and circumstances suited to the Indian society,[26] in several cases the courts refused to apply the rules of English Law on the ground of their inapplicability to the Indian circumstances.[27] Thus, the Indian Law was supplanted and supplemented by the common law and statute law of England.

After the grant of *Diwani* in 1765, when the East India Company took the administration of criminal justices, it continued to administer criminal justice according to Mohammedan criminal law "It was applied in Bengal, in Madras and later on in the other parts of India, though not in Bombay, to Hindus as well as Muslims".[28] Gradually attempts were made by the Company to alter and reform the criminal law and cruel Mohammedan punishments by *Lord Hastings* in 1773 and *Lord Cornwallis* in 1790. *The Charter of 1833* introduced a single legislation for the whole of British India. The English criminal law as stood in 1837 was sanguinary and discriminate with regards to punishment and it could hardly be said to be an improvement upon the Mohammedan criminal law. In the words of Lord Macaulay, it was so defective that it could be reformed only by being entirely taken to pieces and reconstructed.[29] The penal law was codified in 1860. The second half of the 19th century may be described as statutory period in which many enactments and legislations were made. Between 1860 and 1898 many repeals and replacements were made in the criminal procedure. The first *Code of Criminal Procedure* was passed in 1861 which was repealed and replaced by the *Code of 1872*; that too was repealed and replaced by the *Code of Criminal Procedure 1898*. The Code of 1898 continued to be applied even in free India. However, the Code of 1898 was repealed and replaced by the *Criminal Procedure Code of 1973.*

Besides the enactment of the Code of Criminal Procedure, the law relating to evidence was also codified and the *Indian Evidence Act* was passed in the year 1872. One of the main objects of the *Indian Evidence Act, 1872,* had been to prevent laxity in the admissibility of evidence and to introduce a more correct and uniform rule of practice than was previously in vogue. Besides the Code of Criminal Procedure, in the *Indian Evidence Act, 1872,* also certain rights of accused were recognized. The important and basic rights guaranteed to an accused under the *Criminal Procedure Code, 1898* (as amended in 1973) and the *Indian Evidence Act, 1872,* can be outlined, in brief, as under :

(1) The right of being presumed innocent throughout the trial[30],
(2) Right of defence[31],
(3) Right of being produced before magistrate within a prescribed period[32],
(4) Right to be informed of grounds of arrest[33],
(5) Right to engage counsel [34],
(6) Right to have public trials[35],
(7) Right to cross-examine witnesses[36],
(8) Right against testimonial compulsion[37],
(9) Right against double jeopardy [38],
(10) Right to be released on Bail pending trail[39], and
(11) Right to file Appeal [40].

These existing provisions related to criminal procedure in

vogue prior to the adoption of the Constitution of free India, continued to govern the criminal procedure even after Independence and adoption of the Constitution except that some of them were doubly guaranteed by the Constitution in the form of Fundamental Rights and by making them inviolable by the Constitution itself. Although the genesis of the constitutional guarantees to an accused has been mainly the principles of natural justice and concept of personal liberty, some of these guarantees are also based on the declarations/conventions made at international level. Thus, before examining the constitutional guarantees available to an accused, it would be more appropriate to examine first the important developments which had taken place at international level.

D. HUMAN RIGHTS OF ACCUSED RECOGNISED AT INTERNATIONAL LEVEL

In order to provide certain basic rights to an accused for the purposes of restoring the dignity of a human being and protecting him from inhuman behaviour when he is taken into custody, the following two important and noteworthy declarations were made at international level:

(1) Universal Declaration of Human Rights, 1948, and

(2) International Covenant on Civil and Political Rights, 1966.

In addition to the above stated two declarations, several other international instruments were made at different levels from time to time which substantiated and strengthened the basic principles laid-down by these two documents.[41] Out of these, the following three are noteworthy:

(2) United Nations Standard Minimum Rules for the Treatment of Prisoners, 1955;

(4) United Nations Standard Minimum Rules for the Administration of Juvenile Justice (The Beijing Rules), 1985; and

(5) United Nations Rules for the Protection of Juveniles Deprived of their Liberty, 1990.

While the Rules of 1955 make provisions for certain rights to prisoners under arrest or awaiting trial, the latter Rules of 1985 and 1990 make special provisions for the protection of Juveniles deprived of their liberty (i.e., Juvenile accused). An examination of the relevant provisions of these instruments may be useful.

1. Universal Declaration of Human Rights, 1948 and Rights of Accused

The Universal Declaration of Human Rights, 1948, (hereinafter referred to as the Declaration) besides providing in general certain rights restoring the dignity of every human beings like, the rights of personal liberty, equality before law and the right against any discrimination to every human being; also contained a few provisions pertaining to the rights of an accused.

Article 3 of the Declaration provides that "Everyone has the right to life, liberty and security of person."

Article 5 of the Declaration provides that, "No on shall be subjected to torture or to cruel, inhuman or degrading treatment or punishment". This Article is directly related to the rights of an accused against custodial violence, either during the custody of police or judicial custody.

Article 7 of the Declaration states that "All are equal before the law and are entitled without any discrimination to equal protection of the law."

Article 9 of the Declaration declares that " No one shall be subjected to arbitrary arrest, detention or exile." According to *Article 10 of the Declaration* an accused has the Right of Fair and Public Trial and also a right to be heard by impartial tribunal, in the determination of his rights, and of any criminal charges against him. Article 10 of the Declaration is as under:

> "Every one is entitled in full equality to a fair and public hearing by an independent an impartial tribunal, in the determination of his rights and obligations and of any criminal charge against him."

Article 11(1) of the Declaration provides that, "Every one charged with a penal offence has the right to be presumed innocent until proved guilty according to law in a public trial at which he has had all the guarantees necessary for his defence." Further, *Article 11(2) of the Declaration* provides that, "No one shall be held guilty of any penal offence on account of any act or omission which did not constitute a penal offense, under national or international law, at the time when it was committed or shall a heavier penalty be imposed than the one that was applicable at the time the penal offence was committed."

On the basis of the above mentioned provisions of the Universal Declaration of Human Rights,1948, the various rights of an accused recognized under the Declaration can be classified thus:

1. Right of accused to equality before law;
2. Right of accused to life, liberty and security;
3. Right of accused against torture or inhuman punishment;
4. Right of accused to have a fair and public trial;
5. Right of accused to be protected against ex-post laws; and
6. Right of accused to be presumed innocent.

Nowadays, the above rights of accused persons have been provisioned at the world level. It had been expected through this Declaration that every country or state shall make provision of these rules in its own law. It may be said that being an accused, a person cannot enjoy all the human rights but on the other hand, it is also necessary that he should not be deprived of the minimum personal liberties. Thus, a proper balance is to be maintained while imposing restrictions on his freedom and on the exercise of his right of personal liberty.

2. International Covenant on Civil and Political Rights, 1966 and Rights of Accused

Part III of the International Covenant on Civil and Political Rights, 1966 , (hereinafter referred to as "the Covenant") contains the various provisions granting various human rights to accused. *Article 6 of the Covenant* deals with the 'inherent right to life of every human being'; *Article 7 of the Covenant* protects a person from 'torture or to cruel, inhuman or degrading treatment or punishment' and also from 'medical or scientific experimentation without his consent'; *Article 9 of the Covenant* provides every person a 'right to liberty and security' and makes various rules to be followed at the time of arrest and *Article 14 of the Covenant* prescribes various procedures with a view to protect an accused. Out of 21 Articles of Part III, Article 9 and Article 14 of the Covenant deal with rights of accused directly and have also formed the basis of various provisions of the Constitution of India and also judicial decisions. *Article 9 of the Covenant* provides that :

1. Everyone has the right to liberty and security person. No one shall be subjected to arbitrary arrest or detention. No one shall be deprived of his liberty except on such grounds and in accordance with such procedure as are established by law.
2. Anyone who is arrested shall be informed, at the time of arrest, of the reasons of his arrest and shall be promptly informed of any charges against him.
3. Anyone arrested or detained on a criminal charge shall be brought promptly before the judge . . .and shall be entitled to trial within a reasonable time or to release. It may not be the general rule that persons awaiting trial shall be detained in custody, but release may be subject to guarantees to appear for trial, at any other stage of the judicial proceedings, and, should occasion arise, for execution of the judgement.
4. Anyone who is deprived of his liberty by arrest or detention shall be entitled to take proceedings before a court in order that that court may decide without delay on the lawfulness of his detention and order his release if the detention is not lawful.
5. Anyone who has been the victim of unlawful arrest or detention shall have an enforceable right to compensation.

Article 14 of the Covenant provides, *inter alia*, for the following procedural safeguards:

1. (a) All persons shall be equal before the courts and tribunals;
   (b) Everyone shall be entitled to a fair and public hearing by a competent, independent and impartial tribunal established by law;
   (c) The press and the public may be excluded from all or part of a trial for reasons of morals, public

order or national security in a democratic society or when the interest of the private lives of the parties so require;

(d) Any judgement rendered in a criminal case shall be made public except where the interest of juvenile persons otherwise requires or the proceedings concern matrimonial disputes or the guardianship of children;

2. Everyone charged with a criminal offence shall have the right to be presumed innocent until proved guilty according to law;
3. In the determination of any criminal charge against him, everyone shall be entitled to the following minimum guarantees, in full equality:
   (a) To be informed promptly and in detail in a language which he understands of the nature and cause of the charge against him;
   (b) To have adequate time and facilities for the preparation of his defence and to communicate with counsel of his own choosing;
   (c) To be tried without undue delay;
   (d) (i) To be tried in his presence, and to defend himself in person or through legal assistance of his own choosing; (ii) to be informed, if he does not have legal assistance, of this right; (iii) and to have legal assistance assigned to him, in any case where the interest of justice so require, and without payment by him in any such case, if he does not have sufficient means to pay for it;
   (e) To examine, or have examined, the witnesses against him and to obtain the attendance and examination of witnesses on his behalf under the same conditions as witnesses against him;
   (f) To have the free assistance of an interpreter if he cannot understand or speak the language used in court;
   (g) Not to be compelled to testify against himself or to confess guilt.

4. In the case of juvenile persons, the procedure shall be such as will take account of their age and the desirability of promoting their rehabilitation;
5. Everyone convicted of a crime shall have the right of his conviction and sentence being reviewed by a higher tribunal according to law;
6. When a person has been finally convicted of a criminal offence and when subsequently his conviction has been reversed or he has been pardoned on the ground that a new or newly discovered fact shows conclusively that there has been a miscarriage of justice, the person who has suffered punishment as a result of such conviction shall be compensated according to law, unless it is proved that the non-disclosure of the unknown fact in time is wholly or partly attributable to him.
7. No one shall be liable to be tried or punished again for an offence for which he has already been finally convicted or acquitted in accordance with the law and penal procedure.of each country.

Article 15 of the Covenant contains the principle of non-applicability of ex-post facto laws when it provides that:

> "No one shall be held guilty of any offence on account of any act or mission which did not constitute a criminal offence, under national or international law, at the time when it was committed.
>
> No heavier penalty be imposed than the one that was applicable at the time when the criminal offence was committed. If, subsequent to the commission, provision is made by law for the imposition of the lighter penalty, the offender shall benefit thereby."

Article 26 of the Covenant is also worth mentioning which provides that:

> All persons are equal before the law and are entitled to equal protection of the law. . . .the law shall prohibit any discrimination and guarantee to all persons equal and effective protection against discrimination on any ground such as race, colour, sex, language, religion, political or other opinion, national or social origin, property, birth or other status."

This Article of the Covenant is similar to Article 14 of Constitution of India.It is also worth mentioning that most of the provisions of the Covenant mentioned above have found place either in the Indian Constitution or in the Indian Statutes regulating criminal justice administration or in both

3. United Nations Standard Minimum Rules for the Treatment of Prisoners, 1955 and the Rights of the Accused

In addition to the Universal Declaration of Human Rights, 1948, and the International Covenant on Civil and Political Rights, 1966, the United Nations had adopted in the year 1955 the *"Standard Minimum Rules for the Treatment of Prisoners, 1955"*[42] (referred hereinafter to as 'Standard Minimum Rules') for providing certain rights to 'prisoners under arrest' or 'prisoners awaiting trial'. In these Rules though the word "Accused" was not used, certain rights were provided in the Rules to the 'prisoners under arrest' or 'prisoners awaiting trial' which are naturally covered under the term "accused".

Rule 84(1) of the Standard Minimum Rules, provides that: 'persons who are not convicted and are kept in police custody or detention and waiting for trial shall be known as 'untried prisoners'. It is the right of unconvicted and untried prisoners, that they shall be trusted as innocent persons. *Rule 84(1) of the Standard Minimum Rules* provides that 'Unconvicted person shall be presumed to be innocent until the charges has been proved'.

Rule 85 of the Standard Minimum Rules provides that: 'untried prisoners' should not be kept with convicted prisoners' According to *Rule 86 of the Standard Minimum Rules,*"Untried prisoners shall sleep singly in separate rooms, with the reservation of different local custom in respect of the climate."

Rule 87 of the Standard Minimum Rules, recognizing the right of untried prisoner to procure their food at their own expense states that: " Within the limits compatible with the good order of the institution, untried prisoners may, if they so desire, have their food procured at their own expense from the outside, either through the administration or through their family or friends. Otherwise, the administration shall provide their food".

Rule 88 of the Standard Minimum Rules provides for rights of untried prisoners relating to their dress. While Clause (1) of the said Rule provides that: "An untried prisoner shall be allowed to wear his own clothing if it is clean and suitable", clause (2) the Rule provides that :"If the untried prisoner is so poor that he cannot arrange his dress material, then it shall be the duty of that institution to provide to untried prisoners a dress different from the dress provided to the convicted prisoners."

Rule 89 of the Standard Minimum Rules ensures the untried prisoner the right to work. It states that : "An untried prisoners shall always be offered opportunity to work, but shall not be required to work. If he chooses to work, he shall be paid for it."

By *Rule 90 of the Standard Minimum Rules,* 'An untried prisoner has been allowed to procure at his own expense or at the expense of a third party such books, newspapers, writing materials and other means of occupation as are compatible with the interest of the administration of justice and security and good order of the Institution.' Further *Rule 91 of the Standard Minimum Rules* provides that: "An untried prisoner shall be allowed to be visited and treated by his own doctor or dentist if there is reasonable ground for his application and he is able to pay any expenses incurred".

Right of an untried prisoner to communicate and to be communicated has been recognized by *Rule 92 of the Standard Minimum Rule* which states that: "An untried prisoner shall be allowed to inform immediately his family of his detention and shall be given all reasonable facilities for communicating with his family and friends, and for receiving visits from them, subject only to restrictions and supervision as are necessary in the interest of the security and good order of the institution." According to *Rule 42 of the Standard Minimum Rules,* " so far as practicable, every prisoner shall be allowed to satisfy the needs of his religious life by attending the services provided in the institution and having in his possession the books of religious observance and instruction of his denomination".

Right to 'apply for free legal aid' has been recognised to an untried prisoner by *Rule 93 of the Standard Minimum Rules* which provides that: "For the purpose of his defence, an untried prisoner shall be allowed to apply for free legal aid where such aid is available, and to receive visits from his legal advisor with a view to his defence and to prepare and hand over to him confidential instructions. For this purposes, he shall, if he so desires, be supplied with writing material. Interview between the prisoner and his legal advisor may be within the hearing of a police or Institution's official."

It may be noted from the above stated various Rules that various rights recognized by these Rules are intended to provide safeguards against inhuman behaviour to the accused including a female accused also who is under arrest or awaiting trial and is kept under custody. Since persons awaiting trial do not fall in the category of convicted persons, they have been given certain additional facilities compared to a convicted person. These Rules also recognize the fact that an accused person behind the bar is also a human being and, therefore, he cannot be denied basic essential facilities available to an human being in the form of fundamental or human rights such as food, clothing, medical treatment, communication, accommodation, legal assistance and other freedoms with reasonable limitations.

4. International Instruments with regard to the Special Rights of Juvenile Accused (known as Juvenile Delinquent)

As had been pointed out earlier, Article 14(4) of the International Covenant on Civil and Political Rights, 1966, provides that 'in the case of juvenile persons, the procedure shall be such as will take account of their age and the desirability of promoting their rehabilitation.' All societies of the civilized world recognize that special conditions are necessary for children to blossom into adults and lead a meaningful and socially productive life. It is an undisputed fact that juveniles are prone to deviant behaviour and are likely to take to crime more as a demonstration of defiance. In case the juveniles are also governed by the same standards and provisions of criminal justice system which are applicable to adults, possibilities are likely to cause, permanent damage to the personality of juveniles may be caused. Therefore, at international level, a special system of criminal justice tempered with compassion and understanding was advocated for delinquent juveniles and the United Nations framed the following two Rules:

(a) United Nations Standard Minimum Rules for the

Administration of Juvenile Justice (The Beijing Rules), 1985; and

(b) United Nations Rules for the Protection of Juveniles Deprived of their Liberty,1990.These Rules deserve brief discussion.

(a) United Nations Standard Minimum Rules for the Administration of Juvenile Justice (The Beijing Rules), 1985

In order to ensure uniformity of practices and procedures in case of trial of juvenile accused, *"The Beijing Rules"* were recommended for adoption by the 7th United Nations Congress on the 'Prevention of Crime and the Treatment of Offenders' held at Milan from 26 August to 6 September 1985 and were adopted by the General Assembly Resolution 40/33 of 29 November 1985. These rules, *inter-alia,* deal with fundamental perspectives of the juvenile justice, aims of juvenile justice, age of criminal responsibility, scope of discretion at all levels of juvenile justice administration, investigation and prosecution, detention pending trial, adjudication and disposition, legal counsel, parents and guardians, guiding principles in adjudication and disposition , various disposition measures, avoidance of unnecessary delay, need for professionalism and training and non-institutional treatment. The detailed examination of these rules is proposed to be made later on while examining the rights of juvenile accused (commonly known as delinquent juvenile).

(b) United Nations Rules for the Protection of Juveniles Deprived of their Liberty, 1990

In addition to the "Beijing Rules" adopted in the year 1985, the General Assembly of the United Nations adopted by its Resolution no. 45/113 of December 14, 1990, the United Nations Rules for the Protection of Juveniles Deprived of their Liberty, 1990 (hereinafter referred to as the 'Rules for the Protection of Juveniles'. *Rule 1 of the 'Rules for the Protection of Juveniles'* states that : "The juvenile justice system should uphold the rights and safety, and promote the physical and mental well-being, of juveniles. Imprisonment should be used as a last resort." The objectives of these Rules have been described in *Rule 3 of the 'Rules for the Protection of Juveniles'* as under:

"The Rules are intended to establish minimum standards accepted by the United Nations for the protection of juveniles deprived of their liberty in all forms, consistent with human rights and fundamental freedoms, and with a view to counteracting the detrimental effects of all types detention and to fostering integration in society."

Part III of the *'Rules for the Protection of Juveniles'* specifically deal with "Juveniles under arrest or awaiting trial (untried)" and contains Rule 17 and Rule 18. The *'Rules for the Protection of Juveniles'* also provide detailed provisions, in reference to the management of various juvenile facilities. *Rule 17* of the *'Rules for the Protection of Juveniles'* provides, *inter alia* , the following rights to Juveniles who are under arrest or awaiting trial (untried)[43]:

1. They shall be presumed innocent,
2. Only in exceptional cases or circumstances, detention before the trial shall be made,
3. All efforts should be made to apply alternative measures,
3. In case there are unavoidable circumstances regarding the detention of untried juvenile, the court shall give priority to speedy process to insure the shortest possible duration of detention, and
4. Untried detained juveniles should be separated from convicted juveniles.

'Right of legal counsel' and 'Right to apply for free legal aid', 'Right to work and continue education and training' and 'Right to receive and retain materials for their leisure and recreation' have been enshrined in *Rule 18* of the *'Rules for the Protection of Juveniles'*. Rule 18, *inter alia,* provides the following rights to Juvenile detainees:

(a) Juveniles should have the right of legal counsel and be enabled to apply for free legal aid, where such aid is available, and to communicate regularly with their advisers. Privacy and confidentiality shall be ensured for such communications;

(b) Juveniles should be provided, where possible, with opportunities to pursue work, with remuneration, and continue education or training, but should not be required to do so. Work, education or training should not cause the continuation of the detention;

(c) Juveniles should receive and retain materials for their leisure and recreation as are compatible with the interests of the administration of justice.

In reference to the 'Management of Juvenile Facilities', Rules have been made in Part IV of the *'Rules for the Protection of Juveniles'* with regard to: (a) Maintenance of records;[44] (b) Admission, registration, movement and transfer;[45] (c) Classification and placement;[46] (d) Physical environment and accommodation;[47] (e) education, vocational training and work;[48] (f) Recreation;[49] (g) Religion;[50] (h) Medical care;[51] (i) Notification of illness, injury and death;[52] (j) Contacts with the wider community;[53](k) Limitations of physical restraint and the use of force;[54] (l) Disciplinary procedures;[55] (m) Inspection and complaints;[56] and (n) Return to the community.[57] Part V of the *'Rules for the Protection of Juveniles'* contains the Rules with regard to "Personnel".[58] With regard to the physical environment and accommodation during detention the following provisions have been made providing special rights to juveniles:

(i) Juveniles deprived of their liberty have the right to facilities and services that meet all the requirements of health and human dignity;[59]

(ii) The design of detention facilities for juveniles and the physical environment should be in keeping with the rehabilitative aim of residential treatment, with due regard to the need of the juvenile for privacy, sensory stimuli, opportunities for association with peers and participation in sports, physical exercise and leisure-time activities;[60]

(iii) The design and structure of juvenile detention facilities should be such as to minimize the risk of fire and to ensure safe evacuation from the premises;[60]

(iv) There should be an effective alarm system in case of fire, as well as formal and drilled procedures to ensure the safety of the juveniles;[60]

(v) Detention facilities should not be located in areas where there are known health or other hazards or risks;[60]

(vi) Sleeping accommodation should normally consist of small group dormitories or individual bed rooms, while bearing in mind local standards;[61]

(vii) During sleeping hours there should be regular, unobtrusive supervision of all sleeping areas, including individual rooms and group dormitories, in order to ensure the protection of each juvenile;[61]

(viii) Every juvenile should in accordance with local or national standards, be provided with separate and sufficient bedding, which should be clean when issued, kept in good order and changed often to ensure cleanliness;[61]

(ix) Sanitary installations should be so located and of a sufficient standard to enable every juvenile to comply, as required, with their physical needs in privacy and in a clean and decent manner;[62]

(x) Every detention facility shall ensure that every juvenile receives food that is suitably prepared and presented at normal meal times and of a quality and quantity to satisfy the standards of dietetics, hygiene and health and, as far as possible, religious and cultural requirements;[63] and

(xi) Clean drinking water should be available to every juvenile at any time.[63]

E. HUMAN RIGHTS OF ACCUSED RECOGNISED AND GUARANTEED AT NATIONAL LEVEL

As has been pointed out earlier, Universal Declaration of Human Rights, 1948, recognized certain basic human rights of an individual, including an accused. The Code of Criminal Procedure enacted in 1898 (as amended in 1973) also contained many provisions giving various rights to an accused. The Indian Constitution, in tune with the international endeavours, provided four basic principles to govern the criminal justice system, viz , (i) presumption of innocence, (ii) prevention of ex-post facto operation of criminal law, (iii) protection against double jeopardy and(iv) due process concept. Over and above, the 'right of equality and equal protection of laws', has been guaranteed to every citizen as a fundamental right.[64] The main rights of an accused which have been recognized and guaranteed by the Constitution may be stated as under:

(i) Right of Equality and Equal Protection of Laws;
(ii) Right against Ex-Post-Facto Operation of Law;
(iii) Protection against Double-Jeopardy;
(iv) Protection against Self-incrimination;
(v) Right to have freedom from unwanted arrest and matters incidental thereto;
(vi) Right to legal defence;
(vii) Right to have a public and Speedy Trial;
(viii) Right relating to Pre-trial detention and matters incidental thereto; and
(ix) Right to approach higher judicial authority for filing appeal, etc.

1. Right of Equality and Equal Protection of Laws

The 'concept of equality' as enshrined in Article 14 of the Constitution of India prohibits the State from denying equality before the law or the equal protection of the laws to any person on the ground of caste, creed, faith, race, religion, birth and place. The effective derivative source of the doctrine in the criminal justice is Article 21 of the Constitution of India which provides that: "No person shall be deprived of his life or personal liberty except according to procedure established by law." In a criminal trial, there are two parties : the state and the individual. However, both the parties are unmatching in their strength and resourcefulness, in which the individual, i.e., accused, is placed in a disadvantageous position. The role of the doctrine of equality becomes more significant in the context of the rights of a person who happens to be an accused of having committed a crime. This doctrine aims to achieve equality amongst unequal in prohibiting every kind of unjust, undeserved and unjustified inequalities in the administration of justice.[65] As the "right of equality" and the "equal protection of the laws" are to be secured through the instrumentalities of the state, the possible state actions do not conflict with the fundamental right of equality guaranteed against the state.[66]

2. Right against Ex-Post Facto Operation of Criminal Laws

An ex-post facto law is a law which imposes penalties retrospectively, i.e., on acts already done, and increases the penalty for such acts.[67] Clause (1) of Article 20 imposes a limitation on the law-making power of the legislature and prohibits the legislature to make retrospective criminal laws. However, it does not prohibit imposition of civil liability retrospectively, i.e., with effect from a past date.[68] Article 20 (1) runs as under:

> "No person shall be convicted of any offence except for violation of a law in force at the time of the commission of the act charged as an offence, nor be subjected to a penalty greater than that which might have been inflicted under the law in force at the time of the commission of the offence."

3. Protection against Double Jeopardy

Clause (2) of Article 20 of the Constitution recognises another important Human Right as a fundamental right of every citizen when it provides that: "No person shall be prosecuted and punished for the same offence more than once". This clause embodies the common law rule of *'nemo debt vis vexaria'* which means that 'no man should be put twice in peril for the same offence'. If he is prosecuted again for the same offence for which he has already been prosecuted he can take complete defence of his former conviction.[69] This right is also provided in the *Criminal Procedure Code,1973.*

4. Protection against Self-Incrimination

Clause (3) of Article 20 provides that "No person accused of any offence shall be compelled to be witness against himself." In other words, this Article prohibits all kinds of compulsions to make a person accused of an offence a witness against himself.[70] In this context, the Supreme Court in the case of ***M.P.Sharma v. Satish Chandra***[71], had observed that this right embodies three essentials, viz., (a) It is a right pertaining to a person who is "accused of an offence"; (b) It is a protection against "compulsion to be witness"; and (c) It is a protection against such compulsion relating to his giving evidence "against himself." This right can also be said to be the 'Right to Silence'. It may be mentioned that while the Criminal Procedure Code enjoins an accused person to answer truthfully the questions put to him by an investigating officer, Article 20 (2) gives him protection against self-incrimination. This principle is also contained in Article 14(g) of the *International Covenant on Civil and Political Rights, 1966.*

5. Right to have Freedom from unwanted Arrest and matters Incidental thereto

The arrest of a person has serious implications as it amounts to depriving him of his personal liberty. Protection of 'personal liberty of an individual' is his basic Human Right and, thus, in order to protect this human right relating to dignity of a person while arrest, the Supreme Court has interpreted Article 21 of the Constitution in favour of the accused. In India, arrest can be made with a warrant or without one. In the former case, there is already application of mind by a judicial authority, while in the latter case, such arrested person is required to be brought within 24 hours of arrest before the judicial authority. Clauses (1) and (2) of Article 22 guarantee the following rights to the persons who are arrested under an ordinary law:

(a) the right to be informed, as soon as may be, of ground of arrest;
(b) the right to be produced before a Magistrate within 24 hours; and
(c) the freedom from detention beyond the said period except by the order of the Magistrate.[72]

(a) The right to be informed of grounds of arrest

This right guaranteed by the Constitution to an accused to know the grounds of his arrest enables him to prepare for his defence. The delay in informing the grounds of arrest must be justified by reasonable circumstances. The Supreme Court in the case of ***State of M.P. v. Shobharam,***[73] has held that 'this right cannot be dispensed with by offering to make bail to the arrested person'. Further,the Supreme Court by its two leading judgments given in the cases of ***Joginder Kumar v. State of U.P.,***[74] and ***D.K. Basu v. State of West Bengal***[75], have laid down certain guidelines which should be invariably followed by the police and other officers arresting a person during investigation. These guidelines are proposed to be discussed in detail later on.[76]

(b) Right to be Produced Before a Magistrate

Clause (1) of Article 22 of the Constitution also provides that the arrested person must be produced before the Magistrate within 24 hours of his arrest excluding the time necessary for the journey from the place of arrest to the court of the magistrate. The time can be extended beyond 24 hours only under the judicial custody. It affords a possibility, if not an opportunity, for immediate release in case the arrest is not justified.[77]

(c) No Detention Beyond 24 Hours Except by Order of the Magistrate

It is also provided that if there is a necessity of detention beyond 24 hours, it is only possible under judicial custody. The expressions 'arrest' and 'detention' in Articles 22 (1) and (2) were held not to apply to a person arrested under a warrant issued by the court on a criminal or quasi-criminal complaint or under security proceedings.[78] Article 22 is not designed to give protection against the act of the executive or order of non-judicial authorities but applies to a person who has been accused of a crime or of offence of criminal or quasi-criminal nature or of some act prejudicial to the state or public interest.[79] Exception to clause (3) of Article 22 provides two exceptions to the rule contained in clauses (1) and (2) and the rights mentioned above are not available to an enemy, alien and a person arrested and detained under a Preventive Detention Law.

6. Right to have Legal Defence

'No person who is arrested shall be denied the right to consult and to be defended by a legal practitioner of his choice' - is the mandate enshrined in Article 22(1) of the Constitution. This right is also granted by Section 303 of the Code of Criminal Procedure, 1973. It has been held by the courts that this right to have a lawyer of his choice accrues to the arrested person from the time of his arrest. The accused may refuse to have a lawyer but the court has to provide an amicus curie to defend him in serious cases. The Supreme court in the case of ***Hussainara Khatoon v.***

Home Secretary, Bihar[80] has held that 'it is the Constitutional right of every accused person who is unable to engage a lawyer and secure legal services on account of reasons such as poverty, indigence or incommunicado situation, to have free legal services provided to him by the State; and the State is under a constitutional duty to provide a lawyer to such person in the case of a criminal trial. If an accused is not represented by any lawyer and he has not refused to avail the facility of free legal services provided by the State, the trial itself may be vitiated as contravening Art. 21 - "Protection of life and personality liberty."[81]

Article 39-A was added in the 'Directive Principle of State Policy' by the *42nd Constitution Amendment Act, 1976*, and a duty was imposed upon the State 'to ensure that the operation of the legal system promote justice on a basis of equal opportunities' and the State 'shall, in particular, provide free legal aid, by suitable legislation or schemes or in any other way, to ensure that opportunities for securing justice are not denied to any citizen by reason of economic or other disability'. The Supreme Court of India has declared now the 'Right to Free Legal Aid' and 'Right to Speedy Trial' as Fundamental Rights guaranteed under Article 21 of the Constitution of India. The accused need not apply for the same and the right to legal aid is implicit in the requirement of reasonable, fair and just procedure prescribed by Article 21; the failure to provide free legal aid to an accused at the State cost, unless refused by the accused, would vitiate the trial. [82] In order to fulfill the obligation imposed by Article 39-A, in the year 1987, the *Legal Services Authorities Act, 1987*, was enacted under which provisions were made to establish Legal Aid and Services Authorities at District, State and National levels for the purposes of providing legal aid and services. However, the necessary Rules were not framed by the Government and the implementation of the Act was delayed for a decade and the same could be implemented throughout India only in the year 1997.

7. Right to have a Public and Speedy Trial

The principle of openness of judicial proceedings acts as a check against caprice or vagaries and builds up confidence of the public in judicial administration. The right to have public trial is implit in Articles 14, 19(1)(a) and 21 of the Constitution and in the Criminal Procedure Code.

It is rightly said that 'Justice delayed is justice denied'. Though there are no specific provisions either in the Constitution or in the Code of Criminal Procedure for ensuring a speedy trial, the Supreme Court of India has held that this right is implicit under Article 21 of the Constitution.[83] Firstly, in the famous case concerning the trial of juvenile delinquents, namely, ***Sheela Barse v. Union of India,*** [84] the Supreme Court announced the time-schedule for the conclusion of a criminal trial of a juvenile accused. At that time, the Supreme Court showed his unwillingness to fix any time schedule for the conclusion of the trial of an adult accused. Later on, in a significant judgement delivered in ***Abdul Rehman Antuley v. R.S.Nayak,***[85] the detailed guidelines for speedy trial of an accused in a criminal case were laid down by the Supreme Court but the Supreme Court declined to fix any time limit for conclusion of a trial of offences. However, later on, the Supreme Court after four years, deviating from its old stand that 'it was not practical to fix any time limit', had laid down in the case of ***Common Cause v. Union of India,***[86] certain guidelines providing the time limit for conclusion of the criminal trial of an adult accused in specified cases. The right to speedy trial encompasses all the stages, namely the stage of investigation, inquiry, trial, appeal, revision and re-trial. [87]

8. Rights relating to Pre-Trial Detention and matters Incidental thereto

Many rights of an accused during custody – police or judicial – during trial have been recognized by the Supreme Court as implicit in Article 21 of the Constitution. An accused person is also a human being and, therefore, when he is in custody, during trail or awaiting for trial for any reason, his human dignity should be protected. In the case of ***Sunil Batra (No.2) v. Delhi Administration***[88] the learned ***Justice Krishna Iyer,*** delivering the majority judgement, has held that the '*integrity of physical person and his mental personality is an important right of a prisoner,* and must be protected from all kinds of atrocities'. It was opined that 'under trials were presumably innocent until convicted and the practice of keeping under trials with convicts in jails offended the test of reasonableness in Article 19 and fairness in Article 21 of the Constitution'. It was also held that 'the accused persons, in pre-trial or during trial detention, are entitled to *fair and decent treatment by way of comforts, medical attention*, etc., so that their humanity is not degraded and dignity is not offended. The Supreme Court had also granted to an accused an important right against *handcuffing*; the learned ***Justice Krishna Iyer*** opined in the case of ***Prem Shanker v. Delhi Administration***[89] that "Handcuffing is *prima facie* inhuman and, therefore, unreasonable, is overharsh and at the first flush, arbitrary. Absent fair procedure and objective monitoring, to inflict 'irons' is to resort to zoological strategies repugnant to Article 21". Further, in the case of ***Kishore Singh v. State of Rajasthan,***[90] the Supreme Court has held that the use of *third degree method* by police is violative of Article 21 and directed the Government to take necessary steps to educate the police so as to inculcate a respect for the human person. Similarly, *torture and ill treatment of women suspects in police lock up* have also been held to be violative of Article 21.[91] The monetary compensation has also been awarded by the Supreme Court in appropriate cases where there have been violations of the constitutional rights of accused or convicts.[92] By the landmark judgement delivered in ***Nilebati Behera v. State of Orissa,***[93] compensation of Rs. 1,50,000 was awarded by the Supreme Court to the mother of the accused who died in the police custody due to beating. In ***D.K. Basu v. State of West Bengal,*** [94] the Supreme Court while pronouncing a landmark judgement on 'rights of an arrestee', 'duties of police at the time of arrest', 'custodial deaths' and 'powers of Courts in the matter of torture to arrestee' had declared that the Court is empowered to award monetary compensation to an arrestee for the torture during the period of detention. These rights are proposed to be discussed in detail in subsequent chapters.[95]

9. Right to Approach Higher Judicial Authority by way of Filing Appeal, etc.

An appeal to the Supreme Court in Criminal matters has been envisaged by the Constitution of India. Articles 132 and 134 of the Constitution provide for an appeal to the Supreme Court on the 'certificate of fitness' granted by the High Courts and also for an appeal to the Supreme Court by special leave granted by it under Article 136 of the Constitution; but the appeal by special leave may be filed only when the certificate applied for filing an appeal has been refused by the High Court.

In the preceding pages, a modest effort an attempt has been made to discuss the need, evolution and nature of various rights of an accused available under statutory law and/or guaranteed by the Constitution. These rights have been enumerated in brief. Due to the limitation of time and space it is not feasible to examine the various aspects of all the rights available to an accused in detail. Hence, in the subsequent chapters of the present book it is proposed to discuss some basic fundamental rights which are available to an accused at different stages, i.e., prior to arrest, after arrest, during police and judicial custody, prior to trial and during trial. In the chapter to follow, firstly, it is proposed to discuss some fundamental rights of an accused which are available to him at every stage during the period he remains an accused (i.e., from the date of formal accusation levelled against him till he is finally convicted and punished or acquitted by the competent Court).

REFERENCES

1. Jacques Maritian, 'The Rights of Man', London, 1944, p. 37.
2. Varadchriar, S., 'The Hindu Judicial System', (1946), p. 938.
3. In Gautam, IX, 21-22; it is said:

   कर्षक, वणिक, पशुपाला कुमुदि कर्वः स्पेस्वे वर्गे ।

   तेभ्योयथधिकर्महन्प्रत्यव्यवहारित्व धर्म व्यवस्थाः ।।
4. Arthasastra, IV Chapter 9.
5. Sukranity, IV, 5, 114-17.
6. Katyayana on Brihaspati, Verse 496.

   कुलादिभिर निस्किवेपि न संतोषं गतत्सुयः

   विक्रय तत्क्रतम राजा कुक्रतम पुनरूद्धारेत्।।
7. Narads by Katyayana, Verse 295.
8. Pita Maha quaoted in Vyavhara Nirya p. 15.
9. Medhatithi, Manu, VII, 60; Gautam XIII, 8.
10. Abdur Rahim, 'Principles of Mahamadan Jurisprudence', p. 59.
11. Manucci, II, p. 198.
12. See Manrique, I, p. 424.

13. J.R.A.S., London, 1910, p. 764, Travels of Lee, p. 194, Al Badaoni II, pp. 76, 97.
14. *Ibid.*, Travels of Lee, p. 194; Badaoni refers to a Hindu Vakil, Rai Arzani of Khan Aman, Vol. II, pp. 76,97; Akhbarati - Darbar Mullah, 4th Oct. 1693. The following cases were argued by lawyers: 1. Amin Khan v. Manucci, (Theft), Storia II p. 198. 2. State v. Mirja Beg Kotwal, (Murder), Quvam Uddin argued the case, pp. 257-258, Khafi Khan II.
15. Saran, 'The provincial Government of Mughals', Allahabad, 1941, p. 377.
16. Collections, cited in Ahmed, M.B., 'Administration of Justice in Medieval India', Aligarh, 1941, p. 232.
17. Sotoia, I, pp. 174-175.
18. Vide Kotwal Mirza Beg v. State, Khafi Khan, II, p. 257.
19. See, Monrique I, 'Travels in India' (1629-43) edited by Eckford Luard and Father H. Hosten, p. 425.
20. See, Kitabul Ikhtyar, p. 59.
21. Vide, Aurangzeb's order.,
22. Ahmad M.B., 'The Administration of Justice in Medieval India', 1941, Aligarh, p. 180.
23. Badaoni, I, p. 187.
24. See Kitabul Ikhtiyar M.S., Add. 22714 F. 35, Fighe Firoz Shahi Vide (Collections) State v. Suleman, Cited by Ahmad, M.B., *op.cit.*
25. Fatwa III, Kitab Abdul Quazi, Luuck. Ed., pp. 519-20.
26. Waghela v. Sheik, 1887, 14 I.A. 89 of p. 96.
27. Mayor of Lyons v. East India Co., (1836) I Moore, Ind. App. 175.
28. Rankin, 'Background to Indian Law', 1846, p. 164.
29. Macaulay's letter to Lord John Russel, Jan. 19, 1837.
30. Indian Evidence Act, 1872, ss. 102 and 105.
31. Criminal Procedure Code, 1898, ss. 251-A, 256, 257: Now, ss. 240, 243, 247 of amended Criminal Procedure Code, 1973.
32. *Ibid.*, ss 60, 61: Now, ss. 56, 57 of amended Criminal Procedure Code, 1973.
33. *Ibid.*, ss. 173(4) and 251-A (i) : Now ss. 50, 173 of amended Criminal Procedure Code, 1973.
34. *Ibid.*, ss. 340(i): Now ss. 303 and 304 of amended Criminal Procedure Code, 1973.
35. *Ibid.*,ss. 352 :Now ss. 327 of amended Criminal Procedure Code, 1973.
36. Indian Evidence Act, 1872, ss. 137, 138, 143 & 144.
37. Criminal Procedure Code,1898, ss. 342(2) an 342(A): Now ss. 313 and 315(i) of amended Criminal Procedure Code, 1973.

38. *Ibid.*, s. 403: Now s. 300(1) of amended Criminal Procedure Code, 1973.
39. *Ibid.*, ss. 426, 496, 497: Now ss. 389, 436, 437, and 438 of amended Criminal Procedure Code, 1973.
40. *Ibid.*, s. 371 (3): Now s. 363 of amended Criminal Procedure Code, 1973.
41. Among the international instruments relating to criminal justice, mention can be made of the following:
    Convention against Torture and Other Cruel, Inhuman or Degrading Treatment or Punishment, 1984; Convention on the Rights of the Child,1989; Declaration against Torture, 1975; The Code of Conduct for Law enforcement Officials, 1979; Safeguards Guaranteeing protection of the Rights of Those Facing the Death Penalty, 1984; Principles on the Effective Prevention and Investigation of Extra-Legal, arbitrary and summary Executions, 1989; Principles for the Protection of Persons with Mental Illness and the Improvement of Mental Health Care, 1991; Declaration on the Protection of All Persons from Enforced Disappearance,1992; The Convention for the Protection of Human Rights and Fundamental Freedoms,1950; Body of Principles for the Protection of All Persons under any Form of detention or Imprisonment,1988; American Convention on Human Rights, 1969; and the African Charter on Human and Peoples Rights,1969 – to mention a few. See, *Compilation*, Vol. 1.
    See also, Upadhyay, C.M., 'Human Rights in Pre-Trial Detention', A.P.H. Publication, New Delhi,1999.
42. The United Nations Standard Minimum Rules for the Treatment of Prisoners,1955, 'Compilation', Vol. I, p. 243.
43. The United Nations Rules for the Protection of Juveniles deprived of their Liberty, 1990, 'Compilation', Vol. 1. Rule 17 runs as under: Juveniles who are detained under arrest or awaiting for trial (untried) are presumed innocent and shall be treated as such. Detention before trial shall be avoided to the extent possible and limited to exceptional circumstances. Therefore, all efforts shall be made to apply alternative measures. When preventive detention is nevertheless used, Juvenile courts and investigation bodies shall give the highest priority to the most expeditious processing of such cases to ensure the shortest possible duration of detention. Untried detainees should be separated from convicted Juveniles.
44. *Ibid.*, Rules 19 and 20.
45. *Ibid.*, Rules 21 to 26.
46. *Ibid.*, Rules 27 - 30.
47. *Ibid.*, Rules 31 - 37.

48. *Ibid.*, Rules 38 - 46.
49. *Ibid.*, Rule 47.
50. *Ibid.*, Rule 48.
51. *Ibid.*, Rules 49 - 55.
52. *Ibid.*, Rules 56 - 58.
53. *Ibid.*, Rules 59 - 62.
54. *Ibid.*, Rules 63 - 65.
55. *Ibid.*, Rules 66 - 71.
56. *Ibid.*, Rules 72 - 78.
57. *Ibid.*, Rules 79 and 80.
58. *Ibid.*, Rules 81 - 87.
59. *Ibid.*, Rule 31.
60. *Ibid.*, Rule 32.
61. *Ibid.*, Rule 33.
62. *Ibid.*, Rule 34.
63. *Ibid.*, Rule 37.
64. Article 14 of the Constitution of India provides that : "The State shall not deny to any person equality before the law or the equal protection of the laws within the territory of India."
65. Chaturvedi, A.N., 'Rights of Accused under Indian Constitution', Ist Edn. 1984, Deep & Deep Publications, New Delhi, p. 61.
66. *Ibid.*, at p. 60.
67. Hathi Singh Manufacturing Co. v. Union of India, A I R 1960 S.C. 923.
68. Pandey J.N., 'Constitutional Law of India', 1994, Central Law Agency, Allahabad, p. 158.
69. *Ibid.*, at pp. 159-160.
70. *Ibid.*, at p. 161.
71. A I R 1954 SC. 300.
72. Pandey J.N., 'Constitutional Law of India', 1994, Central Law Agency, Allahabad, pp. 192-193.
73. A I R 1966 S.C. 1910.
74. (1994) 2 SCALE Vol. II No. 7. 662.
75. A I R 1997 S.C. 610.
76. See, *Infra*, Chapter Three.
77. Pandey, J.N., 'Constitutional Law of India', 1994, Central Law Agency, Allahabad, p. 93.
78. *Ibid.*
79. *Ibid.*
80. A I R 1979 S.C. 1377.
81. Suk Das v. Union Territory of Arunachal Pradesh, (1986) 2 SCC 401. See also, M.H. Hoskot v. State of Maharashtra, A I R 1978 S.C. 527.

82. Suk Das v. Union Territory of Arunachal Pradesh, (1986) 2 SCC 401
83. Hussainara Khatoon (No.I) v. Home Secretary, State of Bihar, A I R 1979 S.C. 1360 followed in Kadra Pahadiya v. State of Bihar, A I R 1982 S.C.1167. See also, the cases of Hussainara Khatoon (No. 2), A I R 1979 S.C.1369 and Hussainara Khatoon's Case (No.3), A IR 1979 S.C. 1377.
84. A I R 1986 S.C. 1773.
85. A I R 1992 S.C. 1630.
86. (1996) 6 SCC 775.
87. A. R. Antuley v. R. S. Nayak, A I R 1992 S.C. 1630.
88. Sunil Batra (No. 2) v. Delhi Administration, A I R 1980 S.C. 1579.
89. A I R 1980 S.C. 1535. See also, Sunil Gupta v. State of M.P., (1990) 3 SCC 119.
90. A I R 1981 S.C. 625.
91. Sheela Barse v. State of Maharashtra, (1983) 2 SCC 96.
92. See, Rudal Singh v. State of Bihar, (1983) 4 SCC 141, Bhim Singh v. State of J.K., (1985) 4 SCC 677, State of Maharashtra v. Ravikant S Patil, (1991) SCC 373, People's Union for Democratic Rights v. Police Commissioner, Delhi Police Headquarter, (1989) 4 SCC 730.
93. (1993) 2 SCC. 746.
94. A I R 1997 S.C. 10.
95. See, *infra*, Chapters Three and Four.

Three

Human Rights of "Accused" Related to Arrest (Right to Know the Ground of Arrest, Powers of Arresting Authority and Right to be Produced before the Magistrate within Stipulated Time)

Attempts were made in the preceding chapters to examine the basis and evolution of various human rights of an accused and it was found that these rights are available to, and can be availed of by, an accused immediately from the time he becomes an accused, i.e., the date when the former allegation is levied against him, and continue to be available to him throughout the period he remains an accused, i.e., the date on which the final acquittal or conviction of the accused is made. Out of these various rights, some of the rights are guaranteed by the Constitution and some are available under the Code of Criminal Procedure and some are available under both – the Constitution and the Code of Criminal Procedure. Further, out of these various rights, some rights are available to an accused which are related to his arrest or detention (at the time of and after arrest) whereas some rights are available to him at every stage till his final acquittal or conviction. In this Chapter, it is proposed to discuss those rights of an accused which are related to his arrest / detention during police custody and the other rights which are available to him at every stage will be the subject matter of the next chapters. The main rights of an accused related to his arrest and detention during police custody are:

1. Right to Know the Grounds of Arrest;
2. Right to Know the Power of the Arresting Authority; and
3. Right to be Produced before the Magistrate within a Stipulated Time.

A. RIGHT OF ACCUSED TO KNOW THE GROUNDS OF ARREST

The *Criminal Procedure Code 1973,* contains several provisions with regard to the arrest of persons in Chapter V of the Code which deal with, *inter alia,* when police may arrest without warrant,[1] arrest on refusal to give name and residence,[2] arrest by private person and procedure on such arrest,[3] arrest by Magistrate,[4] protection of members of the Armed forces from arrest,[5] arrest how made,[60] search of place entered by person sought to be arrested,[7] pursuit of offenders into other jurisdiction,[8] no unnecessary restraint,[9] person arrested to be informed of grounds of arrest and of right to bail,[10] search of arrested person,[11] power to seize offensive weapons,[12] examination of accused by medical practitioner at the request of police officer,[13] examination of arrested person by medical practitioner at the request of the arrested person,[14] procedure when police officer deputes subordinate to arrest without warrant,[15] person arrested to be taken before Magistrate or Officer in Charge of Police Station,[16] person arrested not to be detained more than twenty four hours,[17] police to report apprehensions,[18] discharge of person apprehended,[19] and power, on escape, to pursue and re-take[20]. Out of these rights, the most important right which has been guaranteed as a 'fundamental right' of an accused by the *Constitution of India* as well as by Article 9(4) of the *International Covenant on Civil and Political Rights, 1966,* is the *Right to Know the Grounds of Arrest.* It is also pertinent to point out that the old *Criminal Procedure Code of 1898* did not contain any provision in this regard; a new provision has been made in the new *Criminal Procedure Code of 1973* recognising this right in the form of a duty of every police officer or other person arresting any person without warrant.

1. Genesis of the Right of an Accused to be Informed of Grounds

A democratic social order while conceding to the state the coercive power to use the criminal process against an individual also improvises ways and mean to protect the individuals so that the exercise of authority does not tend to become tyrannical. The criminal jurisprudence requires that in order to afford a person - accused of a crime - an opportunity to advance his defence at the earliest opportunity, he should be informed of the grounds of his alleged implication in the crime. This concept is enshrined in *Article 22(1) of the Constitution of India* and now, this right has become a constitutionally guaranteed right and is inviolable by ordinary law of the land.[21] This right has always been regarded as vital and fundamental for safeguarding personal liberty in all legal systems where the Rule of Law prevails. For instance, the VI Amendment to the United States Constitution contains similar provision and so does Article 34 of the Japanese Constitution of 1946. In England, whenever an arrest is made without a warrant the arrested person has a right to be informed not only that he is being arrested but also of the reasons and grounds.[22]

Under the ancient Criminal Procedure which differed from modern Criminal Procedure, persons after their arrest were kept in confinement more or less secret till their trials and they could not prepare for their defence as they had no information of the grounds of arrest and moreover of evidence against them. During the confinement, they were subjected to cruel treatments and tortures in order to extort admissions and confessions of guilt justifying for their arrest.[23] From time to time men have fought against arbitrary arrest and detention, i.e., measures of despotism. It was one of the grievances of the English Barons against King John in 1215 that prompted the inclusion of the following public opinion in the *Magna Carta* that[24]: "no free man shall be taken or imprisoned . . . except by the legal judgement of his peers or by the law of the land". The bitter reaction against this arbitrary arrest and detention led to the French Revolution which resulted in the *Declaration of the Rights of Men and Citizens of 1789* which incorporated that: "No man should be accused, arrested or held in confinement, except in cases determined by the law, and according to the forms which it has prescribed."[25]

In the United States of America, a person can be arrested by the police without warrant only when in the presence of the police a crime is committed, or there is an apprehension that the perpetrator might flee, or there is a 'probable cause' to do so. A 'probable cause' is not mere suspicion, or conjecture. Probable cause can be equated with the phrase, 'reasonable grounds' entailing sufficient evidence that a particular suspect is guilty of a particular crime. The arresting officer must take the arrested suspect to a judicial officer without unnecessary delay so that the object and validity of arrest may be judged by an independent impartial authority.[26]

The origin and development of this rule was deliberated upon by the *House of Lords* in 1947 in the case of ***Christie v. Laachinsky*** [27] and Lord Viscount Simson observed thus :

1. "If a policeman arrests without warrant upon reasonable suspicion of felony, or of other crime of a sort which does not require a warrant, he must in ordinary circumstances inform the person arrested of the true grounds of arrest.
2. "He is not entitled to keep reason to himself or to give a reason which is not the true reason. In other words, a citizen is entitled to know on what charge or on suspicion of what crime he is seized."
3. "The requirement that the person arrested should be informed of the reason why he is seized naturally does not exist, if the circumstances are such that he must know the general nature of the alleged offence for which he is detained."
4. "There is no need to explain the reasons of arrest if the arrested man is caught red-handed and the crime is patent to high Heaven."

2. Right of an Accused to be Informed of Grounds as Guaranteed by the Constitution of India

If the policemen are allowed to hold the suspects indefinitely and question them, they will naturally try to persuade the suspects to confess guilt. For, confession is the easiest and most satisfactory solution of a crime and also the justification of the arrest of the accused. It means the persuation may often take the form of "third degree" method of treatment. For this reason, the requirement for prompt furnishing of grounds of arrest and detention has been prescribed under Article 22(1) of the Constitution which provides that " No person who is arrested shall be detained in custody without being informed, as soon as may be of the grounds for such arrest."

Article 22 of the Constitution of India contains two parts. The first part is contained in clauses (1) and (2) which put limitations upon the Union and State legislatures in enacting any procedural law not in conformity with the enshrinement of clauses (1) and (2) of Article 22 for the deprivation of personal liberty of an accused. Thus, the ordinary law to which the limitations apply are that the arrested person must be informed of the grounds of his arrest as soon as may be[28] and that he must be produced within 24 hours of his arrest before the nearest Magistrate,[29] and that he must have an opportunity to consult and to be defended by a legal practitioner of his choice.[30] The second part contained by clauses (4) and (7) is excluded by clause (3) of Article 22 of the Constitution of India from the general principles contained by the first two clauses of that Article and those cover the special law of preventive detention and as such are in contradiction to the ordinary law set out in the first two clauses of the Article.

While moving Article 15-A in the Draft Bill of the Constitution (which corresponded to Article 22) with a view to make the 'Right of an accused to know the grounds of his arrest' as an integral part of the fundamental right, *Dr. B.R. Ambedkar* observed thus [31] :

> "Article 15-A merely lifts from the provisions of the Criminal Procedure Code two of the most fundamental principles which every civilized country follows as principles of international justice. It is quite true that these two provisions contained in clause (1) and clause (2) already to be found in the Criminal Procedure Code and thereby probably it might be said that we are really not making any very fundamental change. But we are as contend making a fundamental change because what we are doing by introduction of Article 15-A is to put a limitation upon the authority both of Parliament as well as of the provincial legislature not to abrogate these two provisions, because they are now introduced in our Constitution itself."

It is pertinent to note that this right could not be claimed by an accused immediately after his arrest in the pre-Constitution period. This right was protected and claimable by an accused under Section 173 of the Criminal Procedure Code, 1898, only when the police report was filed after the completion of investigation into the commission of an offence; of course, trial of the accused could not be held in the absence of the copy of the charge sheet before starting his trial in the court. However, after the incorporation of this right under clause (1) of Article 22 of the Constitution, a new section was included in the new *Cr. P. C.,1973,* which added a new vista in the promotion of human rights and personal liberty of an accused. As per Section 50(1) of the *Cr. P. C., 1973* : "Every Police Officer or other person arresting any person without warrant (other than in preventive detention measures) shall forthwith communicate to him full particulars of the offence for which he is arrested or other grounds for such arrest." Section 50 (2) of the *Cr. P. C., 1973,* provides that 'if the arrest is made without a warrant in a bailable case, the accused should be informed of his right to be released on bail after furnishing sureties.' With the recognition of this new right in the *Cr. P. C., 1973,* the protection and preservation of civil liberty of the Indian citizens has been well recognised by the law relating to Criminal Procedure. However, this new provision of the *Cr. P.C., 1973,* only covers the cases of arrest of an accused without warrant. This does not confer a right to be informed of the grounds of arrest to an accused arrested with warrant. No such distinction, i.e., arrest with warrant and arrest without warrant, has been made in the Constitutional provision contained in Article 22(1) of the Constitution.

3. Definition of 'Arrest' and its various types in the context of the Right of an Accused to be Informed of Grounds

'Arrest' under English Law has been defined as "the restraining of the liberty of a man's person in order to compel obedience to the order of the court of justice or to prevent the commission of crime or to ensure that a person charged or suspected of a crime may be forthcoming to answer it. To arrest a person is to restrain him of his liberty by some lawful authority."[32] The new *Encyclopaedia Britannica* states arrest as " . . . If arrest occurs in the course of criminal procedure, the purpose of the restrain is hold the person for answer to a criminal charge or to prevent him from committing an offence. . ."[33] According to the *Corpus Juris Secundum,* an arrest is the "taking, under real or assumed authority, custody of another person for purpose of holding or detaining him to answer a criminal charge or civil demand".[34] The expression arrest has been defined in *Wharton's Law Laxicon*, thus :

> "The restraining of liberty of a man's person in order to compel obedience to the order of a Court of Justice, or to prevent the commission of a crime, or to ensure that a person charged or suspected of a crime may be forthcoming to answer it."[35]

Section 46(1) of the *Criminal Procedure Code, 1898*, retained by the new Code provides that : "In making an arrest the police officer or other person making the same shall actually touch or confine the body of the person to be arrested, unless there be a submission to the custody by word or action".

Thus, the arrest is made in relation to the commission or prevention of a crime and submission to a criminal charge or civil demand. The word "arrest" is a comprehensive term and is inclusive in effect and character as it appears in Article 22(1) of the Constitution. The Punjab High Court held that in view of the comprehensive meaning of the word "arrest" used in Article 22(1) and (2), 'an abducted person apprehended under the provisions of Section 4 of the *Abducted persons (Recovery and Restoration) Act of 1949* for the purposes of being delivered to the custody of an officer-in-charge of a camp was an arrested person and thus was held entitled to the protection of Article 22 though no offence was committed or was alleged to have been committed.[36] However, the decision of the Punjab High Court has been reversed by the Supreme Court and while considering the definition of 'arrest' for the first time in the context of Article 22(1) and (2), the Supreme Court held that 'the application of Article 22(1) and (2) in the cases of arrests made under warrants was not necessary. Where arrests are made under warrants issued by the magistrates there had already been the application of judicial mind and the arrested person was made acquainted with grounds of arrest before it was actually effected; while in arrest otherwise than under warrants the compliance of Article 22(1) and (2) was mandatory in order to ensure "the immediate application of a judicial mind to the legal authority of the person making the arrest and the regularity of the procedure adopted by him".[37]

A person may be deprived of his personal liberty by arrest or detention in the following various ways:

1. Arrest and detention of a person made for his trial for an offence committed by him. Such arrest and detention may be either (a) on a warrant issued by a magistrate, or (b) by the police without warrant;
2. Arrest and detention of a person made after conviction under a sentence passed by a Court;
3. Arrest and detention of a person made under preventive detention law;
4. Arrest and detention of a person made under the preventive provisions of chapter VIII of the Code of Criminal Procedure;
5. Arrest and detention of a person made under an order of a civil court in aid of civil process; and lastly.
6. Arrest and detention of a person made under various statutes without any accusation of a crime or criminal conduct.

After the decision given in *Ajaib Singh's case* it was held again by the Supreme Court in ***Collector of Malabar v. Erimmal Ebrahim Hazee***[38] that 'before a person could be said to be "arrested" within the meaning of Article 22(1) and (2) of the Constitution, a double test had to be satisfied. First, that the arrest should be by the executive and not by an order of the court under a warrant of arrest issued by a court; and second, that it must be on an accusation of some offence or some prejudicial activity on the part of the arrested person.' Later on, in the case of ***State of U.P. v. Abdul Samad***[39] , the Supreme Court in its majority judgment although did not decide this question of arrest under Article 22(1) as it was unnecessary in the particular circumstances of the case, *Justice Subba Rao,* in his dissenting judgment stated that the arrest and detention of a foreigner for the purpose of deportation was not outside the scope of Article 22(2). Mr. Justice Hidaytullah also later on in the case of ***State of M.P. v. Shobharam,*** [40] opined that 'arrest is arrest whatever may be the reasons for it and the first part of Article 22(1) enjoins a duty on an arresting person to tell the grounds of arrest if made otherwise than under a warrant ; and if it is made under a warrant, the warrant must itself inform the arrested person with the grounds of arrest. In the same case, *Justice Bachhawat* and *Justice Shelat* also, in the context of enabling an accused to look for the second enshrinment of Article 22(1) - the right to counsel - expressed an opinion of doubt as to the exhaustiveness of the test laid down in *Ajaib Singh's case*. It maybe argued that the whole language of Article 22(1) of the Constitution revolves round the right to counsel. A question arises as to how can that right be attached to one kind of arrest and detention and will be denied to another kind of arrest and detention, i.e., arrest otherwise than under a warrant and under those statutes which do not impute any crime or criminal conduct on the part of the arrested person. The Constitution framers were well versed in legal knowledge and aware of these types of arrest and detention; had they intended to exclude same type they would have done so in sub-Article 22(3) as they had done in respect of alien enemy and preventive detention detenus.[41]

It is submitted that the conclusion of the Supreme Court in the *Ajaib Singh's case* that 'apprehension of an abducted person under the provisions of Section 4 of the *Abducted persons (Recovery and Restoration) Act of 1949* for the purposes of being delivered to the custody of an officer-in-charge of a camp was not an arrest' is correct but the observations made by *Justice S.R. Das,* that 'Articles 22(1) and (2) come into play only when the arrest is made by an executive authority and not by judicial authority' is unfortunate from the point of view of human rights of an arrested person. The reason given by the learned justice for this observation was that in the case of arrest effected under a warrant application of judicial mind is made; however, it is submitted that the learned judge erred in equating the application of judicial mind *ex-parte* and on hearing both the sides for and against. On the basis of the observations made by the Supreme Court in latter cases, it may be summed up that the decision in *Ajaib Singh case* is not a final word and further consideration is necessary. The word "arrested" occurring in Article 22(1) should be given in amplitude of wide connotation, so as to include all arrests excepting those made in pursuance of a conviction for the purpose of serving out the sentence of imprisonment pronounced by a judicial tribunal. The expression 'arrest and detention' used in clause (1) of Article 22 of the Constitution is meant to apply to all arrests and detentions made under any law - may it be punitive or preventive or under any civil process or under any revenue recovery process. Narrowing down by any rule of construction and interpretation of statute the scope and ambit of the Constitutional minimum requirement to be followed after arrest and detention shall amount to violation of inviolable right guaranteed by the Constitution to an accused and the Constitutional enshrinement would be robbed of its effect in letter and also in spirit.

4. Minimum Time Limit prescribed for Informing the Grounds of Arrest to an Accused

While the arrested person is entitled to be furnished with the grounds of his arrest as per Article 22 (1), he cannot expect a minimum time limit guaranteed to him. The expression, "as soon as may be" used in Article 22 (1) means "as nearby as is reasonable in the circumstances of a particular case". The same expression occurs in clause (5) of Article 22 also which is exclusively, been made applicable to the arrests and detentions made under preventive detention measures. However, the expression occuring in both the clauses of the Article is one and the same and means one and the same thing. Therefore, the time limit to furnish the grounds of arrest and detention to an accused shall depend on the circumstances and fact situations of a particular case and shall differ from case to case. However, this type of uncertainty of the time limit for being informed of the grounds of arrest has been removed and the time has been made certain by using the expression "forthwith" in the newly added Section 50 (1) of the *Cr.P.C., 1973,* which is applicable in the cases of arrest made without warrant.

5. Meaning of the Expression "Grounds of Arrest" in the context of Constitutionally Guaranteed Right of an Accused

The interpretation of the expression 'grounds of arrest' to be furnished to an accused becomes relevant because the grounds must be sufficient so as to enable the accused to avail of the second privilege enshrined in Article 22(1) ,i.e., the 'Right to Counsel'. In this context, it has been held by the Supreme Court in *Shibban Lal*

Saxena v. State of U.P.,[42] that 'if one of the two grounds was irrelevant or was wholly illusory, the detention order as a whole would be vitiated.' The various views / opinion expressed by the judiciary in this regard can be summed up as under:

(a) Where good grounds were mixed up with vague, indefinite and bad grounds, the arrest and detention could not be said to be in accordance with the procedure established by law;[43]

(b) Grounds must particularise the offence so as to enable the petitioner to make adequate representation against his arrest and detention and in the absence of such particularisation, the grounds would be vague, indefinite and irrelevant;[44]

(c) The expression "to be informed of the grounds of arrest and detention" does not mean the full disclosure of facts giving rise to a reason or cause of arrest and detention and withholding of the facts was not in contravention of the Constitution rights of the accused;[45]

(d) Arrest of the railway porters on the Railway station - platform housing them in jail and on the following day in the premises of the jail their conviction after conducting summary trial without being informed of the grounds of their arrest was an invasion of the constitutional right of the porters;[46]

(e) It is not necessary for the arresting authorities to furnish full details of the offence but it should be somewhat similar to the charge framed by the court for the trial of a case;[47]

(f) It is the duty of the Magistrate to ask the accused person, brought before a Magistrate under Section 167 of the *Cr. P. C., 1973*, whether he has been informed of the grounds of arrest;[47]

(g) A mention in the warrant that the accused was being wanted in connection with certain offence for which he was arrested is sufficient compliance of Article 22(1)[48].

In the case of ***Vimal Kishore v. State of U.P.,***[49] Mr. Justice M. C. Desai, of Allahabad High Court, while holding the communication of grounds to be insufficient, explained the nature of "grounds to be furnished" as enshrined under Article 22(1) of the Constitution in the following words[50]

> "If a person is arrested on a warrant the grounds or reasons for arrest of the warrant is read over to him, that is sufficient compliance with the requirement that he should be informed of the grounds of his arrest; if he is arrested without warrant, he must be told why he has been arrested. If he is arrested for committing an offence, he must be told that he has committed a certain offence, for which he would be placed on trial. In order to inform him that he has committed certain offence, he must be told of the acts done by him which amount to the offence. . . He must be informed of precise act done by him for which he would be tried; informing him merely of the law applicable to that act would not be enough."

In the case of ***In re Madhu Limaye***,[51] the arrest and detention of Madhu Limaye and his companions was held illegal and without the authority of law because they had not been informed of the grounds of arrest. In this case the petitioners applied for the issue of a writ of *habeas corpus* by addressing a letter through jail and complained that their detention and confinement in jail was unconstitutional (violation of Article 22(1) of the Constitution) and without the compliance of legal provision. In the return reply filed by the State this assertion was neither controverted nor anything was stated in this regard. Assumingly, the authorities tried to invoke all kinds of the provisions like Sections 151, 107/117 of the Criminal Procedure Code apart from Section 188 of the Penal Code and since no arrest could be affected for an offence under Section 188 of I.P.C. by the Police Officers without proper orders, these officers had been naturally reluctant to comply with the mandatory requirements of Article 22(1) of the Constitution and no reasons of their arrest were told to them.

It is pertinent to point out that there is nothing special in reference to the right of a female accused to be informed of grounds; the same provision and process applicable to a male accused, is applied in the case of female accused. However, special provision had been made for delinquent Juveniles under the *Juvenile Justice Act 1986*. According to Section 19 of this Act , 'where a Juvenile is arrested, the officer-in-charge of Station shall, as soon as may be, send information to the parents, guardian and the probation officer regarding such arrest and direct him to be present at the juvenile court before which the juvenile will appear.' Although this section does not specify as to what should be the contents of this information, impliedly it would include the information regarding the place of arrest, the place of juvenile court where the juvenile will be produced, time and date when such juvenile will be produced and brief description of the arrest. Although the *Juvenile Justice Act,* 1986 , has now been replaced by the *Juvenile Justice (Care and Protection of Children) Act, 2000,* similar requirements have been retained in the *J.J. Act, 2000* also. The detailed examination of these special provisions are proposed to be made separately.[52]

B. RIGHT OF AN ACCUSED TO KNOW THE POWER OF THE ARRESTING AUTHORITY

In addition to the recognition of the right of the accused 'to know the grounds of arrest', as discussed above, the *Criminal Procedure Code, 1973,* also gives an additional right to an accused vide Section 55, i.e., right to know the power of the arresting person to arrest the accused. By this section which is applicable when arrest is made by an officer-in-charge of a police station or any police officer making an investigation or any officer subordinate to him, a duty is imposed upon the superior officer to deliver an order in writing to the officer required to make the arrest specifying : (a) the person to be arrested, and (b) the offence or other cause for which the arrest is to be made. Further, the officer so directed to make the arrest is also under a statutory duty: (a) to notify to the person to be so arrested the substance of the order, and (b) if so required by such person, to show him the order.This section is, however, related to the arrest made without warrant.

In case an arrest is to be made under a warrant of arrest, Section 75 of *Cr. P.C., 1973,* imposes a duty upon the police officer or other person executing a warrant of arrest to notify the substance thereof to the person to be arrested and also to show such person the warrant so that he may read it and know the grounds of arrest and power of the police officer or other person arresting him. It is to be noted that the provisions of Section 55 of *Cr. P.C., 1973,* empowering a person to be arrested to know the power of the arrester is not applicable in the case in which arrest can be made by any police officer without an order from a Magistrate and without a warrant as has been specified in Section 41 of the *Cr.P.C., 1973.* An additional right to an accused has been provided with regard to arrest by this section.

In this context, the judgment given by the Madras High Court in ***In re Appaswami Mudaly***[53] is relevant in which it has been held that 'a man is entitled to know, when a constable is arresting him, that under what power he is acting and if the constable states that he acts under certain power, which the man knows he has not got, the man so arrested is entitled to object to arrest and to escape from custody when he is arrested.' The opinion of Justice Krishnan are worth quoting. He said that :

> When a constable arrests a man and tells him expressly that he is doing so under a particular authority, which he claims to have to arrest him and if such arrest is resisted, it will be for the prosecution afterwards to establish that the constable who arrested the man had power to act under the authority that he claimed to have. It is not sufficient for the prosecution afterwards to say that the constable had authority under some other provision of law. *I think any man who is being arrested, has a right to ask the officer arresting him to show him what power he has to do so. If the arrest is under a warrant it has been held that the man arrested is entitled to ask that the warrant be shown to him to see that he is being properly arrested and that when the warrant is not shown to him and the arrest is made, such an arrest will not be a legal arrest".* (Emphasis added)

C. RIGHT OF AN ACCUSED TO BE PRODUCED BEFORE A MAGISTRATE WITHIN STIPULATED TIME, i.e., TWENTY-FOUR HOURS

1. Genesis of the Right to be Produced before a Magistrate within Stipulated Time

Prior to the adoption of the Indian Constitution, Sections 60 and 61 of the *Criminal Procedure Code, 1898,* provided that a person arrested and detained by a police officer without or with warrant must be produced before a magistrate; under the former provisions of the Code 'within twenty-four hours' and under the latter provisions, 'without unnecessary delay' from the time of arrest. Since the privileges of this kind contained in the Criminal Procedure Code could be taken away or abridged by the Legislature any time, the Constituent Assembly expressed dissatisfaction in relation to deprivation of personal liberty in accordance with the procedure established by law proposed to be embodied in Article 21 of the Constitution. In order to make these rights inviolable by an ordinary law of the land, the 'right of being produced before a nearest magistrate within twenty-four hours without unnecessary delay was Constitutionally guaranteed by Article 22(2).

2. Right of an Accused to be Produced before a Magistrate within Stipulated Time as Guaranteed by the Constitution of India

Article 22 (2) of the Constitution of India provides another procedural safeguard to an accused in the form of a fundamental right that : "Every person who is arrested and detained in custody shall be produced before the nearest Magistrate within a period of twenty-four hours of such arrest excluding the time necessary for the journey from the place of arrest to the court of the Magistrate" It is further provided by the same Article that "no such person shall be detained in custody beyond the said period without the authority of a Magistrate." Thus, the maximum time limit for which the police can keep a person under detention is twenty-four hours at his own authority ; even if the arrest and detention is *malafide* and contrary to law, the arresting officer may not be liable to be sued for damages for false imprisonment. Detention beyond twenty-four hours without being produced and authorised by a Magistrate shall be illegal.[54] In this connection actual time of arrest is material in order to judge whether the police authorities did or did not comply with the Constitutional requirments of Article 22(2) of the Constitution.[55] This right has been recognized with three fold objectives in mind[56]:

(i) To prevent arrest and detention for the purpose of extracting confessions or as a measure of compelling people to give information;

(ii) To afford an early recourse to a judicial officer independent of the police on all questions of bail or discharge; and

(iii) To prevent police stations being used as they were prisons.

3. Right of an Accused to be Produced before a Magistrate within Stipulated time under Criminal Procedure Code, 1973

'In every civilized society 'personal liberty' of an individual is protected by law and law does not permit detention of any person unless there is legal sanction for it. Section 56 of the *Code of Criminal Procedure, 1973,* requires that "a police officer making an arrest without warrant shall, without unnecessary delay and subject to the provisions herein contained as to bail, take or send the person arrested before a Magistrate having jurisdiction in the case or before the officer-in-charge of a police station". Further, Section 57 of the *Cr. P.C., 1973,* prohibits a police officer from detaining the arrested person for more than 24 hours, exclusive of the time necessary for the journey from the place of arrest to the magistrate's court.[57] Sections 56 and 57 of the *Cr. P. C., 1973,* come into play only when a person is arrested without a warrant. In case a person is arrested under a warrant of arrest, the provisions of Section 76 of the *Cr. P. C., 1973,* are applicable which require the police officer or other person executing warrant of arrest 'to bring the person arrested, without unnecessary delay, before the court before which he is required by law to produce such person.' It is to be noted that although no time is given in these sections, only the expression 'without unnecessary delay' has been used but it has been provided that such delay shall not, in any case, exceed twenty-four hours from the time of arrest exclusive of the time necessary for the journey from the place of arrest to the Magistrate's Court. As had been earlier stated, the right of an accused granted under Sections 56 or 57 or 76 regarding the production before a Magistrate within a stipulated time has also been Constitutionally recognized and guaranteed by Article 22(2) which are inviolable by ordinary legislative enactments.

4. Distinction between Constitutional Provision and Provisions of Criminal Code

In order to understand the scope of statutory right in conjunction with the Constitutional right, a distinction should be made between Article 22(2) of the Constitution and Sections 56 and 57 of the *Cr. P. C., 1973*. The language used in Sections 56 and 57 is "arrested without warrant", while the phrase used under Article 22(2) is "arrested and detained" and is without any qualification. Secondly, the word "every person" used in the Article means all persons without any distinction. Thirdly, the word "Magistrate" used in the said Article is qualified by the word "nearest" whereas in the provision of the Code, the word "Magistrate" is generally qualified by the term jurisdiction. These differences by the Constitutional guarantee of fundamental right from the Criminal Procedure are of very great importance. Thus, the right of being produced before a Magistrate within 24 hours from the time of arrest guaranteed by the Constitution is extendable to all arrests and detentions whether with a warrant or without a warrant.

Sections 41(1) and (2) of the *Cr. P. C., 1973*, empower any police officer to arrest any person who has been concerned in a cognizable offence or against whom a reasonable complaint has been made or a credible information is received or a reasonable suspicion exists of his having been so concerned. Police officer can arrest such person without an order from a Magistrate and without a warrant.[58] Though this section gives a very wide power of arrest in cognizable offences yet it is not without limitations. Definite knowledge and information is required of a police officer before embarking to act under the provisions of Section 41. The law did not intend to give a license to every policeman moving about on the road to arrest and search any person at his own sweet will merely upon some suspicion of his own which may have no reasonable foundation at all.

5. Judicial Interpretation Regarding the Application of the Constitutional Right of the Accused

The deprivation of personal liberty otherwise than according to the procedure established by law has been protected by Article

21 of the Indian Constitution. The expression "procedure established by law" does not mean in accordance with the principles of natural justice but the expression means here the "procedure established by positive state made law" i.e., the law enacted[58] by the Parliament or State Legislature and that should be within its legislative competence. Now the law and the procedure both should be reasonable, fair and just.[59] The law should be valid one and must not be inconsistent with the Fundamental Rights guaranteed under Part III of the Constitution. Before a person can be deprived of his personal liberty, all the requirements of the Constitution and of any other law that may be applicable to the case, must be strictly complied with.[60]

The arrest and detention must not only be valid at its commencement but also be valid throughout. If the detention is valid *ab initio,* it may cease to be so if some provision of law of the Constitution is violated subsequently and in that case the person so detained shall be entitled to be set at liberty forthwith.[61]

Article 22(2) of the Constitution is applicable only at a stage when a person is first arrested in connection with accusation of an offence, or other prejudicial activities against the interest of the state, but not after such person has been found and adjudged guilty of the offence and is arrested and detained in pursuance of the judgement or order of the judicial tribunal. So also where a person has been convicted and sentenced for the contempt of the House by Legislative Assembly of a state, his production before a Magistrate is not required and if produced would be futile. Magistrate would have no power either to release him on bail or make any other order regarding his custody. Hence, detention without the Magistrate's authority of a member or any person convicted and sentenced for contempt of the House of the Legislative Assembly of a State is not violative of Article 22(2).[62]

An arrest under a warrant of a civil court in execution of decree, and arrest made before judgment under a warrant of a civil court are not arrests so as to attract Article 22(2), for they are made under judicial process.[63] It has been held by the Supreme Court that the arrest and detention of an assessee in a civil prison for his failure to pay income tax dues is not arrest within the meaning of Article 22(2).[64] In ***Gunpati Keshavran Reddy v. Nafisul***

Hasan[65], it was alleged that Mr. Homi Dinshaw Mistry was arrested in Bombay and was taken in custody to Lucknow to be produced before the Speaker of U. P. Legislative Assembly for the answer of a charge of breach of privilege of the House. In the instant case the detenu was accused of an offence and could not be produced before a Magistrate within twenty-four hours of his arrest. Therefore, his detention in the Speaker's Custody beyond the period of twenty-four hours was without the authority of a Magistrate and was held illegal. His release was forthwith, ordered; for it was in flagrant disregard of the Constitutional provisions of Article 22(2) which is pre-emptory in terms that "No such person shall be detained in custody beyond the said period without the authority of a Magistrate".

As has been pointed out earlier, in the case of ***State of Punjab v. Ajaib Singh*** [66], the Supreme Court has held that the custody of a person taken by the executive not on the charge of any offence or any prejudicial activity was no "arrest" within the meaning of Article 22(2). This decision may be correct but the *Obiter Dicta,* made by the Supreme Court in ***Ajaib Singh's case***[67] that 'there was a distinction between arrest with a warrant and arrest without a warrant and that Article 22(2) did not apply to the arrest with a warrant' seems to be far from the sound judicial approach and the Constitutional spirit. The reasons are : (a) The phrase used in Sections 60 and 61 of the Code of Criminal Procedure, 1898 is "arrested without warrant" while the phrase used in Article 22(2) of the Constitution is "arrested and detained" without any qualification; (b) Secondly, the word "Magistrate" used in two provisions of the Code has been suffixed by the expression "jurisdiction", while the word "Magistrate" used in Article 22(2) is qualified by the superlative degree "nearest"; (c) Thirdly, the warrant is secured *ex-parte* and as such the application of judicial mind is one sided; and (d) Lastly, the use of word "every" before "person" in the Article suggests all persons arrested while in the provisions of the Code the word "person" used has no qualifications. For these reasons it is submitted that the right of being produced attaches in both cases - arrest with a warrant, and arrest without a warrant. Similarly, the Calcutta High Court in ***Raj Bahadur v. Legal Remembrancer***[68], held that the removal of a girl from a brothel under Section 13 of the *Bengal Suppression of Immoral Traffic Act, 1933,* was not an arrest. So, also where a female abducted for any unlawful purpose is taken into custody under Section 98 of the *Code of Criminal Procedure,1973,*[69] (Section 100 of *Cr.P.C., 1898*) for restoration to her kith and kin is not an arrest.[70] But where a search warrant was issued to search a person wrongfully confined, it was held that the person if found would be immediately be taken to the Magistrate issuing search warrant for orders.[71]

The word "Magistrate" used in the constitutional provision and in the provision of the Cr. P. C. ,1973, has been interpreted by the judiciary meaning thereby, a Magistrate functioning as a court and not as an executive officer. It has been held that the expression "Magistrate" and "Magistrate's Court" used in Article 22(2) of the Constitution and in Sections 56 and 57 of the *Cr. P. C. ,1973,* are interchangeable and mean one and the same thing. In ***Prabhakar Nath v. Distt. Magistrate***[72], the petitioner, President of the Allahabad University Student's Union arrested and detained under Sections 112 and 117 of the Cr.P.C., was produced before the Magistrate posted at Kotwali functioning as an Executive Magistrate, at odd hours. The Allahabad High Court held that there was no violation of Article 22(2), because while granting a remand, he applied his judicial mind and functioned as a court; and the production of the petitioner before him was before a Court of Magistrate under Article 22(2) of the Constitution.It is submitted that the conclusion of the court might be correct but the *obiter dicta* that the production of an arrested person before a Magistrate who was on duty at Kotwali duty was production before the Court seems to be incorrect because an officer while on executive duty cannot act judicially but without bias and executive bent of mind. In Kotwali a magistrate is surrounded by police officers while sitting in the court he is before public and the environment makes psychologically a substantial difference in his attitude. It has also been held by the Allahabad High Court that a detention made under an order of a Magistrate under Section 123-A of the Code of Criminal Procedure (U.P. Amendment Act), 1898, acting as person designate of State Government under special enactment was illegal.[73]

6. Arrest by Magistrate and Thereafter Grant of Remand

In the case of ***Hariharanand v. The Jailor I/C Dist. Jail, Banaras***[74], a question was raised before the Allahabad High Court that, 'when a Magistrate acting in executive capacity under Section 44 (64 of the former code) of the *Cr. P. C., 1973,* arrests an individual and subsequently remands the arrestee to the custody, will the order of remand to the custody made by the arresting Magistrate be an order of the Magistrate under Article 22(2) of the Indian Constitution?'. In the present case the petitioners were arrested by a Magistrate acting under Section 64 of the Criminal Procedure Code, 1898,[75] for their obstructions to the Harijan's entry into Vishwanath temple which amounted to an offence under Section 6 of the *U.P. Removal of Social Disabilities Act, 1947*. The arresting Magistrate on the same day remanded them to the judicial custody. It was held that they were not produced before a court - within twenty-four hours of the arrest, thus their detention beyond twenty-four hours was held illegal and unconstitutional. The reason given was that the Magistrate while acting in executive capacity had no opportunity of applying judicial mind. Further, since the same person cannot be a judge in his own cause, the Magistrate acting in executive capacity cannot be a court, as contemplated by Section 167 of the Code. Similarly, in ***Bir Bhadra Pratap Singh v. D.M. Azamgarh***[76] the petitioner (accused), an advocate, was arrested in the presence of a Magistrate present at the scene of the incident and was produced before him. The order of remand given by that Magistrate under Section 167 was rightly held illegal, because the Magistrate in this case acted "as a judge in his own cause". There is a distinction between judicial function and executive function of a Magistrate. The judicial function of a Magistrate cannot be restricted within the court premises and so also within the working hours of the court. An order of remand passed under Section 167 of the *Cr. P. C., 1973,* in the early hours of morning, or at odd hours in the night could not be assailed as not passed by him while acting as a court. The function of a Magistrate while remanding to custody under Section 167 of the *Cr. P. C., 1973,* is a judicial one and he has to apply his judicial mind on the arrest and has to consider whether the arrest of the person produced before him is legal, regular and in accordance with law as commanded by Article

22(2) of the Constitution. In ***In re Madhu Limaye***[77], the Supreme Court has observed that the object of Article 22(2) is intended to offer protection against the acts of the executive and other non-judicial authorities; and if the Magistrate acts mechanically without applying his judicial mind in the matter of the arrest of the person produced before him the protection offered by Article 22(2) would be meaningless.

Both under Article 22(2) of the Constitution and Section 167 of the *Cr. P. C., 1973,* the actual production of the accused person before a Magistrate is required for obtaining an order of remand; but neither of the provisions require actual production of the accused before the Magistrate on the subsequent dates of remand. It is submitted that though provisions do not require, yet the production of the accused on the subsequent dates of remand it is desirable to produce the arrested person; for the accused may like to tell about his detention which may draw the Magistrate's judicial mind. Remand to police custody under Section 167 of the *Cr. P. C., 1973,* should be allowed only in special cases and for such limited periods as the necessities of the case might require. The remand should not be granted without sufficient cause being shown for it. It is not necessary that the remand should be granted only by a Magistrate having jurisdiction; any Magistrate can grant remand, this latitude is given to the police. Where the maximum period of remand, i.e., 15 days are allowed, has expired no further remand can be granted under Section 167 of the Code. The object of remand to police custody is to facilitate the investigation of the offence but if the circumstances of the case do not necessitate police lock-up, the Magistrate can send the accused to the judicial lock-up in the very beginning. It is the discretion, which should be judicially exercised always after taking into account the full particulars and circumstances of each case.

7. Duty of the Police Officer to Notify the Arrest to certain Specified Persons

There are some special circumstances in existing statutory law where there is a statutory duty of the police officer to notify the arrest. Section 58 of the *Cr. P.C., 1973,* provides thus:

"Officers in charge of police station shall report to the

> District Magistrate or, if he so directs, to the Sub-Divisional Magistrate, the cases of all persons arrested without warrant, within the limit of their respective stations whether such persons have been admitted to bail or otherwise."

Section 19(a) of the *Juvenile Justice Act, 1986*, provided that 'the parent or guardian of the child, if he can be found, shall be informed of the arrest and be directed to be present at the children's court before which the child will appear'. Rule 229 of the *Procedure and Conduct of Business in Lok Sabha* provides thus:

> When a member is arrested on criminal charge or is detained under an executive order of the Magistrate, the executing authority must inform without delay such fact to the Speaker. As soon as the arrest, detention, conviction or release is effected, information should invariably be sent to Government concerned concurrently with the intimation sent to Speaker/Chairman of the Legislative Assembly/ Council/Lok Sabha/Rajya Sabha. This should be sent by Telegram and also by post."

Although an accused, when arrest, has been given a Constitutional right to communicate with his counsel, he has not been given any right to communicate with other person. Communication with the outside world is important for protection of a detainee's rights and is also an important aspect of humane treatment. In view of the importance of the right to communicate, the *U.K. Police and Criminal Evidence Act, 1984*, by Section 56 has recognized the right of arrested persons to have some intimated.[78] The Supreme Court , while holding that such right is inherent in Articles 21 and 22(1) of the Constitution and as such should be recognized and scrupulously protected issued several guidelines to be followed by the police officer or person arresting an accused.[79] These guidelines will be discussed later on.

To conclude, it may be said that the requirement of production of an accused within 24 hours is a healthy provision which enables the Magistrates to keep check over the police investigation and its scrupulous observance by the police is vital for the protection of human dignity and human rights of the pre-trial detainees. For this obvious reason, the Supreme Court has also strongly urged upon the State and its police authorities to ensure the enforcement of this requirement.[80] Where it is found disobeyed, they should come down heavily upon the erring police personnel; the Bombay High Court has held that if a police officer fails to observe the requirement of producing the accused within 24 hours before the Magistrate, he would be guilty of 'wrongful detention'.[81] The rights discussed in the preceding pages are very important rights affecting the human dignity of an accused and, therefore, they must be given full effect in practice. For this purpose the Supreme Court has issued several guidelines from time to time to be followed in the cases of arrest or detention of an accused[82] and they need to be mentioned before concluding the discussion.

D. GUIDELINES ISSUED BY THE SUPREME COURT TO BE FOLLOWED IN ALL CASES OF ARREST OR DETENTION

Before the discussion on the rights of an accused relating to arrest and detention is concluded, reference of two noteworthy judgements delivered by the Supreme Court in *Joginder Kumar v. State of U.P.*[83] and in *D.K. Basu v. State of West Bengal*,[84] (along with *A.K. Jauhari v. State of U.P.*)- decided on 18.12.96- is essential. For the effective enforcement of various fundamental rights granted to an accused, the following requirements were prescribed by the Supreme Court in *Joginder Kumar v. State of U.P*[85] :

(i) An arrested person being held in custody is entitled, if he so requests to have one friend, relative or other person who is known to him or likely to take an interest in his welfare told as far as practicable that he has been arrested and where is being detained;

(ii) The Police Officer shall inform the arrested person when he is brought to the police station of this right; and

(iii) An entry shall be required to be made in the Diary as to who was informed of the arrest. These protections must be held to flow from Articles 21 and 22(1) and be enforced strictly.

The Court further observed that 'it shall be the duty of the Magistrate before whom the arrested person is produced, to satisfy himself that these requirements have been complied with.' Further, 'the above requirements were in addition the rights of the arrested persons found in the various Police Manuals.' Departmental instructions should be issued that 'the attesting police officers record the reasons for making the arrest in the case diary'- the Supreme Court observed.

The case of ***D.K. Basu v. State of West Bengal***[86] decided by the Supreme Court three years later, dealt in detail with certain rights of an accused at the time of arrest along with the aspect of awarding compensation to the arrestee for torture to him during police custody. In this case, the Executive Chairman, Legal Aid Services, West Bengal, a non-political organization, on 26th August, 1986, addressed a letter to the Chief Justice of India drawing his attention to certain news items published in the *Telegraph* newspapers dated 20, 21 and 22 of July, 1986 and in the *Statesman* and *Indian Express* dated 17th August, 1986 regarding deaths in police lock-ups and custody. It was stated in the letter that efforts are often made to hush up the matter of lock-up deaths and thus the crime goes unpunished and "flourishes". It was requested that the letter along with the news items be treated as a writ petition under "public interest litigation" category. The letter was treated as a writ petition and notice was issued on 9.2.1987 to the respondents. In response to the notice, the State of West Bengal filed a counter. The respondents characterised the writ petition as misconceived, misleading and untenable in law. While the writ petition was under consideration, a letter addressed by Shri Ashok Kumar Johri on 29.7.1987 to the Hon'ble Chief Justice of India drawing the attention of the court to the death in police custody of one Mahesh Bihari of Pilkha, Aligarh was received. The letter was also treated as a writ petition and was directed to be listed along with the writ petition filed by Shri D.K. Basu. In this case , the learned *Justice Dr. Anand,* while deliberating the various rights of as person who is arrested called such person as "arrestee" instead of "accused" and laid down various requirements stated as under to be followed in all cases of arrest or detention as preventive measures till legal provisions are made which are stated as under:[87]

1. The police personnel carrying out the arrest and handling the interrogation of the arrestee should bear accurate, visible and clear identification and name tags with their designations. The particulars of all such police personnel who handle interrogation of the arrestee must be recorded in a register.

2. The police officer carrying out the arrest of the arrestee shall prepare a memo of arrest at the time of arrest and such memo shall be attested by at least one witness, who may be either a member of family of the arrestee or a respectable person of the locality from where the arrest is made. It shall also be countersigned by the arrestee and shall contain the time and date of arrest.
3. A person who has been arrested or detained and is being held in custody in a police station or interrogation centre or other lock up shall be entitled to have one friend or relative or other person known to him or having interest in his welfare being informed, as soon as practicable, that he has been arrested and is being detained at the particular place, unless the arresting witness of the memo of arrest is himself such a friend or a relative of the arrestee.
4. The time, place of arrest and venue of custody of an arrestee must be notified by the police where the next friend or relative of the arrestee lives outside the district or town through the legal aid organisation in the district and the police station of the area concerned telegraphically within a period of 8 to 12 hours after the arrest.
5. The person arrested must be made aware of this right to have someone informed of his arrest or detention as soon as he is put under arrest or is detained.
6. An entry must be made in the diary at the place of detention regarding arrest of the person who has been informed of the arrest and the names and particulars of the police officials in whose custody the arrestee is.
7. The arrestee should, where he so requests, be also examined at the time of his arrest and major and minor injuries, if any, present on his / her body, must be recorded at that time. The "inspection memo" must be signed both by the arrestee and the police officer effecting the arrest and its copy provided to the arrestee.
8. The arrestee should be subjected to medical examination by a trained doctor every 48 hours during his detention

in custody by a doctor on the panel of approved doctors appointed by Director, Health Services of the concerned State or Union Territory. Director, Health Services should prepare such a panel for all Tehsils and Districts as well.

9. Copies of all the documents including the memo of arrest, referred to above, should be sent to the *Illaqa* Magistrate for his record.
10. The arrestee may be permitted to meet his lawyer during interrogation, though not throughout the interrogation.
11. A police control room should be provided at all district and state headquarters, where information regarding the arrest, and the place of custody of the arrestee shall be communicated by the officer causing the arrest within 12 hours of effecting the arrest and at the police control room it should be displayed on a conspicuous police board.

The Supreme Court held that : "The requirements, referred to above flow from Articles 21 and 22(1) of the Constitution and need to be strictly followed. These would apply with equal force to the other governmental agencies also to which a reference has been made earlier". It was further declared that: 'These requirements were in addition to the Constitutional and statutory safeguards and did not detract from various other directions given by the courts from time to time in connection with the safeguarding of the rights and dignity of the arrestee'.

The Supreme Court, keeping in mind the serious miseries of the arrest faced by an accused (arrestee), took a strong view in the case of the non-compliance of the aforesaid requirements and held that the 'concerned official responsible for such non-compliance shall be liable for departmental action. In addition to such action, he shall also be liable to be punished for contempt of court and the proceedings for contempt of court may be instituted in any High Court of the country, having territorial jurisdiction over the matter'.[88]

In this context, the Supreme Court felt that "creating awareness about the rights of arrestee would be a step in the right direction to combat the evil of custodial crime and bring in transparency and accountability." It was hoped by the Supreme Court that 'these requirements would help to curb, if not totally eliminate, the use of questionable methods during interrogation and investigation leading to custodial commission of crimes'. In order to create awareness not only amongst the arrestees but also amongst the personnel exercising the power of arrest, the Supreme Court directed that 'the requirements mentioned aforesaid should be forwarded to the Director General of Police and the Home Secretary of every State/ Union Territory and it shall be their obligation to circulate the same to every police station under their charge and get the same notified at every police station at a conspicuous place. It would also be useful and serve larger interest to broadcast the requirements on the *All India Radio* besides being shown on the National Network of *Doordarshan* and by publishing and distributing pamphlets in the local language containing these requirements for information of the general public.

The judgement delivered by the Supreme Court and the directions contained therein can be said to be historic and progressive step towards securing the freedom of an individual and prohibiting the violation of Human Right /Fundamental Right of an accused except in a manner permitted by law. It is gratifying to note that now at every police station these directions in local language are exhibited at conspicuous place. Further, the National Human Rights Commission of India has also published small pamphlets containing various rights of an accused including the guidelines issued by the Supreme Court for creating mass awareness and legal literacy.

In the preceding pages, the three most important rights of an accused relating to arrest were examined. However, two more rights are available to an accused after his arrest, i.e., Right to secure the services of counsel and get free legal aid and Right to be released on Bail. As these rights are available to an accused not only at the time of arrest but are available to him at every stage from the time of arrest till the final acquittal or conviction, they are proposed to be discussed separately in the next chapter.

REFERENCES

1. Criminal Procedure Code, 1973, section 41.
2. *Ibid.*, section 42.
3. *Ibid.*, section 43.
4. *Ibid.*, section 44.
5. *Ibid.*, section 45.
6. *Ibid.*, section 46.
7. *Ibid.*, section 47.
8. *Ibid.*, section 48.
9. *Ibid.*, section 49.
10. *Ibid.*, section 50.
11. *Ibid.*, section 51.
12. *Ibid.*, section 52.
13. *Ibid.*, section 53.
14. *Ibid.*, section 54.
15. *Ibid.*, section 55.
16. *Ibid.*, section 56.
17. *Ibid.*, section 57.
18. *Ibid.*, section 58.
19. *Ibid.*, section 49.
20. *Ibid.*, section 60.
21. Constitution of India, 1950, Article 22(1) : "No person who is arrested shall be detained in custody without being informed, as soon as may be, of the grounds for such arrest nor shall be denied the right to consult and to be defended by, a legal practitioner of his choice."
22. Chaturvedi A.N., "Right of Accused under Indian Constitution,' 1984, Ist Edn., Deep & Deep Publication, New Delhi, p. 215.
23. Stephen Sir J.F., 'A History of Criminal Law of England,' Vol. I. London 1983, pp. 227 and 345.
24. Homer D. Crotty, 'Magna Carta-myth and reality', Los Angeles Bar, Bull 40, 366 (1964-65).
25. Chafee, Z., 'Documents on Fundamental Human Rights,' I; Harvard, 1951. See also. Alan Barth, 'The Price of Liberty', New York, 1961, p. 11.
26. Chaturvedi A.N., 'Rights of Accused under Indian Constitution,' 1984, Deep & Deep Publication, pp. 216-217.
27. 1947 1 All E.R. 567.
28. Criminal Procedure Code, 1973 S. 50(1) : "Every Police Officer or other person arresting any person without warrant shall forthwith communicate to him full particulars of the offence for which he is arrested or other grounds for such arrest".

29. Criminal Procedure Code, 1973, (but not applicable to preventive detentions under clause (4) to (7) of Article 22 by clause (3), Constitution of India, 1950.
30. Criminal Procedure Code, 1973, Section 303.
31. Constituent Assembly Debates, Vol. IX, pp. 1496-7.
32. Earl Jowitt, 'The Dictionary of English Law', Vol. 1, (1959) 152.
33. 15th edition, Vol. 1 at p. 540.
34. Corpus Juris Seeundum, Vol. V. p. 285 quoted Ajaib Singh v. State of Punjab, 1952 Cr. L.J. 1313 at p. 1332 (Punj.) (F.B.).
35. Wharton's Law lexicon, quoted in *Ibid.*
36. Ajaib Singh v. State of Punjab, 1952 Cri L.J. 1313 at p. 1324 (Punjab): A I R Punj. 309 (F.B.)
37. State of Punjab v. Ajaib Singh 1953 Cr. L.J. 180 at p. 185 (S.C.); see also. Raj Bahadur v. Legal Remembrencer, A I R 1953 Cal. 522; 1953: Cri. L.J. 1187.
38. A I R 1957 S.C. 688 p. 691.
39. A I R 962 S.C. 1506 at pp. 150910.
40. State of M.P. v. Shobharam, AIR. 1966 S.C. 1910 at pp. 1916-17, 22.
41. Chaturvedi A.N., 'Rights of Accused under Indian Constitution,' 1984, Deep & Deep Publication, New Delhi, p. 224.
42. AIR 1954 S.C. 179 : 1954 Cr. L.J. 456.
43. Prem Dutta v. Supdtt. Central Prison, 19 Cr. L.J. 685 (All); See also Abdul Ghani v. State, A I R 1955 J. & K 38 : Cr. L.J. 1953 (F.B.).
44. Sitaram Kishore v. State, A I R 1956 Pat. 1 : 1956 Cri L.J. 86.
45. Prem Nath v. Union of India. AIR 1958 Punj 56.
46. A I R 1956 All. 641.
47. Gabinding Pao Kabui v. U.T. Manipur, AIR. 1963 Manipur 12 at p. 14.
48. Kali Charan v. State, A I R 1955 All. 462.
49. A I R 1956 All. 56: Cri L.J. 13.
50. *Ibid*, at p. 61; Oak J. in a separate judgement held the same view.
51. A I R.1982 S.C. 53.
52. See, *infra*, Chapter
53. A I R 1924 Madras 555.
54. Mst. Bhagwan v. State, AIR. 1973 Pepsu 33.
55. Sharvan Kumar v. Supdt. Dist. Jail. AIR. 1957 All. 189 at p.191.
56. Upadhyaya, Chandra Mohan, 'Human Rights in Pre-trial detention', A.P.H. Publishing Corporation, New Delhi,1999, p. 82.
57. Cr. P. C.,1973, section 57: "No Police Officer shall detain in custody a person arrested without warrant for a longer period than under all the circumstances of the case is reasonable, and such period shall not, in the absence of a special order of a magistrate under

section 167, exceed twenty-four hours exclusive of the time necessary for the journey from the place of arrest to the magistrate's court."

58. A.K. Gopalan v. State of Madras, A I R 1950 S.C. 27.
59. Maneka Gandhi v. Union of India, A I R 1978 S.C. 597. This decision overrules the concept of law laid down in A.K. Gopalan v. State of Madras, A I R 1950 S.C. 237.
60. In re Madhu Limaya, A I R 1969 S.C. 1014 at pp. 1018-19, See also, Narayan Singh v. State of Punjab, A I R 1952 S.C. 106.
61. State of Bombay v. Atma Ram, A I R 1951 S.C. 164.
62. Keshav Singh v. Speaker, Legislative Assembly, A I R 1965 All 349 at pp. 354-55. See, also State of Punjab v. Ajaib Singh, A I R 1953 S.C. 10.
63. Chaturvedi A.N. Rights of Accused under Indian Constitution, 1984, Deep & Deep Publication, Rajouri Garden, New Delhi 110027, p. 272.
64. Collector of Madras v. Erimmal Ebrahuim Hazee, A I R 1957 S.C. 91: Hallai v. B.M. Desai, A I R 1956 S.C. 20.
65. A I R 1954 S.C. 638 : 1954 Cr. L. J. 1704.
66. A I R 1953 S.C. 10 : 1953 Cr. L. J. 180.
67. State of Punjab v. Ajaib Singh, A I R 1953 S.C. 10.
68. *Ibid.*
69. A I R 1953 Cal. 522 at p. 523 : 1953 Cr. L. J. 1187.
70. See, *supra*, notes 67 and 69.
71. *Ibid.*
72. A I R 1960 All. 467 : 1969Cr. L. J. 1049.
73. Harpal Singh v. State, A I R 1950 All. 562.
74. A I R 1954 All. 601 at p. 605.
75. Criminal Procedure Code, 1973, section 44 (1).
76. A I R 1959 All. 384.
77. A I R 1969 S.C. 1014 at p. 1019.
78. Section 56 of the U.K. Police and Criminal Evidence Act, 1984 provides that: "Where a person has been arrested and is being held in custody in a police station or other premises, he shall be entitled, if he so requires, to have one friend or relative or other person who is known to him or who is likely to take an interest in his welfare told, as soon as is practicable except to the extent that delay is permitted by the section, that has been arrested and is being detained there."—Code C, Para 3.1, and Para 5.1.
79. Joginder Kumar v. State of U.P., (1994) 2 SCJ 230.
80. Khatri v. State of Bihar, (1981) 1 SCC 627.
81. Sharifbai v. Abdul Razak, A I R 1961 Bom. 42.

82. See, Joginder Kumar v. State of U.P., (1994) 2 SCJ 230; D.K. Basu v. State of West Bengal, (1997) 1 SCC 416, Francis Coralie Mullin v. Union Territory of Delhi, (1981) 1 SCC 608.
83. Joginder Kumar v. State of U.P., (1994) 2 SCJ 230, at p. 237
84. D.K. Basu v. State of West Bengal, A I R. 1997 614.
85. Joginder Kumar v. State of U.P., (1994) 2 SCJ 230 at pp. 236-237.
86. D.K. Basu v. State of West Bengal, A I R. 1997 614.
87. *Ibid.*, at 623.
88. *Ibid.*, at 623-624.

Four

Human Rights of "Accused" Available at Every Stage

(Rights to Engage Counsel, to Apply for Free Legal Aid and to be Released on Bail)

In the preceding chapters attempts were made to examine basis and evolution of various human rights of an accused and also the rights available to an accused under the Constitution of India and the Criminal Procedure Code as soon as he is arrested or detained like : (a) Right to know the grounds of arrest (b) Right to know the power of the arresting authority and also (b) Right to be produced before the magistrate within a stipulated time including the Right to Communicate. In addition to those rights, already discussed, there are two more valuable rights which are available to, and can be availed of by, an accused immediately from the time he becomes an accused, i.e., the date when the former allegation is levied against him, and continue to be available throughout the period a person remains an accused, i.e., the date on which the final acquittal or conviction of the accused is made; these rights are: (a) Right to seek the services of counsel and right to apply for free legal aid and (b) Right to be released on bail.The first right is related to the recognised Human Right of "Free and Fair Trial" and the second right is related to the infringement of the "Fundamental Right of Personal Liberty" guaranteed to an accused by the Constitution of India. In this chapter it is proposed to examine the above mentioned two rights of an accused in detail which are available to him before, or at the time of or even after the arrest and detention of the accused during police custody or judicial custody and some time till final acquittal or conviction, as the case may be.

A. RIGHT OF AN ACCUSED TO HAVE THE SERVICES OF COUNSEL AND FREE LEGAL AID

1. Genesis of the Right to have the Services of Counsel and Free Legal Aid in India

Right of an accused to have the Services of Counsel in India has been recognized from ancient times. During Hindu and Muslim rules, the cases of an accused having been defended by *Pundits* and *Maulvis* have been found.[1] However, it may be said that in the modern times the right of an accused to have the services of counsel, at international level, has its origin to *Article 10* of the *Universal Declaration of Human Rights,1948,* by which every State has been charged with a duty to ensure to an accused 'A Fair and Public Hearing' and *Article 14.3 (d)* of *International Covenant on Civil and Political Rights,1966,* and at national level to *Article 22(1)* of the *Constitution of India* which declares that 'no person who is arrested shall be denied the right to consult and to be defended by a legal practitioner of his choice'. It is worth mentioning that prior to the Constitutional guarantee, this right of an accused was protected by section 340(1) of the *Code of Criminal Procedure, 1898* (now Section 303 of *Criminal Procedure Code, 1973,* referred to hereinafter as Cr.P.C.,1973) which provided that 'any person accused of an offence before a Criminal Court or against whom Criminal proceedings were instituted under this Code could as of right be defended by a pleader'. Further, *Article 39-A* of the Constitution which was inserted later on by the *42nd Constitutional Amendment Act, 1976,* provides for the 'right to free legal aid' to indigent person. Section 304 of *Cr.P.C. 1973,* also provides that 'where in a trial if the accused is not represented by a pleader due to insufficient means the Court shall assign a pleader for his defence at the State expenses'. Due to the importance of these rights, the apex court of India has declared that at any stage, if an accused remains undefended by a lawyer, the entire criminal proceeding would be vitiated.[2] Thus, these two aspects require examination in more details.

2. Right to Consult a Counsel of One's Own Choice

The right to have the services of counsel guaranteed by *Article 22(1)* includes 'right of consultation with a lawyer of one's own choice'. This right is also protected under Section 303 of the *Cr.P.C., 1973* and extends and attaches to the accused not only since his arrest and detention under any punitive law but also extends to attach to any accused person under circumstances of near custodial interrogation[3] if desired for one to be presented by his side at the time of his examination. This right must not be abused and should be granted subject to reasonable restrictions as to time and convenience of the police authorities no less than that of the party seeking interview. In this connection, ***Medgavkar, J.***, of Bombay High court has observed thus [4]:

> "If the ends of justice is justice and the spirit of justice is fairness, then each side should have equal opportunity to prepare its own case, and to lay its evidence fully, freely and fairly before the Court. This necessarily involves preparation. Such preparation is far more effective from the point of view of justice, if it is made with the aid of skilled legal advice—advice so valuable that in the gravest of Criminal trials when life undertakes the prosecution of the prisoner also provides him, if poor, with such legal assistance".

Section 126 of the *Indian Evidence Act, 1872*, also provides for all communications to be privileged made between client and his counsel and , therefore, all communications between an accused and his legal advisors will be privileged and confidential.[5] His right of communication is transgressed in his removal and confinement to a place unknown to his relations and friends which shall amount to violation of his right of legal assistance.[6]

Choice of legal assistance of a lawyer is a personal matter of an accused person; if he does not desire that he should be represented by a lawyer, no one can impose upon him a lawyer. But while considering his desire of not to be represented by a lawyer, due weight should be given to his competency. In a case, the petitioners were produced before the Magistrate from the police custody at 7 P.M. and immediately after Court working hours the trial took place and concluded at 8.30 p.m. and since at that time the accused persons could not get assistance of a lawyer for their defence, they pleaded guilty and were convicted; it was held that their plea of guilty in a trial held after the Court hours in the absence of legal assistance could not be regarded as of voluntary violation on their part.[7] Such trial had deprived the petitioner of their right of legal assistance which resulted in the failure of justice. The ground given by the Magistrate that he was pre-occupied with his executive duties and so for the sake of expedious trial he held the trial at night hurrying through it in the manner, could in no circumstances be countenanced and justified.[8]

3. The Legal Aid - A Constitutional Imperative

The Constitution of India in its *Article 39-A* has provided that the opportunities for securing justice are not denied to any citizen by reason of economic or any other disabilities. A comprehensive report on legal aid was submitted in May, 1973 by the *Krishna lyer Committee* appointed by the Government of India by an order dated 27-10-1972. *Mr. Justice Krishna lyer* of the Supreme Court (as he then was), headed the Committee. As a consequence of the Report of the Committee , a new *Article 39-A* was added in the Directive Principles of State Policy of the Constitution by the *42nd Constitutional Amendment Act, 1976*, making a provision for 'free legal aid to ensure that opportunities for securing justice should not be denied to any citizen by reason of economic or other disabilities'. However, no concrete steps were taken in this regard for providing various schemes of legal aid and, therefore, a second Committee was appointed by the Government of India- headed by *Mr. Justice Bhagwati* - to look after the earlier Committee's Report and both *Mr. Justice Bhagwati* and *Mr. Justice Krishna lyer* were members of the Committee; and the Committee submitted a comprehensive report containing various recommendations on the basis of which the Central Government of India and the State Governments made several schemes for providing legal aid and advise to the poor. The main idea of framing the schemes for legal aid and advice to the poor was to provide legal literacy thereby to create legal awareness among the people. One of the important aims and objects of these schemes was to achieve social justice and to reduce social disparity by providing free legal aid to the weaker sections of the society and by encouraging and promoting settlement by conciliation in legal proceedings. For the effective implementation of these Schemes, the Central Government formed a 'Committee For Implementing Legal Aid Schemes' (CILAS) at national level, 'State Legal Aid Boards' at State level and 'District Legal Aid Committees' at the District Level. Thereafter, a new legislation, namely, *Legal Services Authorities Act, 1987*, was enacted but the implementation of the same was delayed for ten years for want of necessary Rules and ultimately in the year 1997, the Act was implemented and various Legal Services Authorities were established at District and State Level throughout India to implement the schemes of legal aid and *Lok Adalat*. At Central level, National Legal Services Authority was established.

4. Right of Accused to be Defended by a Counsel

It is now well settled law that "free aid to indigent and poor accused" springs form Article 21 of the Constitution[9]. Besides, Article 39-A also provides for "equal justice and free legal aid". After a catena of legal decisions, it is now a settled duty of the State to provide free legal aid for ensuring equal justice amongst those citizens who are unable to engage lawyers in their litigations by reason of their economic disabilities. Section 304 of Criminal Procedure Code, 1973, also provides that 'where in a trial if the accused is not represented by a pleader due to insufficient means the Court shall assign a pleader for his defence at the State expenses'. The combined and effective forces of Section 304 Cr. P.C., Article 21 and that of Article 39-A are quite consistent with that of Article 22(1). The 'Court shall assign a pleader for his defence at the expenses of State' and 'an arrestee has a right to consult and be defended by a legal practitioner of his choice' have different meaning. While both – the provisions of Cr. P. C. and the Constitution - are for ensuring and securing justice to an accused, it was held earlier by the Supreme Court that 'the right to be defended by a legal practitioner of his choice' could only mean a right of the accused to have the opportunity to engage a lawyer and does not guarantee an absolute right to be supplied with a lawyer by the State[10]. In ***Janardan Reddy v. State of Hyderabad***[11], the Supreme Court observed that:

> "It cannot be laid down as a rule of law that in every capital case where the accused is unrepresented, the trial should be held vitiated and that a Court of appeal or revision is not

> powerless to interfere if it is found that the accused was so handicapped for want of legal aid that proceedings against him may be said to amount to negation of a fair trial."[12]

In ***Tara Singh v. State,***[13] the Supreme Court has held that 'the right of an accused to be defended by a pleader did not extend to a right in an accused to be provided with a lawyer by the State or by the police or by the Magistrate *suo-moto*. It is a privilege given to him and the duty is cast upon the accused to ask for a lawyer if he desires to engage one for himself or to get his relations to engage one for him.'

Access of justice is an integral part of social justice enshrined in the Preamble of the Constitution. On this basis the Supreme Court, later on, held in the case of ***Hussainara Khatoon v. Home Secretary, State of Bihar,***[14] that 'in view of our Indian society of which poor and weaker section constitute larger part of it, *free legal service is inalienably element of reasonable, fair and just procedure* for without it person suffering from economic or other disabilities would be denied of justice.' Legal Aid is 'really nothing else but equal justice in action and in fact is delivery system of social justice - intended to reach justice to common man. This is a Constitutional right of every accused person who is unable to engage a lawyer.[15] The State is under a mandate to provide a lawyer to an accused person if the circumstances of the case and the needs of justice so required, provided of course the accused person does not object to the provision of such a lawyer. The State's obligation starts when the accused was produced first time before the Court of Magistrate. That is the stage at which an accused needs competent legal services. The Magistrate or Session Judge, before whom the accused appears, is under an obligation to inform the accused that 'if he is unable to engage the services of a lawyer on account of poverty or indigency, he is entitled to obtain free legal aid at the cost of State.'[16] Legal assistance to a poor or indigent accused who is arrested and put in jeopardy of his life or personal liberty is a Constitutional imperative / mandate not only by Article 39-A but also by Articles 14 and 21 of the Constitution. In ***Sheela Barse v. State of Maharashtra,***[17] the apex court held that 'it is a *sine qua non* of justice and where it is not provided, injustice is likely to result.' In this case the Supreme

Court directed the State Government regarding protection of women prisoner and the legal assistance. In ***M.M. Hoskot v. State of Maharashtra,***[18] the Supreme Court held that 'persons who are in prison shall be given legal aid at the expense of the State by the Court assigning counsel.' An accused who is lodged in a jail does not know to whom he can turn for a help in order to indicate his innocence or defend his Constitutional or legal right or to protect himself against torture and ill-treatment or oppression and harassment at the hand of his custodians. It is, therefore, absolutely essential that legal assistance must be made available to prisoners in jail whether they may be under trial or convicted prisoner. Hence, in the case of ***Hussainara Khatoon (II) v. Home Secretary, State of Bihar,***[19] the Supreme Court held that the 'right to free legal services is an essential ingredient of reasonable, fair and just procedure for a person accused of an offence and it must be held implicit in the guarantee of Article 21.'

5. Trial Outside the Court Premises: Legal Aid and Assistance of Lawyer

Legal assistance of lawyer is generally not available in case a trial of a criminal case is held outside the Court premises and its working hours. In such a case the Court's duty is to explain the circumstances to the accused and possibly the trial. In ***Hansraj v. State,***[20] the accused persons were summarily tried within jail precincts on 30-3-1955 and were convicted and sentenced under sections 120 and 121 of the Act. They were neither informed as to the date of trial and with their rights to be furnished with grounds and to be defended by lawyers under Section 340 (now Section 303), Criminal Procedure Code, 1989 and Article 20(1) of the Constitution nor were told that if they made any statement which was damaging to their interest the same statement might be used against them. It was held that the trial was vitiated as they were denied their right under Article 22(1) and (2) of the Constitution. However, in a summons case, the petitioner, on his plea of guilty, was tried and convicted for allegedly possessing illicit liquor by a mobile Court outside Court premises and also outside its working hours. The plea of legal assistance was rejected on the ground that in a summons case 'speedy trial' is the interest of all concerned.[21]

It may be submitted that the procedure needs a change with regard to the right to counsel in summons cases. By hurrying through the procedure and by non-compliance of the substantive right, justice is denied rather than done. The Criminal Jurisprudence and the Constitution impose a duty upon the trial Court to, specifically, inform the accused of their rights irrespective of the nature of the case. Now it is well settled principle of law that 'even when no request comes from the accused, it is the duty of the Court to apprise the accused specifically of his Constitutional rights in the interest of justice and confidence in its administration.'

6. Right to Counsel is Continuum

The only condition necessary for availability of right to counsel is the formal arrest of a person; before invoking this right, his detention after arrest is not necessary. The right to be defended by a legal practitioner of choice is a continuing right and is not lost by virtue of the arrested person's release on bail bond or personal bond.[22] The Allahabad High Court rightly held that in order to show that the right to be defended by counsel conferred by Article 22(1) has been violated, it was not necessary to show that person arrested was actually denied the right of defence; it was sufficient that the impugned act itself denied that right to him.[23]

In the case of ***State of M.P. v. Sobharam***[24], the Supreme Court discussed the availability of the right to be defended by a legal practitioner of his choice in any trial of the crime when the punishment is only fine and there is no danger to personal liberty of the accused. The majority consisting of Justice Bachawa, Justice Shelat and Justice Hidayatullah, held that in such a case, the right is not lost by virtue of the release of the arrested person on bail or personal bond, Section 63 of the Act. Mr. Justice Hidaytullah, speaking for the majority had observed thus [25]:

> The rights given by Article 22(1) and (2) are absolute in themselves and do not depend on other laws. There is no force in the submission that if there is only punishment of fine and there is no danger to personal liberty the protection of Art. 22(1) is not available. Personal liberty is invaded by arrest and continues to be restrained during the period of a person is on bail and it matters not whether there is or is

not a possibility of imprisonment. A person's arrest and put on his defence against a criminal charge, which may result in penalty, is entitled to the right to defend himself with the aid of counsel and any law that takes away this right offends against the Constitution.

However, dissenting with the majority view, Chief Justice A.K. Sarkar, and Justice J.R. Mudholkar, observed that[26]:

> "where a person is subjected to a trial under a law which does not provided for and order resulting in the loss of his personal liberty, he is not entitled to the Constitutional right to defend himself at the trial by a legal practitioner. The reason is that Arts. 21 and 22 of the Constitution are concerned only with giving protection to personal liberty".

The minority view - that when a person is released on bail his personal liberty is not at stake - seems to be incorrect for the simple reason that even the person so released also runs the risk of conviction and punishment, if he is not properly defended. Therefore, the majority view being expressed by Justice Hidayatullah seems to be perfectly in accord with the Constitutional spirit.

It may be summed up that the choice of consultation and representation by a pleader is a personal lookout of the accused; neither the State can deny it to him nor the State can offer it to him by assigning a lawyer generally in all cases. Of course, the assignment of a pleader to an indigent accused has now been a statutorily recognised right. Section 304 of the *Criminal Procedure Code, 1973* fortified by compulsive directive of *Article 39-A of the Constitution* is a good vista regarding indigent accused and it should be given full effect. The right to counsel is a continuing right and the rule that the right accrues only since the time of arrest needs extension of wide amplitude so that it accrues in all connected legal proceedings immediately after formal accusation is launched lodging of the formal report or complaint of accusation, and continues till the finality of the verdict of guilt and innocence.

7. Legal Positions Prevalent at Present With Regard to the Right to be Represented by Lawyer in a Criminal Proceedings

There had been a difference of opinion as to when services of lawyer is to be provided to an accused by the Court at the State expense. The provision of the *Code of Criminal Procedure*, although imposed a duty upon the Magistrate to appoint a lawyer at the State expenses, this duty was only to be exercised when a demand for a lawyer was made by the accused facing trial. In other words, if no such demand was made the trial court was under no obligation to provide free legal aid. This legal position prevailed even after the adoption of the Constitution and the Supreme Court also in its earlier Judgements had upheld that the duty to provide a lawyer to an accused by the Magistrates and Session Judges arose only when a demand was made by the accused. However, the attitude of the Supreme Court had gradually changed since the insertion of Article 39-A in the Directive Principles of State Policy regarding equal justice and free legal aid which had been a significant landmark and revealed a movement in the proper direction and a retreat of the judiciary from the traditional attitude. With a view to achieve the objective of Article 39-A, the Supreme Court of India delivered its revolutionary judgment in ***Hussainara Khatton v. State of Bihar***[27] in the year 1979, and the 'Right of Free Legal Aid and Services' was given the status of 'Fundamental Right'. The rule laid down in the year 1979 was expanded in the year 1981 by another landmark judgment given in ***Khatri v. State of Bihar,***[28] which imposed a duty upon the state to provide free legal service to the accused not only at the stage of trial but also at the stage when he was first produced before the Magistrate, and also when he was remanded from time to time. A duty to inform about this new fundamental right to every accused was also cast upon every Magistrate and Session Judge in the country. However, the different pronouncements of Supreme Court did not make it clear whether the right to legal assistance was confined only to poor, downtrodden and indigent accused or was available to every accused. Ultimately, the journey of legal assistance started in 1979 from the judgement given in *the case of Hussainara Khatoon* - declaring the human right to legal assistance as fundamental right of poor, downtrodden and indigent accused, witnessed many landmark pronouncements concerning the enforcement and implementation of basic human rights by the apex court of India and had finally ended in the judgement delivered in ***Suk Das v. Union of India,***[29] in which the Supreme Court emphatically declared again that : "Free Assistance at State cost is a fundamental right of person accused of an offence which may involve jeopardy to his life or personal liberty and this fundamental right is implicit in the requirement of reasonable, fair and just procedure prescribed by Article 21."

The Supreme Court also finally settled that : "The exercise of this fundamental right is not conditional upon the accused applying for free legal aid and, hence, cannot be denied if the accused failed to apply for it." It was observed by the Supreme Court that: "Illiteracy, poverty, ignorance of right and entitlements under the law and absence of legal awareness are responsible for the deception, exploitations and deprivation of rights and benefits of the poor in this land. It would be mockery of the legal aid programme if it were to be left to the poor, ignorant and illiterate accused to ask for free legal service."[29]

While declaring the 'right to legal assistance' as the backbone of the right of fair trial, the Supreme Court had also declared through its various pronouncements that 'it is Constitutional obligation of the State to see that there is no violation of the fundamental right of such person, particularly when he belongs to the weaker section of the community as he is unable to wage a legal battle against a strong and powerful opponent who is exploiting him. As the guardian of the fundamental rights of the people, the Supreme Court has reserved powers of the widest amplitude to ensure the protection of the Constitutional rights including right to legal aid / assistance.'[29]

Thus, the 'right to legal aid' to the poor and downtrodden has been accepted by the judiciary as the backbone of the 'human right to fair trial' and the approach of the Indian judiciary towards the implementation of this human right has been realistic and praiseworthy. It is now well settled that the duty of the Magistrate and Session Judge, before whom an accused is presented, to provide the services of a lawyer at the expense of the State is not dependent on the demand to be made by the accused and any trial would be vitiated if the accused remains unrepresented by a lawyer. The only exception to this rule is - when the accused himself refuses to accept the services of a lawyer provided to him at the cost of the State.

B. RIGHT OF AN ACCUSED TO BE RELEASED ON BAIL

The 'right to be released on bail' has nowadays become a very important right in the armoury of an accused. It is one of the foremost recognized social defences under criminal laws of any civilized society for preserving an individual's personal dignity. This right is available to an accused at any stage of legal proceedings starting from the date of formal accusation before arrest till the final conviction; in other words, it may be claimed before arrest after arrest, during trial and also at the time of consideration of appeal against conviction of the accused by trial court. As this right is one of the fundamental rights of an accused, it requires examination in detail.

1. Definition and Concept of Bail

The term 'bail' has nowhere specifically defined in the statutes relating to criminal law. The *Code of Criminal Procedure*, the *Oxford Dictionary*[31] and the *Law Lexicon*[32] define bail as 'security for appearance of prisoner on giving which the accused is released pending investigation, inquiry, trial or appeal. Webster's Dictionary defines bail as : "The process by which a person is released from custody."[33] In *Blackstone's Commentaries* on the *Laws of England* it has been observed that[34] :

> "That interest of the arrest being only to compel an appearance in court at the writ, that purpose is equally answered whether the sheriff detains his person or takes sufficient security for his appearance called bail (from the French word Baillor, to deliver) because the defendant is bailed or delivered to his sureties upon their giving security for his appearance."

The expression 'bail bond' and 'recognizance' are interchangeable and the import of these terms practically identical effect. According to the American Jurisprudence, the Court has power to release an individual accused of crime without bail or on his own recognizance.

The concept of bail, historically speaking has deep roots in Anglo-American laws. In medieval England, the need to enlarge an under-trial prisoner from the disease ridden jails while waiting for the delayed trials conducted by travelling justices was considered as a custom. The custody of the prisoners was given to reputed third parties of their own choice who undertook the responsibility for assuring their appearance at trial. If the accused did not appear, his surety would stand trial in his place.[35] In administration of criminal justice, the state has to adjust two conflicting demands of the society : on the one hand, it has to shield the individuals from the hazards of the alleged criminal trial and on the other, the jurisprudential canon of the innocence of the accused is to be upheld. The pre-trial detention leads to far grave consequences. Though the accused is presumed innocent till proven guilty, he suffers deprivations of liberty of life, loses his job, if any, and is deprived of an opportunity to work for himself and his family and that falls heavily on the innocent members of his family, is deprived of his contribution in the preparation of his defence and lastly the cost of his maintenance in jail saddles upon the public exchequer.[36] He is subjected to the "stress and distress" of prison life and he feels psychologically and morally more depressed than after conviction in the jails. In the present bail system, either the poor accused for the release "has to fall back on touts and professional sureties or to suffer detention. The consequences of both these are grave. On the one hand, the poor accused is fleeced of his money by touts and professional sureties and on the other hand, he is deprived of his liberty without trial and conviction."[37]

In this connection it may be pertinent to know the position regarding grant of bail in England which is different from the one of India, the U.S.A. and Canada. In England, bail does not involve the provision of some form of security that can be released or the obtaining of a bond which guarantees payment. It is simply a recognizance which is an undertaking by the accused that in case he does not appear at the Court he will become indebted to the Crown to the extent of a specified sum of money, big or small, having regard to the circumstances. The system, therefore, works in the same way irrespective of the poverty or wealth of the accused. *The Criminal Justice Act of 1967* restricts the Magistrates' power to refuse bail to specified situations. The Act also allows a grant of bail to be subject to conditions such as surrender of passport or reporting to the police.[38] In the United States the practice is emerging that the accused should ordinarily be released either on order to appear or on his own recognizance bond if judicial enquires reveal that the accused has roots and standing in his community unless substantial risk of non-appearance is shown.

2. Right of Accused to be Released on Bail under Indian Law

(a) Provisions of Criminal Procedure Code, 1973

According to Section 50(2) of *Cr. P.C. 1973*, in case an accused is arrested by a police officer without warrant, it is his right that he should be informed that he is entitled to be released on bail and that he may arrange for sureties on his behalf. Section 436 of the *Cr. P.C. 1973*, enacts that a person arrested without a warrant on the allegation of having committed a *bailable offence*, as a matter of right, shall be released on a bail bond with or without surety either while in the custody of the officer immediately after his arrest or when such person appears or is brought before the Court at any stage of the Criminal proceedings. Section 437 of the *Cr. P.C. 1973*, provides that to enlarge an arrestee who committed a *non-bailable* offence is a matter of judicial discretion; such person may or may not be released on bail. But if there are reasonable grounds to believe that such arrestee is guilty of an offence punishable with death or imprisonment for life, the arrestee shall not be released on bail unless the arrestee is below 16 years of age, or is a women or is sick or infirm. Recently, the Supreme Court in the case of ***Chandra Swami v. Central Bureau of Investigation,*** [39] has held that when a case does not cover the clause (i) or (ii) of Section 437, ordinarily a person who is suspected to having committed offence would be entitled to bail under Section 437(1). As the provision of the Section 437(1) speaks of release on bail of person below 16 years of age (Juvenile) and women, it cannot be said that a small boy or a *pardanashin* women should be refused to be released on bail and be allowed to languish "stress and distress" of jail for want of sureties.

Section 438 of the Cr. P. C.,1973, empowers a High Court or a Court of Sessions to grant a bail to a person apprehending arrest on an alleged accusation of a *non - bailable offence*. These Courts, on the application of a person, may direct that in the event of such arrest, the applicant shall be released on bail subject to the conditions amongst others in the light of the facts of a particular case that :

(a) the person shall make himself available for interrogation by police officer as and when required;

(b) The person shall not directly or indirectly on inducement, threat, or promise to any person acquainted with the facts of the case to dissuade him from disclosing such facts to the Court or to any police officer;

(c) shall not leave India without the previous permission of the Court; and

(d) such other conditions as may be imposed under sub-section (3) of Section 437 of the Code as if the bail is granted under that section.

Recently, Justice Thomas of the Supreme Court in ***Bimal Krishna Kundu v. State of Andhra Pradesh,***[40] has laid down the following guidelines with regard to the he powers of Court to grant anticipatory bail:

"(i) Section 438 applies to all non-bailable offences and not merely to offences punishable with death or imprisonment for life;

(ii) The applicability of the section is not confined to offences triabale exclusively by the Court of Sessions;

(iii) There is no indication in section 438 for justifying a hiatus to be made among non-bailable offences vivisecting those punishable with death or imprisonment for life and those others punishable with less than life imprisonment. No doubt such a classification is indicated in Section 437 (1), but that section is concerned only with pre-arrest bail."

By the *Amendment Act of U.P., 1976* [Act 16 of 1976]; application of Section 438 has been omitted in the State of Uttar Pradesh with effect from 1-5-76. In the state of West Bengal a provision has been added to Section 438 by the *West Bengal Act 47 of 1981*, (vide Section 3 effective from 24th Dec. 1982) which runs as under :

"provided that where the apprehended accusation relates to an offence punishable with death, imprisonment for life or imprisonment for a term of not less than seven years, no final order shall be made on such application without giving the State not less than seven day's notice to present its case".

The following principles of law as laid down in Cr. P.C. 1973, with regard to provision of bail can be stated :

(i) Section 436(1) of the *Cr. P. C., 1973*, speaks of bail but the provision thereof makes contradiction between 'bail' and 'personal bond' without sureties in bailable offence. Here bail is suggestive of 'with or without sureties'; but bail bond under Section 436(2) of the Code covers own bond;

(ii) Section 444(1) of *Cr. P. C., 1973*, provides for both the bond of the accused and the undertaking of the surety. Thus, to read bail as including only cases of release with sureties will stultify the importance of this sub-section;[41]

(iii) Sub-section (2) or (3) of Section 441 of the Code dispel the doubts reflected in sub-section (1) and the word 'bail' has been used in a generic sense intending to cover bond "with or without sureties".[41]

(iv) Section 389 of the *Cr. P. C., 1973*, provides for release of a convicted person by the appellate court on bail or on his own bond. Thus, an under-trial cannot be worse off than a convict.

(v) The Supreme Court's power to enlarge a prisoner is very wide and contains no limitations. Law which is meant for the service of life must interpretatively rise to the occasion for liberties.

Overriding consideration and principles in adjudication or granting bail which are common in case of Sections 437 (1) and 439 (1) appears sometimes are[42] :

(1) the nature and gravity of the circumstances in which the offence is committed,

(2) The position and status of the accused with respect to the victim and the witness,

(3) The likelihood of the accused fleeing from justice or repeating the offence, or jeopardizing his own life being faced with grim prospect of possible release in the case, or tampering with witness,

(4) History of cases as well as its investigation and other relevant grounds which, in so many variable factors, cannot be exclusively set out, and

(5) The Court has not to investigate facts and comments on merit.

'A Committee consisting of judges, lawyers, members of Parliament and other legal experts reported that a liberal policy of conditional release without monetary sureties or financial security and release on one's own recognizance with punishment provided for violation would reform the bail system and would help the poorer sections of society to get equal justice under law.'[43]

(b) Special Right of an Accused to be Released on Bail Under Section 167(2) of Cr. P. C. 1973

According to Proviso (a) to Section 167 (2) of the *Cr. P. C.,1973*, an accused can claim release by furnishing bail before the completion of investigation and the filing of charge sheet. After the filing of the *charge sheet* the power of granting bail is, however, only under Section 437.[44] An accused under the proviso to section 167(2) acquires statutory right to be released on bail on default of prosecution in not filing charge-sheet within the prescribed period of 90 days and this right is absolute , as it is a "legislative command" and not Courts' discretion.[45]

In ***Hussainara Khatoon v. State of Bihar*** [46], the Supreme Court has held that 'it is desirable for the Magistrate that on the very day, the period of 60/90 days expires and when no charge-sheet has been filed, they should without waiting for written application to be moved by the under trial for his bail, specially inform the accused that he has a right to be released on bail under the proviso of Section 167 of *Cr. P.C.,1973*, and also ask him (the accused) whether he is prepared to furnish bail, and his (accused) reply shall be recorded and shall form part of the remand papers. If the answer of the under trial accused is in positive, the Magistrate shall pass the order of his bail on the remand paper disclosing the amount and number of sureties' and release the accused after furnishing the bail as ordered. It has been held in another case that 'no written application for bail is necessary; intimation showing willingness to furnish bail can be oral and Court is not empowered to refuse bail for want of written application.'[47] Where charge sheet has not been filed within 90 days or 60 days, as the case may be, the accused is entitled to released on bail.[48]

(c) Right of an Accused to be Released on Bail After Conviction Pending Appeal

Under Section 389 (3) of *Cr.P.C., 1973*, an accused who is convicted of bailable offence by Magistrate, the convicting Magistrate can order release of such person on bail when he intends to present an appeal against the order of such conviction provided that:

(a) such convicted person is on bail at the time when he is convicted,

(b) such accused or convicted is sentenced for a term not exceeding three years, and

(c) the offence for which such person has been convicted is a bailable one.

The power under Section 389 (3) is restricted to trial court and it enables the trial court to suspend sentence and grant bail to a convicted person for such limited period as will afford sufficient time to present an appeal and obtain order from the appellate court under Section 389 (1) for which he has to satisfy to trial court. But the jurisdiction of trial court to suspend sentence under Section 389 is limited only to cover cases under coming under clauses 3(1) and 3(2) of Section 389 and, therefore, a prayer under Section 389 (3) in the cases where the sentence awarded is imprisonment for life and / or the conviction is for non-bailable offence can be rejected by the trial court.[49] Pendency of an appeal is *sine qua non* for a convict to invoke Section 389 so also to exercise jurisdiction under sub-sections (1) and (2) of the section.[50]

Section 389(1) seems to be a rider to the other clauses of the section. Since pending any appeal by a convicted person, the appellate court which includes High Court in view of Section 389(2) may, for the reason to be recorded in writing, order that 'the execution of the sentence or order appealed against be suspended and, also, if he is in confinement, that he be released on bail or on his own bond' suggest that session court as an appellate Court cannot only suspend the execution of the sentence but it can also release the accused who is in custody either on bail or on his personal bond or recognization. In furtherance to above, under Section 389(1), an appellate court can even release a convicted person who is not on bail and has been sentenced to imprisonment for a term exceeding 3 years either on bail or on his personal bond [51]. Under Section 389, pending an appeal by a convicted person the appellate court can order the suspension of "the execution of the sentence or the order appealed against". The words suspension of "execution of the sentence" or "order appealed against" are of wide connotation and that the appellate Court in exercise of the jurisdiction under Section 389 of *Cr.P.C.,1973*, is empowered to even direct suspension of the order of conviction, hence no limitation can be read in Section 389 of the Code of 1973.[52]

5. Right of a Juvenile Accused to be Released on Bail

As has been observed earlier, according to the proviso of Section 437(1) of *Cr.P.C. 1973*, the Court is empowered to release a person who is under the age of 16 years or a woman or sick or infirm person even if he has been accused of an offence punishable with death or imprisonment for life or he has been accused of an offence which is a cognizable offence and he had been previously convicted of an offence punishable with death, imprisonment for life or imprisonment for seven years or more or he had been previously convicted on two or more occasions of a non-bailable, or guilty of cognizable offence. However, in spite of the grant of this special power to the trial court with regard to the release of a juvenile or a woman accused, the power is still discretionary. The *Juvenile Justice Act, 1986* (referred to hereinafter as JJ Act, 1986), made revolutionary changes with regard to bail and custody of delinquent juvenile accused (a boy who has not attained the age of 16 years and a girl who has not attained the age of 18 years) declares the provisions of the Code of Criminal Procedure, 1973, or any other law for the time being in force in cases of juveniles with regard to the grant of bail and custody of juvenile were made inoperative Section 18 of the *JJ Act, 1986* which provided *inter alia* as under:

1. Any juvenile brought before a Juvenile Court shall be released on bail with or without surety except in the following three conditions:

(a) When such release is likely to bring the juvenile accused into association with any known criminal, or

(b) Such release is likely to expose him to moral danger, or (c) His release would defeat the ends of justice;

2. Such bail can be granted by the officer-in-charge of the police station or by the juvenile court;
3. In case the bail is not granted and the juvenile accused is not released by the officer-in-charge of the station, such accused shall not be kept in a police station in the lock-up or jail even during the period of presenting such accused before the juvenile court;
4. In such a case where a juvenile accused has been arrested but not released on bail at the police station, the officer-in-charge shall cause him to be kept in an observation home or a place of safety but in no case such accused will be kept in the police lock-up or the jail;
5. When a juvenile accused is brought before a juvenile court and the court does not release him on bail due to the reasons mentioned above, the juvenile court shall not commit such accused to prison and shall send him to an observation home or a place of safety for such period during the pendency of the inquiry regarding him;
6. The aforesaid provision are applicable to a juvenile accused irrespective of the fact that he is arrested or detained for a bailable or non-bailable offence carrying any quantum of punishment.

It is to be pointed out here that the *JJ Act, 1986,* had been repealed and a new Act has been enacted in the year 2000, namely, the *Juvenile Justice (Care and Protection of Children) Act, 2000.* By this Act also, the similar provisions with regard to the release of a juvenile accused on bail have been retained except that now under the new Act, the age of boy has been raised from 16 to 18 years and a 'delinquent juvenile' (boy or girl) is now named as 'juvenile in conflict with law'. The detailed deliberation of this aspect and matters related thereto are proposed to be made later on while discussing the rights of juvenile accused.[53]

4. Judicial Interpretation of the Right of an Accused to be Released on Bail

'Releasing a person on bail should be the normal practice and refusal to do so should be an exception' – is the general attitude of the Indian judiciary. Besides prohibition of the deprivation of a person of his liberty unless his guilt is proved, the liberal but judicious use of the bail technique in releasing a person on bail has the side advantage of avoiding over crowding in the jails, to some extent.

The Supreme Court in ***Hussainara Khatoon v. State of Bihar,***[54] has held that 'the unreasonable pre-trial detention, without caring to hold trial or to conclude it, is the violation of fundamental right granted by Article 21 of the Indian Constitution.' Further, where the accused is known to the community he should be let off on personal bond with or without monetary consideration instead of with money surety. In ***Hussainara Khatoon (1) v. Home Secretary, State of Bihar,***[55] Mr. Justice Bhagwati, had pointed out that ' the Bail system, as being administered in the criminal court today, is extremely unsatisfactory and needs drastic change. . . .There are several consideration which deter an accused from running away from justice and risk of financial loss is only one of them and that too not a major one. . . Moreover, the bail system causes discrimination against the poor since the poor would not be able to furnish bail on account of their poverty while the wealthier persons otherwise similarly situated would be able to secure their freedom because they can afford the furnish bail. . . . This discrimination arises even if the amount of the bail fixed by the Magistrate is not high with money sureties.'

In ***Moti Ram v. State of M.P.,***[56] in which a poor mason was required to provide a surety of Rs. 10,000, the Supreme Court referring to the *Manhattan Bail Project of the U.S.A.* and pointing out that an excessive bond amount may cause injustice to poor people, reminded the magistracy of the country that monetary bail was not a necessary element of the 'criminal process' and urged that 'if a Magistrate was satisfied after an inquiry into the condition and background of the accused that he had his roots in the community and was not likely to abscond, the accused could be released on order to appear on his own recognizance.' The Supreme Court ordering to release the petitioner on his own bond of a sum of Rs. 1,000 concluded the judgement with 'an after word' that 'We leave it to parliament to consider whether in our socialist republic, with social justice as its hallmark, monetary superstition not other relevant consideration like family ties, roots in the community, membership of stable organization, should prevail for bail bond to ensure that the 'bailee' does not flee justice. The best guarantee of presence in court is the reach of the law, not the money tag. . . .'

In the case of ***Talab Haji Hussain v. Madhukar Purshottam Mandlar,***[57] it was held that 'if at any subsequent stage of the proceeding, it is found that any person accused of a bailable offence is intimidating, bribing or tampering with the prosecution witness or is attempting to abscond, the High Court may under its inherent power cancel his bail and cause him to be arrested and commit him to judicial custody for such period as it thinks necessary to secure the ends of justice or to prevent the abuse of process of any court.' The correctness of this view - that the High Court can in a proper case, under Section 482 cancel the bail given to an accused and re-arrest him- was challenged in ***Ratilal Bhanji v. Asstt. Customs Collector, Bombay,*** [58] on the ground that the cancellation of bail in bailable offence under the inherent powers of the High Court was in violation of Article 21 of the Constitution. The Supreme Court, rejecting the contention and reaffirming the Talab Haji Hussain rationale, held that the 'cancellation of bail was in accordance with the procedure established by law' as the jurisdiction of the High Court 'springs from the overriding inherent powers of the High Court and can be invoked in exceptional cases, only when the High Court is satisfied that the end of justice will be defeated unless the accused is committed to custody.'[59]

Bidding farewell to the established past practice that 'a person once found guilty and sentenced to life imprisonment cannot be released on bail unless his conviction and sentence were set aside' and releasing the appellant on bail bond, Mr. Justice Bhagwati of Supreme Court observed in ***Kashmira Singh v. State of Punjab***[60] that: "It would be indeed a travesty of justice to keep a person in jail for a period of five or six years for an offence which is ultimately found not to have been committed by him. Can the court ever compensate him for incarceration which is found to be unjustified? Would it be just at all for the court to tell a person : we have admitted your appeal because we think you have a *prima facie* case, but unfortunately we have no time to hear your appeal, you must remain in jail, even though you may be innocent? . . . So long as this Court is not in a position to hear the appeal of an accused within a reasonable period of time, the Court should ordinarily, unless there are cogent grounds for acting otherwise, release the accused on bail in case where special leave has been granted to the accused to appeal against his conviction and sentence." [61] Thus, where special leave to appeal against conviction and sentence has been granted to life-prisoner and there is an inordinate delay in the disposal of such appeal, such life prisoner may be released on bail.

Although various provisions have been made in the Code of Criminal Procedure, 1973, with regard to granting bail, they become meaningless for a poor and downtrodden accused because he is unable to procure the necessary sureties. Realising the pitiable condition of such accused who suffer with poverty and is subjected to atrocities during the police or judicial custody, Mr. Justice P.N. Bhagwati in the case of ***Hussainara Khatoon (I) v. Home Secretary, Bihar,***[62] opined that : "It is a travesty of Justice that the poor, because the bail procedure is beyond their meagre means, have to suffer long years in pre-trial detention. . . .The antiquated procedure perpetuated by the new Code which insists on a bond with a monetary obligation invariably supported by sureties whose solvency must be proved, operated very harshly against the poor, being beyond their means. They are exploited, suffer deprivation and losses and are unable to defend themselves. The discriminatory nature of the bail system becomes all the more acute by reason of the mechanical way in which it is customarily operated. Hence to eliminate the evil effects of justice, it is imperative that the bail system should be thoroughly reformed so that it should be possible for the poor, as easily as the rich, to obtain pre-trial release without jeopardising the interests of justice". Advocating for suitable reforms in the law relating to bail, the learned Justice Bhagwati in the said case suggested and opined that : "It is high time that our Parliament realises that risk of monetary loss is not the only deterrent against fleeing from justice, but there are also other factors which act as equal deterrents against fleeing. Ours is a socialist republic with social justice as the signature tune of our Constitution and Parliament would do well to consider whether it would not be in consonant with the ethos of our Constitution that instead of risk of financial loss, other relevant considerations such as family ties, roots in the community job security, membership of stable organisations etc. should be the determinative factors in grant of bail and the accused should in appropriate cases be released on his personal bond without monetary obligation, subject to penalty in case of breach."[63]

Summarising the existing law relating to bail, the learned justices (Mr. Justice Bhagwati and Mr. Justice Koshal) formulated certain guidelines to be followed by the Courts while exercising the discretionary power of granting bail with sureties or on the personal bond of the accused. The Supreme Court opined that till the amendment of the penal law is made by the Parliament, 'even under the law as it stands today, the courts must abandon the antiquated concept under which pre-trial release is ordered only against bail with sureties. That concept is outdated and experience has shown that it has done more harm than good. The new insight into the subject of pre-trial release which has been developed in socially advanced countries and particularly the United States should now inform the decisions of our Courts in regard to pre-trial release.'

The Supreme Court expressed that the court while considering the bail application of an accused for its satisfaction that the accused has his roots in the community which would deter him from fleeing, should take into account the factors concerning the accused, like : (a) The length of his residence in the community, (b) His employment's status, history and his financial condition, (c) His family ties and relationship, (d) His reputation, character and monetary condition, (e) His prior Criminal record including any record of prior release on recognizance or on bail, (f) The identity of responsible members of the community who would vouch for his reliability, (g) The nature of the offence charged and the apparent probability of conviction and the likely sentence in so far as these factors are relevant to the risk of non-appearance, and (h) Any other factors indicating the ties of the accused to the community or bearing on the risk of willful failure to appear.

The learned justices further opined that if the Court is satisfied on a consideration of the relevant factors that the accused has his ties in the community and there is no substantial risk of non-appearance, the accused may, as far as possible, be released on his personal bond. Of course, if facts are brought to the notice of the Court which go to show that having regard to the condition and background of the accused, his previous record and the nature and circumstances of the offence, there may be a substantial risk of his non-appearances of the trial, as for example, where the accused is a notorious bad character or a confirmed criminal or the offence is serious (these examples are only by way of illustration), the Court may not release the accused on his personal bond and may insist on bail with sureties. But in the majority of cases, considerations like family ties and relationship, roots in the community, employment, status etc., may prevail with the Court in releasing the accused on his personal bond and particularly in cases where the offence is not grave and the accused is poor or belongs to a weaker section of the community, release on personal bond could, as far as possible, be preferred. But even while releasing the accused on personal bond it is necessary to caution the Court that the amount of the charge. The decision as regards the amount of the bond should be an individualised decision depending on the individual financial circumstances of the accused and the probability of his absconding. The amount of the bond should be determined having regard to these relevant of the accused for release on bail, the majority of the accused persons would be relieved from the hardship faced by them due to their poverty, ignorance and delayed disposed of criminal cases filed against them, factors and should not be fixed mechanically according to a schedule keyed to the nature of the charge. Otherwise, it would be difficult for the accused to secure his release even by executing a personal bond. Moreover, when the accused is release on his personal bond, it would be very harsh and oppressive if he is required to satisfy the Court-and what we have said here in regard to the Court must apply equally in relation to the police while granting bail-that he is solvent enough to pay the amount of the bond if he fails to appear at the trial and in consequence the bond is forfeited. The inquiry into the solvency of the accused can become a source of great harassment to him and often result in denial of bail and deprivation of liberty and should not, therefore, be insisted upon as a condition of acceptance of the personal bond. We have no doubt that if the system of bail, even under the existing law, is administered in the manner we have indicated in this judgement, it would go a long way towards relieving hardship of the poor and help them to secure pre-trial release from incarceration. It is for this reason we have directed the under trial prisoner whose names are given in the two issues of the Indian Express should be release forthwith on their personal bond. We should have ordinarily said that personal bond to be executed by them should be with monetary obligation but we directed as an exceptional measure that there need be no monetary obligation in the personal bond because we found that all these persons have been in jail without trial for several years, and in some cases for offences for which the punishment would in all probability be less than the period of their detention and moreover the order we were making was merely an interim order. The peculiar facts and circumstances of the case dictated such an unusual course.[64]

It is hoped that if the courts in the country keep in mind the guiding principles enunciated by the Supreme Court, while considering the applications of the accused for release on bail, the majority of the accused persons would be relieved from the hardship faced by them due to their poverty, ignorance and delayed disposal of criminal cases filed against them.

REFERENCES

1. See, *supra*, Chapter 2.
2. Suk Das v. Union of India, 1986 2 SC.C. 401 : AIR 1986 S.C. 991.
3. Per V.R. Krishna lyer, J., in Nandani Satapathy v. P.L. Dani, 1978 Cr. L. J. 968 at p. 990 (S.C.)

4. Moti Bai v. State, 1954 Cr. L. J. 1951 (Raj)
5. See, Steel, W.W., "The Doctrine of Right to Counsel : Its impact on the administration of criminal Justice and legal profession", Southwestern L.J., 23, 488 (1969).
6. Dey v. Emperor, A I R 1935 Cal. 101.
7. Afjal Hussain v. State, A I R 1962 Raj, 216 : 1962 (2) Cri L. J. 496
8. *Ibid.*
9. Francis Coralie v. Union Territory of Delhi ,1981 S.C. Criminal Law Journal 306, (A I R 1981 S.C. 738)
10. Janardan Reddy v. State of Hyderabad. A I R 1951 S.C. 217
11. *Ibid.*
12. *Ibid.*, at p. 222
13. A I R 1951 S.C. 441 : 52 Cri. L.J. 1491
14. A I R 1979 SC 1369.
15. A I R 1979 S.C. 1369, 1374.
16. Khatri & others v. State of Bihar , A I R 1981 SC 928.
17. A I R 1983 378.
18. A I R 1978 S.C. 527.
19. SCC (1980) 99, at p. 105.
20. A I R 1956 All 641 : 1956 Cri. L.J. 1267.
21. Hadu Sahu v. State, A I R 1967 Orissa 37 : 1967 (1) Cri. L.J. 394.
22. Raghubir Singh v. State, A I R 1952 All. 589, (Accused's Counsel has right to be present at the time of identification parade test).
23. Deodat Rai v. State, A I R 1951 All. 718.
24. 1966 Cri. L.J. 1521 (S.C.) : A I R 1966 S.C. 1910
25. *Ibid.*, at p. 1529
26. Per A.K. Sarkar, C.J., *Ibid.*, at p. 1523.
27. A I R 1979. S.C. 1369.
28. A I R 1981. S.C. 928.
29. (1986) 2 SCC 401 : A I R 1986 S.C. 991.
30. Nath, S., "Legal Aid to the poor and downtrodden as the backbone of human right to fair trial - the Indian Approach" - *Proceeding of International Conference of International Congress on Legal Science,* Belgium, 1986.
31. Oxford Dictionary, Ninth Edn. 1995, Oxford University Press :Bombay, p. 95: "Money etc. required as security against the temporary release of a prisoner or accused person pending trial".
32. Law lexicon ,Govt. publication.
33. Webster's Third New International Dictionary.
34. Blackstone's Commentaries on the laws of England, vol. III, Ch. p. 290.
35. Chaturvedy, A. N., 'Rights of Accused under Indian Constitution', 1984 Deep & Deep publication, Delhi, p. 283.

36. Report of the Legal Aid Committee appointed by the Goverment of Gujarat,1971 and Headed by the then Chief Justice of India Mr. Justice P.N. Bhagwati, p. 185.
37. *Ibid,*
38. Sidddique Ahamad, 'Criminology: Problems and Perspectives. p. 330.
39. A I R 1997 S.C. 2575.
40. A I R 1997 S.C. 3589, at p. 3591-3592
41. Moti Ram v. State of M.P., 1978 Cr. L.J. 1703 (S.C.) at p. 1709.
42. Praveen Malhotra v. State (Delhi Admin.), 1990 (2) CCC 321 (D.H.C.) at p.72
43. Quoted in Hussainara Khatton v. Home Secretary, Bihar A I R 1979 S.C. 1360 at p. 1361..
44. Shrawan Hanji Undirwada v. State of Madhya Pradesh, 1976 MLJ 654.
45. Devendra Kumar v. M.P., Cr. L.J. 1992, 1730.
46. 1979 Cr. L.J. 1052 : AIR 1979 S.C. 1377.
47. Uma Shnker v. State of M.P., 1982 Cri. L.J. 1186, at p. 1189.
48. Mohd. Salim Khan v. State of U.P. 1982 Cr. L.J. 1242 : A I R 1982 S.C. 1096.
49. Vaskaran v. State of Kerala, 1987 Cri L.J., 1588.
50. Kochumminno Chcttiar v. State of Kerala, 1977 Cri. L.J.. 1872.
51. Mallik, M.R., 'Law of Bail and Practice', at p. 126.
52. Shanti Behal v. State (Delhi Administration), D.B. Ch. C.C. 1994 (1) 618 (621).
53. See, *infra,* Chapter Fifth.
54. A I R 1979 S.C. 1360, 1369, 1377 : 1979 Cri L.J. 1036 (S.C.).
55. 1980 SCC. 81, at p. 85.
56. 1978 Cr. L.J. 1703 (S.C.) : (1978) 3 SCC 47 : 1978 SCC (Cri) 185.
57. Cr. P.C. 1973, section 482; see also, Talab Haji Hussain v. Madhukar Purshotam Mandkar, Cr. P.C. 1973, A I R 1958 S.C. 376 : 1958 60 Bom. L.R. 465.
58. A I R 1967 S. C. 1639.
59. *Ibid.,* at p. 1640.
60. 1977 Cri L. 1746 : A I R 1977 S.C. 2147.
61. *Ibid.,* at p. 1747.
62. (1980) 1 SCC 81 at p. 82.
63. *Ibid.* at p. 83.
64. *Ibid.* at p. 88.

Five

Human Rights of "Accused" Available during Trial

(Rights to Speedy Trial or Accelerated Hearing Including Speedy Investigation, to be Presumed Innocent, to seek Protection Against Self-Incrimination and also Against Double Jeopardy)

In the previous chapters, after discussing the basis and evolution of human rights of an accused, firstly those rights were examined which are available to him at the time of arrest and after arrest but before the commencement of the trial; thereafter those rights were examined which could be claimed by him at any time starting from the date of the formal accusation till the date of his final conviction. However, such rights of an accused were not discussed which are available to him during trial. In addition to the rights already discussed in the preceding three chapters, an accused has also been granted several other rights even after the commencement of the trial; some of which are guaranteed as Fundamental Rights by the Constitution and some are fundamental to the Administration of Criminal Justice relating to procedure. Due to the limited time and space it is not possible to discuss all the rights in detail which are available to an accused during trial. In this Chapter, it is proposed to discuss only the following rights of an accused which are basic and fundamental to the Administration of Criminal Justice, such as: (i) Right to Speedy Trial or Accelerated Hearing including Speedy Investigation; (ii) Right to be presumed Innocence till finally convicted; (iii) Right to seek Protection against Self Incrimination; and (iv) Right against to seek Protection/Immunity against Double-Jeopardy.

A. RIGHT OF AN ACCUSED TO SPEEDY TRIAL OR ACCELERATED HEARING INCLUDING SPEEDY INVESTIGATION

1. Genesis of the Right of an Accused to Speedy Trial

'Justice Delayed is Justice Denied' is the cry of this century. Although right of an accused to "speedy trial' is not specifically enumerated as a fundamental right in our Constitution, still in view of the personal liberty of an human being which is a precious one guaranteed under Article 3 of the *Universal Declaration of Human Rights, 1948,* which provides that *"every one arrested or detained shall be entitled to trial within reasonable time or to release pending trial"* and so also in accordance with the provisions of Article 21 of the Constitution of India that the deprivation of personal liberty of an human being shall be only in accordance with law, the right to speedy trial has been held implicit in the broad sweep and ambit of Article 21 by the Supreme Court of India in case of ***Maneka Gandhi v. Union of India.***[1] In America, speedy "Trial" is one of the Constitutionally guaranteed rights available to the accused. The United States Congress had already passed 'Speedy Trial Act, 1974', which mandated time limits, ultimately reaching 100 days within which criminal charged must either brought to trial or admonished. In India, the old saying – "Justice Delayed is Justice Denied" has now been coined into a shape after dynamic interpretation of Article 21 of the Constitution in ***Maneka Gandhi's case.***[2] Thus, the recognition of the 'Right of an accused to speedy trial' as a 'fundamental Right' has been granted in India by the judiciary. It may be pointed out that Sections 167, 209 and 309 of the *Cr. P. C.,1973,* have emphasized the importance of expeditious disposal of cases including investigations and trials.

2. Right of an Accused to Speedy Trial as Embedded in the Statutory Law of Criminal Procedure

The main statutory provision which exemplifies the rule of speedy trial is Section 309 of the *Code of Criminal Procedure, 1973* (corresponding to Section 344 of the *Code of Criminal Procedure, 1898*). Clause (i) of Section 309 of the *Cr. P.C. , 1973,* provides that 'in every inquiry or trial, the proceedings shall be held as expeditiously as possible and, in particular, when the examination of witness has once begun, the same shall be continued from day to day until all the witnesses in attendance have been examined, unless the Court finds the adjournment of the same beyond the following day to be necessary for reasons to be recorded.' Clause (2) of Section 309 of the *Cr. P.C. , 1973*, provides that 'if the court after taking cognizance of an offence, or commencement of trial, finds it necessary or advisable to postpone the commencements of, or adjourn, any 'Inquiry' or 'Trial' , it may, from time to time, for reasons to be recorded, postpone or adjourn the same on such terms as it thinks fit, for such time as it considers reasonable, and may by a warrant remand the accused if in custody.'

These provisions indicate that the intention of the Legislature had been to complete the trial or inquiry expeditiously after its commencement and thus indirectly incorporates the concept of a speedy trial or inquiry / investigation. Although a Magistrate has been empowered to grant remand to an accused, the following restrictions are imposed upon this power of Magistrate[3]:

(1) No Magistrate shall remand an accused person to custody under Section 309 (1) for a term exceeding fifteen days at a time;
(2) When witnesses are in attendance, no adjournment or postponement shall be granted without examining them, except for special reasons to be recorded in writing; and
(3) No adjournment shall be granted for the purpose only of enabling the accused person to show cause against the sentence proposed to be imposed on him.

The following two explanations have been provided with regard to the power of a Magistrate to grant remand or adjournment[4]:

(1) If sufficient evidence has been obtained to raise a suspicion that the accused may have committed an offence, and it appears likely that further evidence may be obtained by a remand, this is a reasonable cause for a remand; and
(2) The terms on which an adjournment or postponement may be granted include, in appropriate cases, the payment of costs by the prosecution or the accused.

The Supreme Court has directed in several cases the dropping or discontinuance of proceedings were such proceedings constituted an abuse of process of court or where the ends of justice demanded such a course of action. For instance, in ***Machander v. State of Hyderabad,***[5] it was observed by the Supreme Court that 'while it is incumbent on the Court to see that no guilty person escapes, it is still more its duty to see that justice is not delayed and accused persons are not indefinitely harassed.' While holding that "The scales must be held even between the prosecution and the accused", the Court refused to order trial on account of time already spent and other relevant circumstances of that case. In ***Veerbhadra v. Ramaswami Niackar,***[6] in which a period of five years had already elapsed, the Supreme Court refused to send back proceedings on the ground it would not be just and proper in the circumstances of the case to continue the proceedings after such a lapse of time. Similarly, in ***Chajju Ram v. Radhe Shyam,***[7] the Court refused to direct a re-trial after a period of 10 years and in ***State of U.P. v. Kapil Deo Shukla,***[8] though the court found the acquittal of the accused unsustainable, it refused to order a remand or direct a trial after a lapse of 20 years.

2. Inclusion of the Right to Speedy Investigation as an Integral Part of the Right of an Accused to Speedy Trial

An individual's personal liberty is affected by an arrest. For this reason, Sections 56 and 57 of the *Cr.P.C. 1973,* analogous to Article 22(1) and (2) of the Constitution provide for the production of such person before a Magistrate as soon as possible to determine whether the arrest depriving the personal liberty to the arrested person is justified or not whereas reference of Section 167 under Section 57, emphasises the importance of expeditious disposal of cases during investigation and trials. The entire objects of Sections 56, 57 and 167 of the *Cr.P.C. 1973,* which are *mandatory,* and of Article 22(1) and (2) of the Constitution are fully supported by Article 21 because *quick justice is sine qua non* of Article 21 of the Constitution.[18] Therefore, it has been held by the Supreme Court in several cases that the fundamental rule of speedy trial found under Article 21 of the Constitution is not only exercisable against the actual court proceedings but also against police investigation and speedy investigation and trial are equally mandated by both in letter and in spirit by the *Cr.P.C. 1973*.

In the case of ***Abdul Rehman Antulay etc. v. R.S. Nayak***[9], the Supreme Court pronounced that 'speedy trial flowing from Article 21 of the Indian Constitution, encompasses all the stages namely the stages of investigation, enquiry, trial, appeal, revision and retrial.' In ***Srinivas Pal v. Union Territory,***[10] the court quashed the proceeding against the appellant on the ground of delay in investigation and commencement of trial. In ***State of Andhra Pradesh v. P.V. Pavithran,***[11] the Supreme Court upheld the decision of the High Court quashing the F.I.R. on the ground of inordinate delay in completing the investigation. However, while doing so, the Supreme Court took care to observe that 'while examining the plea of delay in completing the investigation, the Court should have regard to all the relevant circumstances and that it is not possible to formulate any inflexible guidelines or rigid principles of uniform application for speedy investigation nor is it possible to stipulate any arbitrary period of limitation for completing the investigation.' It had been observed in ***Nimoon Sangma v. Government of Meghalaya,*** [12] that 'Sections 167, 209 and 309 of *Cr. P.C., 1973,* emphasize the importance of expeditious disposal of criminal cases including investigation and trials. The umbrella of 'speedy trial rule' which is an integral part of Article 21 is equally available to the accused during investigation, trial (and even post-trial field of capital offences punishable with death).'[20] Speedy investigation and trial are equally mandated by both in letter and in spirit of the Code : therefore, not only unexplained delay in police investigation would plainly falls within the scope of the mandate of rule of speedy trial but also inordinate delay in police investigation itself equally attract the rule and violate Article 21 of the Constitution.[13]

To conclude, it may be said that the Fundamental Right of an accused to speedy trial enshrined in Article 21 of the Constitution is not an application to the proceeding in a Court *stricto sensu* but also includes within its sweep the proceedings of police investigations as well. However, this right may be denied where the accused himself is responsible for delay; for instance in ***Diwan Naubat Rai v. State through Delhi Administration,***[14] the Supreme

Court refused to quash the proceedings because it was found that the accused himself was mainly responsible of the delay of which he was complaining.

4. Recognition of the Right to Speedy Trial as Fundamental Right of an Accused by Judiciary

The right of an accused to speedy trial as a fundamental right is the outcome of the judicial activism of the Supreme Court. In ***Maneka Gandhi's case,***[15] the Supreme Court declared that 'speedy trial is the essence of criminal justice and there can be no doubt that delay in trial by itself constitutes denial of justice. . There can, therefore, be no doubt that speedy trial, meaning thereby reasonable expeditious trial, is an integral and essential part of the fundamental right enshrined in Article 21.' Similarly, in ***Hussainara Khatoon v. Home Secretary, Bihar,***[16] by majority judgment the Supreme Court held that ". . A procedure which keeps much large numbers of people behind bars without trial so long cannot possibly be regarded as reasonable, just or fair trial so as to be in conformity with the requirement of Article 21. The law as enacted by the legislature and as administered by the Courts must radically change its approach to pre-trial detention and insure "reasonable, just and fair procedure".[17] In ***Hussainara Khatoon (II) v. Home Secretary, Bihar***[18]; the Supreme Court held that the 'undertrial prisoners against whom charge sheet had not been filed by the police within the period of limitation provided for in Section 468 could not be proceeded against the prisoners at all and they must be released forthwith. The reason was that any further detention of such persons would have been unlawful and violative of fundamental right enshrined in Article 21'.The observations made by Justice Bhagwati in ***Hussainara Khatoon (III) v. Home Secretary, Bihar***[19], are worth quoting:

> "The State cannot avoid its Constitutional Obligation to provide speedy trial to the accused by pleading financial or administrative inability. The State is under a Constitutional mandate to ensure speedy trial and whatever is necessary for this purpose, has to be done by the State. It is also the Constitutional Obligation of this court as the guardian of the fundamental rights of the people, as a sentinel on the

> quinine, to enforce the fundamental right of the accused to speedy trial by issuing necessary directions to the State which may include taking of positive action, such as augmenting and strengthening the investigation machinery, setting up new courts, building new court houses, providing more staff and equipment to the Courts, appointment of additional judges and other measures calculated to ensure a speedy trial".

In ***State of Bihar v. Uma Shankar Ketriwal*** [20], the Patna High Court ordered the acquittal of the accused on the ground that 'the prosecution commenced in 1963 and still was in progress in 1979, which was an abuse of the process of the Court and should not be allowed to go on further.' The Supreme Court affirmed the decision of the High Court on the ground of inordinate delay and observed thus :

> " . . . the trial has not made much headway even though no less than 20 years have gone by. Such protraction itself means considerable harassment to the accused not only monetarily but also by way of constant attention to the case and repeated appearances in Court, apart from anxiety. It may well be that the respondents themselves were responsible in a large measure for the slow pace of the case in as much as quite a few orders made by the trial Magistrate were challenged in higher courts, but then there has to be a limit to the period for which criminal litigation is allowed to go on at the trial stage. In this view of the matter, we do not consider the present case a proper on for our interference. . ."

Re-affirming the principle of law laid down in ***Hussainara Khatoon's case,***[21] the Supreme Court in ***Kadra Pahadiya v. State of Bihar,***[22] held that 'any accused who is denied this right of speedy trial is entitled to approach this Court for the purpose of enforcing such right.' The significance of the right to speedy trial was reiterated by the Supreme Court in ***T.V. Vatheeswaran v. State of Tamil Nadu***[23] and this right was extended even to post-conviction stage, entitling the accused to ask for lesser sentence of life imprisonment in case of undue delay in carrying out the death sentence. This opinion was based upon the immense psychological, emotional and mental torture a man condemned to death suffers. In *Sheela Barse v. Union of India*[24], a Division Bench comprising Justice Bhagwati and Justice R.N. Mishra, reaffirmed that the 'right to speedy trial was a fundamental right implicit in Article 21 of the Constitution' and observed that 'the consequence of violation of fundamental right to speedy trial would be that the prosecution itself would be liable to be quashed on the ground that it is in breach of the fundamental right'. The learned Justice Bhagwati also deliberated upon the primary reasons for the delayed disposal of the criminal cases and opined that 'one of the primary reasons for delay in the trial of criminal cases is the total inadequacy of judge-strength and lack of satisfactory working conditions for Magistrates and Additional Sessions Judges.' In order to overcome the problem of arrears of criminal cases in the trial courts the learned judges expressed their firm view that 'every State Government must take necessary measures for the purposes of setting up adequate number of Courts providing them the necessary facilities. It is also necessary to set up an Institute of Academy for training of judicial officers so that their efficiency may be improved and they may be able to regulate and control the flow of cases in their respective Courts.'

5. Guidelines Issued by the Supreme Court fixing the Time Limit for Conclusion of Trial to make the Right to Speedy Trial an Effective and Real One

The Supreme Court, for the first time, in *Sheela Barse v. Union of India*[25] fixed the time limit (maximum nine months – 3 months for investigation and 6 months for trial) for conclusion of the trial related to juvenile accused. It held that :

> "So far as a child accused of an offence punishable with imprisonment of not more than 7 years is concerned, a period of three months from the date of filling of the complaint or lodging of the First Information Report shall be deemed to be the maximum time permissible for investigation and a period of six months from the filling shall be the reasonable period within which the trial of the child should be completed".

It was specifically directed by the Supreme Court that if

these time limits are not obeyed, the prosecution against the child were liable to be quashed". It is to be noted that in spite of the recognition of the fact that the consequence of violation of the fundamental right to speedy trial would be that the prosecution itself would be liable to be quashed on the ground that it is in breach of the fundamental right guaranteed under Article 21, the Supreme Court declined to fix a time limit for the trial of the criminal cases relating to adult accused in the instant case. The learned justices expressed that 'the question may have to be considered in some other case where the court may be called upon to examine as to what is reasonable length of time for a trial beyond which the Court would regard that the right to speedy trial is violated.'

For the purposes of making the 'right of speedy trial' of an accused more realistic and effective, the Supreme Court issued certain guidelines, in the year 1992, in the case of ***Abdul Rehman Antulay v. R.S. Nayak***.[26] The main guidelines were as under :

"(1) Fair, Just and Reasonable procedure implicit in Article 21 of the Constitution creates a right in the accused to be tried speedily. . .The fact that a speedy trial is also in public interest or that it serves the societal interest also, does not make it any the less the right of the accused. It is in the interest of all concerned that the guilt or innocence of the accused is determined as quickly as possible in the circumstances.

(2) Right to speedy trial flowing from Article 21 encompasses all the stages, namely, the stage of investigation, inquiry, trial, appeal, revision and retrial. That is how, this Court has understood this right and there is no reason to take a restricted view.

(3) The concerns underlying the right to speedy trial from the point of view of the accused are:

(a) the period of remand and pre-conviction detention should be as short as possible. In other words, the accused should not be subjected to unnecessary or unduly long incarceration prior to his conviction;

(b) the worry, anxiety, expense and disturbance to

his vacation and peace, resulting from an unduly prolonged investigation, inquiry or trial should be minimal; and

(c) undue delay may result in impairment of the accused to defend himself, whether on account of death, disappearance or non-availability of witnesses or otherwise.

(4) At the same time we cannot ignore the fact that it is usually the accused who is interested in delaying the proceedings. As is often pointed out, "delay is a know defence tactic". Since the burden of proving the guilt of the accused lies upon the prosecution, delay ordinarily prejudice the prosecution. Non-availability of witness, disappearance of evidence by lapse of time really work against the interest of the prosecution. In every case, where the Right to Speedy Trial is alleged to have been infringed, the first question to be put and answered is - who is responsible for the delay ? Proceedings taken by either party in good faith, to vindicate their rights and interests, as perceived by them cannot be treated as delaying tactics nor can the time taken in pursuing such proceedings be counted towards delay. It goes without saying that frivolous proceedings or proceedings taken merely for delaying the day of reckoning cannot be treated as proceedings taken in good faith.

(5) While determining whether undue delay has occurred (resulting in violation of right to speedy trial) one must have regard to all the circumstances, including nature of offence, number of accused and witnesses, the work load of the court concerned, prevailing local conditions and so on what is called, the systemic delays. It is true that it is the obligation of the State to ensure a speedy trial and State includes judiciary as well, but a realistic and practicai approach should be adopted in such matters instead of a pedantic one."

In spite of the serious concern shown by the learned Justice Jeevan Reddy towards the consequences of delay in the trial of criminal cases, he refused to draw a time limit beyond which a criminal proceeding would not be allowed to go. He opined that 'in many cases, the accused may himself have been responsible for the delay and therefore he cannot be allowed to take advantage of his won wrong. In some cases, delays may occur for which neither the prosecution nor the accused can be blamed but the system itself is responsible and such delays too cannot be treated as unjustifiable, broadly speaking. Of course, if it is minor offence—not being on economic offence - and the delay is too long, not caused by the accused, different considerations may arise. For the above-stated reasons, Mr. Justice Jeevan Reddy stated that 'it is neither advisable nor feasible to draw or prescribe an outer time limit for conclusion of all criminal proceedings.' He opined that "Any such rule is bound to be qualified one."

It is a matter of co-incident that again the matter relating to delay in the, or pendency of, criminal trial raised before the double bench of the Supreme Court consisting of learned judges Mr. B.B. Jeevan Reddy and Mr. G.B. Majumdar, in ***Common Cause v. Union of India,***[27] - a public interest litigation filed by a registered society "Common Cause". In this case request was made by the petitioner for the following directions with regard to the criminal courts functioning all over the country:

(a) To quash all proceedings against persons accused of offences under the Motor Vehicles Act where the proceedings were initiated more than one year ago and were still pending in any Court in the country;

(b) To direct the unconditional release of the accused and dismissal of all proceedings pending in criminal courts with respect to offences under Indian Penal Code or other penal statutes which have been pending of more than three years from the date of their institution and for which offences the maximum sentence provided under law was not more than six months with or without fine. This direction was sought in respect of all prosecutions whether lodged by police or by the governmental agency or by a private complaint;

(c) To direct the unconditional release of all the accused and dismissal of criminal proceedings against persons who have been in police or judicial custody for a period of more than three years from the date of their arrest or remand to such custody, where the offences alleged were not punishable with more than seven years with or without fine; and

(d) To direct the unconditional release of the accused and dismissal of proceedings against persons accused of offences under Section 309 of the Indian Penal Code (IPC) where the proceedings have been pending in any Court for more than one year from the date of their institution.

A request was also made by the petitioner that 'the aforesaid directions should apply not only to cases pending in courts on the date of the passing of the order but also to cases executed afterwards.'

Deviating from his earlier stand taken four years back in the ***A.R. Antulay's case***[28] that 'it is neither advisable nor feasible to draw or prescribe an outer time limit for conclusion of all criminal proceedings', Mr. Justice Jeevan Reddy, in this case - ***Common Cause v. Union of India,***[29] - with a view to ensure that the 'criminal prosecutions do not operate as engines of oppression', fixed the following time limit in different types of cases pending in criminal courts for conclusion of the criminal trials and for discharging the accused after the expiry of the fixed period :

"(a) Where criminal proceedings are pending regarding traffic offences in any Criminal Court for more than two years on account of non-serving summons to the accused or for any other reason whatsoever, the court may discharge the accused and close the cases.

(b) Where the cases pending in the criminal courts for more than two years under IPC or any other law for the time being in force are compoundable with the permission of the court and if in such cases trial have still not commenced, the criminal court shall after hearing the public prosecutor and other parties represented before it or their advocates, discharge or acquit the accused, as the case may be, and close such cases.

(c) Where the cases pending in criminal courts under IPC or any other law for the time being in force pertain to offences which are non-cognizable and bailable and if such pendency is for more than two years and if in such cases trials have still not commenced, the criminal courts shall discharge or acquit the accused, as the case may be and close such cases.

(d) Where the cases pending in criminal courts under IPC or any other law for the time being in force are pending in connection with offences which are punishable with fine only and are not of recurring nature, and if such pendency is for more than one year and if in such cases trials have still not commenced, the criminal court shall discharge or acquit the accused, as the case may be and close such cases.

(e) Where the cases pending in criminal courts under IPC, or any other law for the time being in force are punishable with imprisonment up to one year, with or without fine, and if such pendency is more than one year and if in such cases trials have still not commenced, the criminal court shall discharge or acquit the accused, as the case may be, and close such cases.

(f) Where the cases pending in criminal courts under IPC, or any other law for the time being in force, are punishable with imprisonment up to three years, with or without fine, and if such pendency is for more than two years and if in such cases trials have still not commenced, the criminal court shall discharge or acquit the accused as the case may be and close such cases."

The learned Justice Jeevan Reddy also directed that:

(i) The period of pendency of criminal cases shall be calculated from the date the accused are summoned to appear in the Court;

(ii) All the criminal courts in India must initiate trial of the offences mentioned above on a priority basis.

(iii) The High Courts should issue necessary directions in this behalf to all the criminal courts under their control and supervision.

(iv) The directions so issued were applicable not only to the cases pending on the date of delivering the judgment but were also applicable to cases which may be instituted thereafter.

It was clarified by the learned Justice of the Supreme Court that the above-stated directions regarding the outer time limit for a criminal trial were not applicable to the cases involving following types of offences :

(1) Corruption, misappropriation of public funds, cheating, whether under the *Indian Penal Code, Prevention of Corruption Act* or any other Statute,
(2) Smuggling, foreign exchange violation and offences under the *Narcotics, Drugs and Psychotropic Substances Act,*
(3) Offences under *Essential Commodities Act, Food Adulteration Act,* Acts dealing with Environment or any other economic offences,
(4) Offences under *Arms Act, Explosive Substances Act, Terrorists and Disruptive Activities Act,*
(5) Offences relating to the Army, Navy and Air Force,
(6) Offences against public tranquility,
(7) Offences relating to public servants,
(8) Offences relating to coins and Government stamps,
(9) Offences relating to elections,
(10) Offences relating to giving false evidence and offences against public justice,
(11) Any other type of offences against the State,
(12) Offences under the Taxing enactments, and
(13) Offences of defamation as defined in Section 499 of IPC, 1860.

In this context, a reference to a landmark judgement of the Allahabad High Court[30] is noteworthy by which the directions to all the subordinate courts and tribunals in Uttar Pradesh have been issued to decide suits, criminal trials, labour disputes, rent control; cases and other cases within a time-frame fixed by the Court. Day to day hearting was also allowed to facilitate early disposal of the cases. In order to reduce huge pendency of cases in subordinate courts and delay in disposal of cases, the Allahabad

High Court also directed all judicial officers 'to devote their energies and time in disposal of the cases falling in the critically old and very old categories, as if a judicial emergency has been imposed and a red alert sounded.' The Court further added that, barring exceptional cases and exigencies, all out effort should be made to dispose of the existing cases of original jurisdiction falling in the category of 'critical cases' within a period of one year, cases falling in the category of 'very old' in two years, ' old cases' in three years and the remaining cases of the 'recent' category within four years period. The appeals and revisions of the 'critically old' category should be decided within six months period, 'very old' within one year, 'old' within 18 months and that of 'recent' category in two years period.

To conclude, it may be said that the directions issued by the Supreme Court are praiseworthy and these directions would reduce the arrears of pending cases relating to the offences punishable with up to 3 years imprisonment and in the times of come such cases will be decided within the maximum period of two years. Thus, the right to have a speedy trial, would be enjoyed by an accused at least in certain specific cases to a limited extent. It seems to be a good beginning in restoring the fundamental right of the accused. This may be said to be a step in the right direction for making the Right of an accused to Speedy Trial effective and real in true sense. However, its effectiveness can only be achieved when these directions of higher judiciary percolate down to the lower rungs of judiciary, police and prison administration and are followed in reality. Despite these revolutionary pronouncements of the Supreme Court and High Courts, the problem of delayed justice remains endemic in the Indian judicial system due to a plethora of reasons like, ever increasing gap between the legal services available and the much higher demand created by the galloping rate of crime, the poor quality of judicial personnel and legal services, the faulty procedures and practices in the administration of criminal justice, overburdened judiciary, unsatisfactory working conditions of judicial personnel and lack of adequate court staff, frequency of adjournments and lawyers' strikes, etc. to mention a few major factors, contributing to inordinate delay in criminal justice. The 'right to be tried without delay or speedy trial' is a highly vulnerable kind of fundamental right and necessary steps are required to be taken for its preservation and protection by all the actors of criminal justice administration, i.e., lawyers, police, judiciary, public and also the accused himself.

B. RIGHT OF AN ACCUSED TO BE PRESUMED INNOCENT TILL FINALLY CONVICTED

Until the charges against an accused are finally proved and he is convicted by a competent court in accordance with the prescribed procedure of law, he has a 'right to be presumed innocent.' This right arises as soon as the formal accusation is levied upon an accused and continues throughout the continuance of the criminal proceeding until the court declares him to be guilty and punishes him. Being the fundamental basic right of the administration of criminal justice this right requires detailed examination.

1. The Concept and Genesis of the Right of an Accused to be Presumed Innocent

As has been pointed out earlier, the principle of 'presumption of innocence' which is a cardinal principle of the human rights law applicable to pre-trial detention of an accused finds a place of pride in Article 11(1) of the *Universal Declaration of Human Rights, 1942,* Article 14(2) of the *International Covenant on Civil and Political Rights, 1966,* and Rule 84(2) of the *Standard Minimum Rules for the Treatment of Prisoners, 1955.* There are two systems, i.e., accusatorial and inquisitorial systems, followed in different parts of the world in administration of criminal justice. The accusatorial system is followed in common law countries, viz., England, Canada, Australia, U.S.A. and India, whereas the inquisitorial system is followed in some European countries like France. In India, where the accusatorial system is followed, the principle of 'presumption of innocence' is followed which requires that pre-trial detainees should be distinguished from convicted persons and should be provided "separate treatment appropriate to their status as unconvicted person."[31] It imposes burden of proof of charge on the prosecution and the accused has the benefit of doubt. Article 43 of the Yearbook of International Law Commission, 1955, provides

provides that 'a person shall be presumed innocent until proved guilty.'[32] Sir Stephen explains the rationale of the 'rule of presumption of innocence' in the following words:

> "In the present day the rule that a man is presumed to be innocent till he is proved to be guilty is carried out in all its consequences. . . . If it be asked why an accused person is presumed innocent . . .the true answer is, not that the presumption is probably true, but that society in the present day is so much stronger than the individual, and is capable of inflicting so very much more harm on the individual than the individual as a rule can inflict upon society, that it can afford to be genersous".[33]

The principle of 'presumption of innocence of the accused' applicable in English Law is applied in India through the statutory law of criminal procedure and evidence and it also gave birth to the rule of immunity from self-incrimination embodied in Article 20(3) of the Constitution which provides that "no person accused of any offence shall be compelled to be a witness against himself."

2. Right of an Accused to be Presumed Innocent as Recognised by Law of Evidence and Interpreted by Judiciary

(a) Privileges Available to an Accused on the Basis of the Doctrine of the Presumption of Innocence

The 'right of an accused to be presumed innocent' is a matter of law of evidence according to which the burden of proof is thrown upon the prosecution to prove the prisoner's guilt beyond all imaginations of reasonable doubt. It gives the present day recognized 'right of benefit of doubt' to an accused of crime. Thus, the presumption of innocence is particularly a warning not to treat certain things improperly as evidence.[34] In practice, the presumption warrants the search for independent evidence. The presumption is also connected with false defence failure of the accused to explain the circumstances adverse to him, testimonial compulsion, coerced admission and confessions, *mens rea*, circumstantial evidence and the strict construction of the statutes relating to the crimes, punishment, procedure and the like. The onus of proving all the ingredients of an offence is always upon the prosecution and it does not shift at any stage to the accused. It is not the part of the prosecution's duty to somehow book the crook; even in cases where the defence of the accused does not appear to be credible or is palpably false, that burden does not become any the less.[35] In the absence of independent evidence where the accused was convicted and sentenced to the extreme penalty of death on the basis of an incorporated evidence of the inmates of the deceased person's family, the Supreme Court have given the benefit of doubt to the accused in the case of ***Ram Lakhan v. State of U.P.***[36] In case a criminal trial concludes into acquittal of the accused, the presumption of innocence is strengthened and is sometimes called a double presumption. The appellate court has expressed regrets and inability in interfering with an order of acquittal in the absence of 'very substantial and compelling reasons.'[37]

It is to be noted that 'the burden of proof' gives rise to the 'burden of proof beyond reasonable doubt' which is the outcome of the 'presumption of innocence'. 'Reasonable doubt' is that state of the case which, after the entire comparison and consideration of all the evidence, leaves the mind of the juror in that condition that they cannot say that they feel an abiding conviction to a moral certainty of the truth of the charge. A 'reasonable doubt' seems to be that doubt for which a cogent reason can be assigned. The Supreme Court has stated in ***Palvinder Kaur v. State of Punjab***[38] that 'a suspicion, however great it may be, cannot take the place of proof and therefore in such cases the accused becomes entitled to the benefit of doubt'; however, it does not mean that on this ground 'the other accused should also be acquitted in relation to whom the remaining portion of the evidence of that witness has been proved'. The similar view has been expressed by the Supreme Court in another case of ***Sat Kumar v. State of Haryana***[39]. However, the Supreme Court has also held that such cases will 'call for a closer scrutiny of the evidence and the Court must feel assured that it is safe to rely upon the witness for the conviction of the remaining accused'. The following valuable privileges are conferred on the accused by the doctrine of presumption of innocence :

(1) He is not bound to confess guilt and to answer any questions and can keep his lips sealed by placing his reliance on the presumption of innocence.

(2) He need not lead any evidence in defence;
(3) He cannot be compelled to be a witness against himself[40] unless he himself voluntarily chooses in writing [41];
(4) no oath can be administered to him[42];
(5) The accused shall not render himself liable to any punishment for his refused questions; but the court may draw an inference from his refusal or answers it deems fit[43];
(6) The accused cannot be convicted on his voluntarily confession extorted from him by using third degree methods of torture, threat to torture and inducement.[44]

It is well settled law on the point that the burden of proof of guilt rests always on the prosecution and this burden when because of certain circumstances requiring explanation from the accused is known as the one which shifts on the accused; nevertheless, it is less rigorous on the accused than on the prosecution. The Supreme Court has held in ***C.I. Emden v. State of U.P.***,[45] that 'it is sufficient if the explanation given by the accused is reasonably probable'. In ***Alamgir v. State of Bihar***,[46] it was held that 'a criminal statute warrants strict constructions and the construction favourable to the accused should be adopted. While putting construction of the relevant words due regard to the context in which they have been sued must be given.' The Supreme Court in ***Tolaram Relumal v. State of Bombay***,[47] has held that 'in case of two possible and reasonable constructions, the court must lean towards that construction which exempts the accused from the penalty. The presumption also extends to a civil case where a criminal act has been alleged to have been committed; for instance in an action on a life insurance policy the presumption is against suicide.'

(b) Limitations on the Privileges of an Accused Available on the Basis of the Doctrine of the Presumption of Innocence

It has been observed that the presumption of innocence also needs effective modification by judicial decisions. A right to keep silence does no more give privilege to tell lies and take up false defences.[48] In ***Pershadilal v. State of U.P.***[49], while construing Section 114 of the *Evidence Act, 1872*, the Supreme Court observed, that : 'Where in a murder charge the accused falsely denied several relevant acts which have been conclusively established, the court would be justified in drawing an adverse inference from this against the accused.' The limits on the privilege of an accused person not to open his mouth has further been explained in ***Deonandan v. State of Bihar***[50]. In this case the appellant accused was charged with murder and was convicted on the basis of only circumstantial evidence which pointed the accused as the probable assailant with reasonable definiteness and in proximity to the deceased as regards time and situation for which the accused did not offer an explanation. The absence of any explanation or false explanations was treated as an additional link in the chain of circumstances which went against the accused. In ***M.G. Agarwal v. State of Maharashtra,***[51] the apex court held that 'a conviction can be reasonably founded on circumstantial evidence and an inference of guilt can be drawn if the proved facts are wholly inconsistent with the innocence of the accused and are consistent with his guilt.' In the case of ***Andhra Pradesh v. I BS Prasad Rao,*** [52] the Supreme Court has gone a step further in holding that 'even if one or more of the circumstances in the chain of circumstantial evidence is inconsistent with the guilt, but the combined effect of the facts is conclusive of the guilt, a conviction will be justified.'

There is a danger to the excessive devolution to the rule of presumption of innocence and to the soothing sentiment that all acquittals are always good regardless of justice to the victim and the community. In the context of escalating crime and escape the doctrine that ' it is better that ten guilty men should escape than one innocent may be convicted' is a false dilemma. In this context the following observations of Justice Krishna Iyer, who has been a strong supporter of Human Rights of accused, made in the case of ***Shivaji Sahabra Babade v. State of Maharashtra,***[53] warn against the excessive reliance on the presumption of innocence:

> The cherished principle or golden thread of proof beyond reasonable doubt which runs through the web of our law should not be stretched morbidly to enhance every hunch, hesitancy and degree of doubt. The excessive solicitude reflected in the attitude that a thousand guilty men go out but one innocent martyr shall not suffer is a false dilemma. Only reasonable doubts belong to the accused. Otherwise

> any practical system of justice will then break down and lose credibility with the community.

However, in ***Kali Ram v. State of H.P.,***[54] the Supreme Court reemphasized the importance of the principle of presumption of innocence in the following words:

> It is no doubt that wrongful acquittals are undesirable and shake the confidence of the people in the judicial system much worse, however is the wrongful conviction of an innocent person. The consequences of the conviction of an innocent person are far more serious and its reverberations cannot but be felt in a civilised society.

(C) Principles of 'Presumption of Innocence' and 'Fair Trial'

'Fair Trial' is the foundation of the adversary system of criminal trial. Although it is difficult to explain the concept with precision as the notion is a relative one, there is now universal consensus on the attributes of fair trial. The principle of presumption of innocence is an essential attribute of fair trial. The rights of the accused in relation to defence and other rights and the venue and the modes of conducting the trial are inextricably related to the notion of fair trial. The presumption ensures a fair trial which is a valuable right of an accused against State which has enormous power and huge resources. Public hearing in open court as embodied in Section 327 of *Cr. P.C., 1973*, is undoubtedly essential for fair administration of criminal justice. Similarly fair trial also requires that all evidence taken in the course of criminal proceedings must be taken in the presence of the accused as per provisions of Section 273 of *Cr. P.C., 1973.* Amongst various procedural safeguards ensuring fair trial, presumption of innocence is one of the important protection available to an accused.

To conclude it may be said that the presumption of innocence of the accused in English Criminal Jurisprudence has basically been the mainstay of this rule in India. The rule casts burden on the prosecution to prove a person guilty and allows the accused to stand by and watch prosecution failing in establishing the charge conclusively and beyond all reasonable doubts. This presumption of innocence gave birth to the rule of immunity from self-incrimination embodied in Article 20(3) of our Constitution, the resembling provision under Section 342 of the *Code of Criminal Procedure, 1898,* did continue and is still in force as per Section 313 of the *Code of Criminal Protection, 1973.* A usefulness of the doctrine of presumption of innocence is that it helps in defending the dignity of an individual in view of the fact that most of the persons accused of crimes are poor, uneducated and sometimes many go undefended.

C. RIGHT OF AN ACCUSED TO BE PROTECTED AGAINST SELF-INCRIMINATION

1. Genesis of the Right of an Accused to be Protected against Self-incrimination

The Constitution of India enshrines in Clause (3) of Article 20 an injunction that "No person accused of any offence shall be compelled to be a witness against himself". This doctrine is known as the doctrine against 'self-incrimination' which has been designed to protect the accused from being compelled by hope or fear to admit facts or deny them. The immunity from self incrimination is based on the presumption of innocence and so long as the presumption remains as one of the fundamental canons of criminal jurisprudence, evidence against the accused should come from sources other than the accused. The doctrine had its origin in the 16th century in England in protest against the inquisitorial methods of the Ecclesiastical courts. The English *Criminal Evidence Act, 1898,* provided that though the accused is a competent witness on his own behalf, he cannot be compelled to give evidence against himself and his failure to give evidence in defence cannot be commented upon. There the protection was also, extended to a witness other than the accused. In the United States of America, the 5th Amendment of the Constitution provides that "no . . . person . . .shall be compelled in any criminal case to be a witness against himself. . .the accused may voluntarily elect to give evidence but if he elects not to give evidence in defence, this fact cannot be considered to his prejudice."[55] Prior to the adoption of the Constitution, this right was recognized in India in Section 342 of the *Criminal Procedure Code, 1898* and presently it exists in Sections 313 & 315 of the *Cr.P.C., 1973* and in Sections 24, 25 and 26 of the *Indian Evidence Act, 1872.* But, prior to the Constitutional provision, it was followed within the limitation of court premises only; later on, when it became the fundamental right in the Constitution its dimensions became wide spread.

In common law countries, the development of the rule against self-incrimination has been impressive. The protection is extended to cover all persons who have been accused on trial or those giving evidence. The privilege has been enlarged to include oral as well as documentary evidence in criminal as well as civil proceedings; and it traverses beyond the confines of the court to the legislative committees and other tribunals. As was pointed out earlier, due to the doctrine of the presumption of innocence of the accused, the burden is placed on the prosecution to prove a person guilty and the accused is allowed to stand by and watch prosecution failing in establishing the charge "conclusively" and "beyond all reasonable doubts". This presumption was impliedly recognized by section 101 of the *Indian Evidence Act, 1872* which provides that 'whosoever desires any court to give judgement as to any legal right or liability dependent on the existence of facts which he asserts, he must prove that those facts exist.' This presumption of innocence also gave birth to the rule of immunity from self-incrimination embodied in Article 20(3) of the Constitution.

2. Statutory Provisions related to the Right of an Accused to be Protected against Self-incrimination

Following the common law, Sections 203 and 204 of the *Criminal Procedure Code of 1861*, provided that no Oath could be administered to an accused and the Magistrate was invested with discretion to examine an accused. Section 250 of the *Criminal Procedure Code, 1872*, compulsorily provided for a general questioning of the accused after the prosecution witness had been examined and Section 345 of this Code prohibited the administration of oath to a person accused of an offence. These provisions were later on introduced in Section 342 of the *Criminal Procedure Code, 1898*, and are now retained in Section 313 of the *Cr.P.C., 1973* which provides thus:

1. In every enquiry or trial, for the purpose of enabling the accused personally to explain any circumstances appearing in the evidence against him the court—

(a) may at any stage, without any previously warning to the accused put such questions to him as the court considers necessary;

(b) shall after the witness for the prosecution have been examined and before he is called on for his defence, question him generally on the case; provided that in any summons case, where the court has dispensed with the personal attendance of the accused it may also dispense with his examination under clause (b).

2. No oath shall be administered to the accused when he is examined under sub-section (1)
3. The accused shall not render himself liable to punishment by refusing to answer such question, or by giving false answer to them.

Further, Section 315(1) of the *Cr. P.C., 1973* reproducing the provisions of Section 342-A of *Cr. P.C., 1898*, provides that :

Any person accused of an offence before a criminal court shall be a witness for the defence and may give evidence on oath in disproof of the charges made against him or any person charged together with him at the same trial : provided that he shall not be called as a witness except on his own request in witness.

Similarly, an accused person cannot be convicted on the basis of a coerced confession of an accused. Section 164(2) of the *Cr. P.C., 1973*, narrates this right of the accused in the following words:

"The Magistrate shall before recording any such confession, explain to the person making it that he is not bound to make a confession and that if he does so, it may be used as evidence against him; and the Magistrate shall not record any such confession unless, upon questioning the person making it he has reason to believe that it is being made voluntarily".

Additional protections have been provided by the *Indian Evidence Act, 1872*. According to Section 24 of the said Act, 'any confession made by an accused is irrelevant if it has been caused by inducement, threat or promise.' Section 25 of the Act provides that 'a confession made by an accused person to a police officer cannot be proved.' Similarly, according to Section 26 of the Act, 'a confession by an accused person while in custody cannot be proved.' After the incorporation of the protection against self-incrimination as a constitutional right in 1950, the vistas of the rule have become more wide open. The Indian Courts have looked into other systems of jurisprudence to ascertain the scope of the rule; particularly the precedents from the United States.[56] While the American Courts, in the interpretation and extension of the Constitutional Right of the accused, have taken a very liberal view of the doctrine of self-incrimination by enlarging its scope to the extent of the "mischief against which it seeks to guard", the various dimensions of this right is still to be determined by the Indian interpretation.

3. Constitutional Right of an Accused to be Protected against Self-incrimination and its Dimensions

The 'right of an accused to be protected against self-incrimination' has been guaranteed under clause (3) of Article 20 of the Constitution which comprehends the application of several rules of evidence and procedure and also confers a privilege to remain silent in matters incriminating against the accused. Article 20(3), thus, consists of the following main components:

(a) a right pertaining to a person "accused of an offence",
(b) a protection against "compulsion to be witness", and
(c) a protection against such compulsion resulting in his giving evidence "against himself".

Physical and mental tormentations and tortures are implicit in a compulsive testimony aimed primarily at getting an easy way to prove the guilt of an accused. Therefore, the Constitution of India expressly forbids the use of evidence tendered by a person who is compelled to be witness against himself. Accordingly, the guarantee against testimonial compulsion incorporated in Article 20(3) can be claimed by a person establishing that if a statement is sought to be tendered in evidence against him, it is liable to expose him to an accusation. The availability of this right and its various dimensions have been discussed in various judgements of Supreme Court and High Courts which require brief examination.

(a) Meaning And Scope Of The Right Of An Accused To Be Protected Against Self-Incrimination

The main principles of law related to the constitutional right of an accused to be protected against self-incrimination based on various judicial decisions may be outlined as under.

(1) In order to avail himself of the protection it is necessary that the person must have stood in the character of an accused at the time when he made the statement. It is not enough that he should become an accused, any time after the statement has been made.[57]

(2) The right protected by Article 20(3) was held available to the petitioner against whom a First Information Report had been lodged and, therein, he had been recorded as an accused.[58]

(2) "To be a witness" is not equivalent to "furnishing evidence" in its widest significance; that is to say, as including not merely making of oral or written statements but also production of documents or giving materials which may be relevant at a trial to determine the guilt or innocence of the accused.[59]

(3) The inherent logic of the doctrine has led the courts to extend protection of Article 20(3) to that kind of documentary evidence, which, if it were oral evidence, would be protected.[60]

(4) Every positive volitional act which furnishes evidence is testimony, and testimonial compulsion connotes coercion which procures the positive volitional evidentiary acts of the person, as opposed to the negative attitude of silence or submission on his part.[61]

(5) The phrase used in Article 20(3) is 'to be a witness' and 'not to appear as a witness' : It follows that the protection afforded to an accused, so far as it is related to the phrase to be witness, is not merely in respect of testimonial compulsion in the court room but may well extend to compelled testimony previously obtained from him. It is available therefore to a person against whom a formal accusation relating to the commission of an offence has been levelled which in the normal course may result in prosecution.[62]

(6) A person could "be a witness" not merely by giving oral evidence, but also by producing documents or by making intelligible gestures in the case of dumb witness[63] or the like according to the expression "to be a witness" used in Article 20(3).

(b) Extension of the Scope of the Protection/Immunity of an Accused Against Self-incrimination

It has been said that To what extent the scope of the protection/immunity of an accused against self incrimination can be extended to cover those cases which are not direct testimony of the accused has been a debatable issue amongst the different High Courts and the Supreme Court. In this context the following situations have evoked judicial interpretation:

1. Utilisation of tape recorded statements obtained by deception and without the knowledge of an accused;
2. Utilisation of specimen writings, finger prints, etc. of an accused;
3. Production of documents through the legal process of 'search and seizure' from the custody of an accused; and
4. Utilisation of statements voluntarily made by an accused.

(1) Utilisation of tape recorded statements obtained by deception and without the knowledge of an accused and the protection / immunity of an accused against self-incrimination

The Supreme Court in the case of ***Usufalli v. State of Maharashtra***[64], has held that 'tape recorded statements even obtained by deception and without the knowledge of an accused are not the testimonial compulsions.' Briefly the facts on this case were briefly thus: A trap was arranged by the police officials by setting the tape recorder in the inner room and fitting the microphone in outer room where the appellant and Sheikh had conversation. Justice Bachawat held that 'the protection of Article 20(3) was not available to the appellant; in spite of the fact that the tape recording was done without the appellant's knowledge and in a deceptive manner, nevertheless the accused was not compelled;

for he was free to speak or not to speak. Therefore, as the testimony was not compelled, Article 20(3) did not apply.'[65] The Supreme Court reiterated the same view in ***R. M. Malkani v. State of Maharashtra***[66] that 'tape recorded conversation was held admissible and in no way it infringed protection against self-incrimination, for the simple reason that the accused was not compelled to make the statement'. In ***Shri N. Sri Ramma Reddy v. Sri V.V.Giri,***[67] the Supreme Court held that 'the tape recorded statements become admissible if (a) the conversation is relevant to the matter in issue, (b) The voice is clearly identified, and (c) The accuracy of the tape recorded conversation is proved by eliminating the possibility of erasing the tape record. A contemporaneous tape record of a relevant conversation is a relevant fact and is admissible under Section 8 of the *Indian Evidence Act, 1872.* It is *'res gestae.'* Just as a photograph taken without the knowledge of the person photographed can become relevant and admissible so does a tape record of a conversation unnoticed by the talkers is relevant and admissible.

(2) Utilisation of specimen writings, finger prints, etc. of an accused and the protection/immunity of an accused against self-incrimination

Taking of 'specimen writings', 'finger prints', etc., and utilization of the same have been held not to be included under Article 20(3) of the Constitution. In ***Ram Swarup v. State*** [68] the accused was directed by the Sessions Judge to give his specimen writing under Section 73 of the Indian Evidence Act, 1872, for being compared by an expert. This order was challenged on the plea that the direction of the Sessions Judge to furnish the specimen writing amounted to compelling to furnish evidence against the accused and, therefore, was hit by Article 20(3) of the Constitution. The Supreme Court held that 'the direction given by the Sessions Judge under Section 73 of the *Indian Evidence Act, 1872,* was not hit by the provisions of Article 20(3) of the Constitution and, therefore, the accused could not refuse to give his specimen writing when ordered by the court to give it'. The court noted the observation of the full bench decision of the Rangoon High Court given in ***Emperor v. Nga Tun Hlaing***[69] that 'the ridges of his thumb are not provided by him any more than the feature of his countenance are provided by him; all that he is asked to do is to display these ridges; for better scrutiny the ridges are linked over and an impression is made on a piece of paper.'

(3) Production of documents through the legal process of 'search and seizure' from the custody of the accused and the protection/immunity of an accused against self-incrimination

There is a distinction between an order of the court by which the accused himself is directed to produce the documents and order of the court by which the police is directed to search and seize the documents in the possession of the accused. Whereas the former amounts of testimonial compulsion under Article 20(3), the latter does not amount to be so because neither search nor seizure are the acts of occupier of the searched property - they are the acts of another, i.e., police to whom he is obliged to submit. As to whether the production of documents through the legal process of search and seizure from the custody of an accused does hit the constitutional privilege was initially discussed in ***M.P. Sharma v. Satish Chandra.***[70] In this case, on the application of the Registrar of Joint Stock Companies, Delhi, an investigation into the affairs of Messers Dalmia Jain Airways Ltd., which went into liquidation on 13-6-1952 with an intention to defraud its shareholders within a short span of six years of its incorporation with an authorised share capital of Rs. 10 crores, revealed the commission of various offences punishable under the Indian Penal Code. After lodging the First Information Report, a search warrant was issued by the District Magistrate. During the search, a number of incriminating documents were seized. The petitioner moved under Article 32 of the Constitution for quashing the search warrant and the return of the documents as the search warrant was in violation of Article 19(1)(f) and Article 20(3) of the Constitution. It was further urged that Article 20(3) not only applied to oral testimony given by an accused in a criminal case pending against him in a court, but also applied to evidence of whatever character if compelled out of a person who was likely to become incriminated thereby as an accused. The arguments were negatived and the Supreme Court held that 'a search and seizure of documents from the possession of the accused made in pursuance of warrants issued under Section

96 of the *Code of Criminal Procedure, 1898* (now Section 93 of the *Cr.P.C., 1973*), was legal and Constitutional. There was no invasion of the fundamental right of the petitioner guaranteed by Article 20(3) of the Constitution consequent upon a legal search and seizure made under Section 96 of that Code of 1898.'[71] Justice Bala Krishna Ayyar quoted *in extenso* the observations made by Justice Somasundaram in a Madras High Court Judgement[72] thus:

> "No Article of the Constitution prohibits either a search under Section 165 of Criminal Procedure Code by the police of premises involved in cognizable offence or the issue of search warrant by a Magistrate whether the offence involved is cognizable or non-cognizable. It is easy to see where a different view would lead us. A person may commit a burglary and keep the loot in an almirah inside his house or he may commit cheating and keep the proceeds thereof in a drawer of his writing desk, and they would all be as safe as if they had been lodged in the Bank of England. The Constitution is not intended to be a charter for the lawless and there is nothing in Article 20 of the Constitution or in any of its other Articles to prohibit the police from searching either the person of the accused or the premises in the manner laid down by Criminal Procedure Code. Nor have the powers of the Magistrate to issue a search warrant in the circumstances set out in the Code been abrogated by the Constitution."

There are conflicting decisions on the point whether 'compelled production of documents under section 94 of *Criminal Procedure Code, 1898*,, (section 91 of the *Cr. P.C.,1973*) was hit by Article 20(3) of the Constitution. The answer of the question by the *High Courts* of *Kerala* [73], *Gujarat*[74] and *Allahabad* [75] had been affirmative that 'the constitutional guarantee under Article 20(3) is not only confined to oral testimony but also extends to any compulsory process for production of evidentiary documents which are reasonably likely to support the prosecution against the accused.' On the other hand, the *High Courts* of the *Madhya Bharat* [76] and *Jammu and Kashmir*[77] had been negative that 'searches conducted under the orders of the court do not tantamount to testimonial compulsion to the accused person so as to amount to an invasion of the guarantee of immunity from self-incrimination contained in Article 20(3) of the Constitution; as neither the search nor the seizure is such an act of the other person to which the occupier is obliged to submit, the legal searches and seizures cannot to be testimonial compulsion within the meaning of the prohibition contained by Article 20(3).' The Division Bench of the Punjab High Court has tried to strike a balance between the two conflicting views in ***State v. Prabhu Singh***[78] by holding that 'an order of the Magistrate requiring the accused to produce a document is hit or not hit by the prohibition would always depend upon the nature of that document; if the document is such, as is not hit by his statement conveying his personal knowledge relating to the charge against him, he may be called upon by the court to produce that document; but if the order relates to a document which contains any statement of the accused based on his personal knowledge, the order for its production will attract the Constitutional bar against his testimonial compulsion.'

The contention that the production of documents at the instance of the court to the party hit the constitutional protection against self-incrimination can be sustained on the basis of the 'use of compulsion by the court' on the party accused of an offence. The criterion of using the search procedure as laid down in ***Gurpurb Singh v. Autar Singh***[79] seems to be the valid criterion because the use of search of documents through the agency of the police is in no way a testimonial compulsion. The conflicting views on the subject has been resolved by the Supreme Court in ***State of Gujarat v. Shyamlal*** [80] where the Court by a Majority of 4 to 1 held that Section 94(1) of the Code of Criminal Procedure, 1898 (now 91 of the Code of 1973) did not apply to an accused. Justice Sikri, speaking for the majority after citing *in extenso* a few early English cases viewed that the Magistrate's order was violative of Article 20(3) of the Constitution, while Justice Shah, dissenting, held otherwise when he observed thus:

> "Testimonial compulsion as guaranteed by Article 20(3) relates to the proceeding pending in the court and does not relate to an order of the police officer made during the investigation and, therefore, he erroneously held that the court would not consider enaction of a police officer calling

upon a person charged with the commission of an offence to produce a document or thing in his possession which infringes the guarantee under Article 20(3) of the Constitution. The reference made by the Session Judge should have been accepted".

(4) Utilisation of statements made by an accused voluntary and the protection/immunity of an accused against self-incrimination

It has been held by the Supreme Court in ***Mohamed Dastagir v. State of Madras***[81], that 'there was no accusation of an offence against the accused at the time when he was asked to produce the currency notes meant to be offered as bribe; therefore, he could not avail himself of the right protected by Article 20(3). No doubt he was asked but he could have very well refused to do so.' It is submitted that the court erred in appreciating the circumstances which had subdued the appellant to a state of fear when he had reproduced the currency notes. Likewise, the seizure of incriminating articles from a person voluntarily surrendering to a magistrate's court is not an act of compulsion.[82] Where a person is found by the police in suspicious possession of some articles and he is asked to explain the possession under Section 124 of the *Bombay Police Act, 1955*, as there was reason to believe that the property was stolen, there could not be any question of the accused being compelled to incriminate himself.[83] The position is precisely the same when an accused is asked to explain the circumstances appearing in evidence against him under Section 342 of the Code of Criminal Procedure 1898 (now 313 of the Code of 1973) at any stage of the proceeding. It is pertinent to note voluntary confession does not attract the constitutional guarantee; only testimony obtained by 'compulsion' would invite the attention of Article 20(3) of the Constitution and 'compulsion' means 'duress' which includes 'threatening', 'beating' or 'imprisoning of the wife, parent or child of a person'. Thus, where the accused makes a confession without any inducement, threat or promise, Article 20(3) does not apply.

To conclude, it may be said that the principle of granting immunity to an accused from self-incrimination is the outcome of the doctrine of presumption of innocence of the accused resulting from the adopted outrageous procedure of the court of star chamber and barbarous punishment awarded to an individual irrespective of the fact that he was guilty or innocent. This principle, in India, though was not recognized in the present form in the very early of the second half of the 19th century, nevertheless, to some extent, received statutory sanction only when provisions were made in the Indian Evidence Act, 1872 and the Code of Criminal Procedure, 1898. The immunity was further strengthened by the Constitutional provision and, in some cases, as has been discussed in the previous pages, it has been converted into a Fundamental Right of an accused guaranteed by Act 20(3) of the Constitution. The rule is also recognised by the provisions contained in the *Cr.P.C., 1973.*

D. RIGHT OF AN ACCUSED TO SEEK PROTECTION/ IMMUNITY AGAINST DOUBLE JEOPARDY

1. Genesis of the Concept of Protection/Immunity against Double Jeopardy

The doctrine of double jeopardy emanating from the common law principles has been universally recognized as an established rule of criminal jurisprudence and reflects the changing criminal law and procedure as well as the political reflect. The concepts of *double jeopardy, autre fois acquit* and *autre fois convict* as well as of *issue estoppel* seem to be the off-shoots of the doctrine of *res-judicata* and these rules in themselves are distinguishable from one another. It is no exaggeration to mention that the application of the principle of *res-judicata* in the form of double jeopardy, autre fois acquit and autre fois convict and issue-estoppel is definitely more essential in criminal trials than in civil actions, because in criminal trials there is always an apprehension of conviction and consequently the person being stigmatised and his freedom being threatened. The *Fifth Amendment of the American Constitution* while incorporating this principle, has laid down that : " . . .Nor shall any person be subjected for the same offence to be twice in jeopardy of life or limb. . ." The words 'jeopardy of life and limbs' indicate that the immunity was restricted to crimes of the highest grade; however, by a gradual process of liberal construction, the courts have extended the scope of the clause to make it applicable to all indictable offences including misdemeanours.[84] Under the law of the United States, in order to be put in Jeopardy there must be a valid indictment or information duly presented to a court of competent jurisdiction, there must be an arraignment and plea, and the law Jury must be impaneled and sworn. The protection is against the peril in which a person is placed by the Jeopardy.[85] The 'double jeopardy clause' of the Fifth Amendment was declared to be a bar to a prosecution for a lesser crime after conviction for a greater offence.[86] The roots of the principle are also found in the common law that 'where a person has been convicted of an offence by a court of competent jurisdiction, the conviction is a bar to all further criminal proceedings for the same offence'.[87]

There is an ancient maxim - *Nimo Bis Debet Puniri Pro Uno Delicto*, which means that 'no one ought to be twice punished for one offence'; sometimes it is also mentioned as *Pro Eadem Cause*, that is 'for the same cause'. *Halsbury's Laws of England* has explained the principle thus[88] :

> "The plea of *autre fois convict* or *autre fois acquit* avers that the defendant has been previously convicted or acquitted on a charge of the same offence as that in respect of which he is arraigned. The question for the jury on the issue is whether defendant previously been in jeopardy in respect of the charge on which he is arraigned, for the rule of law is that a person must not be put in peril twice for the same offence. The test is whether the former offence and the offence now charged have the same ingredients in the sense that the facts constituting the one are sufficient to justify a conviction of the other, not that they relied on by the crown are the same in the two trial. A plea of *autre fois acuqit* is not proved unless it is shown that the verdict of acquittal of the previous charge necessarily involves an acquittal of the latter".

Under English law the rule applies mainly in two cases :

(a) Where the acquittal was for the exact offence charged in the subsequent indictment; or

(b) Where the subsequent indictment is based on the same act or omission in respect of which previous acquittal was made and some statute directs that the accused shall not be tried or punished twice in respect of the same acts or omissions.[89]

The following inquiries are relevant for determining whether or not in a particular case the plea of double jeopardy would be admissible:

(i) Was the accused in jeopardy on the first indictment?
(ii) Was there a final verdict? and
(iii) Was the previous charge substantially the same as the present one?

If the answers to these questions are in the affirmative, the plea of Double Jeopardy will succeed. Final verdict here does not only mean the verdict of conviction but includes the verdict to have been in jeopardy because no conviction upon an invalid charge would be effectual. Therefore, if the plea to jurisdiction taken by the accused succeeds or he gets the previous order quashed, he shall remain liable to be tried again on the same charge. In India this principle was firstly recognized by the *General Clauses Act,1897*; thereafter by the *Criminal Procedure Code, 1898,* by the *Constitution of India* and also by the *Criminal Procedure Code, 1973.*

2. Recognition of the Concept of Protection/Immunity against Double Jeopardy in India and its Judicial Interpretation

In India, firstly, Section 26 of the *General Clauses Act, 1897*,recognised the concept of double jeopardy; thereafter, it was recognised by Section 403 of the *Code of Criminal Procedure, 1898* and the provisions were also retained in Section 300(1) of the *Cr.P.C.,1973.*

Section 26 of the *General Clauses Act, 1897* provided as under.

> "Where an act or omission constitutes an offence under two or more enactments, then the offender shall be liable to be prosecuted and punished under either or any of these enactments, but shall not be liable to be punished twice for the same offence".

Section 300(1) of the *Criminal Procedure Code, 1973,* provides that :

> "A person who has been tried by a court of competent jurisdiction for an offence and convicted or acquitted of such offence shall, while such conviction or acquittal remains in force, not be liable to be tried again for the same offence

nor on the same facts for any other offence of which a different charge from the one made against him might have been made under sub-section (1) of Section 221, or for which he might have been convicted under sub-section (2) thereof".

In sub-sections (2) to (6) of Section 300, certain exceptions to the rule contained in sub-section (1) of Section 300 have been provided. The whole basis of the application of Section 300(1) is that the first trial should have been before a court competent to hear and determine the case and to record a verdict of conviction or acquittal. Under this Section, second trial is barred when the accused is convicted or acquitted, that is, the cause must have been heard and determined. It is also to be remembered that where there are two alternative charges in the same trial, the fact the accused is acquitted of one of them will not prevent the conviction on the other.

There is a distinction between 'Acquittal' and 'Discharge'. Discharge of the accused does not amount to an acquittal. A person is said to be discharged when he is relieved from legal proceedings by an order which does not amount to judgment which is the final order in a trial terminating in either conviction or acquittal of the accused.[90] An order of discharge is not a judgment. Discharge may take place either after the preliminary inquiry or during a trial before a Magistrate before the accused has been called upon to plead. When there is no *prima facie* case against the accused and he has not been put on his defence, nor any charge has been drawn up against him to which he could plead, he should be treated to be discharged and not acquitted. A man, who in law is only "discharged", may again be charged with the same offence if other testimony should be discovered; but a man who has been acquitted can never be put on the trial again for the offence of which he has been acquitted. A discharge leaves the matter at large for all purposes of judicial inquiry and there is nothing to prevent the Magistrate discharging the accused, from inquiring again into the case.[91]

In addition to the recognition of the protection of an accused against double jeopardy by the *Cr.P.C.,1973*, this protection/ immunity has also been guaranteed by clause (2) of Article 20 of the Constitution which provides that : "No person shall be prosecuted and punished for the same offence more than once". The protection guaranteed under Article 20(2) is narrower than the protection available in England and America, presumably may be because of the abolition of jury system from India. In India, the second trial is a bar when a person has not only been prosecuted but punished also for the same offence for which he is prosecuted again. Therefore, there is no bar to a second prosecution in a case where there has been no punishment in the first trial. In ***Smt. Kalawati v. State of Himachal Pradesh***[92], Justice Chandrashekhar Ajyar of the Supreme Court has held that:

> "If there is no punishment for the offence as a result of the prosecution, the sub-section (2) of the Article 20 has no application and secondly, an appeal against an acquittal wherever such is provided by the procedure is in substance a continuation of the prosecution".

Justice Bhagwati of the Supreme Court opined in ***Maqbool Hussain v. State of Bombay,***[93] that:

> "Article 20 (2) incorporates within its scope the plea of 'Autre fois convict' as known to the British Jurisprudence or the plea of 'double jeopardy' as known to the American Constitution but circumscribes it by providing that there should be not only a prosecution but also a punishment in the first instance in order to operate as bar to a second persecution and punishment for the same offence."

With reference to the expression 'competent court', Justice Bhagwati of the Supreme Court observed in the same case that:

> "The words 'before a court of law' or 'judicial tribunal' are not to be found in Article 20(2). But in order to invoke the protection of Article 20 (2), there must have been a prosecution and punishment in respect of the same offence before a court of law or a tribunal, required by law to decide the matter in controversy judicially on evidence on oath which it must be authorised by law to administer and not before a tribunal which entertains a departmental or an administrative enquiry even though set up by a statute but not required to proceed on legal evidence given on oath. The Article contemplates proceedings of the nature of

criminal proceedings before a court of law or a judicial tribunal and the prosecution in this context means an initiation or starting of proceedings of a criminal nature before such a court or tribunal in accordance with the procedure prescribed in the statute which creates the offence and regulates the procedure."[94]

Thus, it may be summed up that Article 20(2) implies three things :

(i) a person must be accused of an offence,
(ii) the proceeding or the prosecution should have taken place before a court or judicial tribunal and should be of judicial character, and
(iii) the prosecution must be in reference to the law which creates the offence and provides for punishment.

3. Limitations on the Protection/Immunity of an Accused against Double Jeopardy

Various exceptions have been provided by Section 300 of the *Cr.P.C., 1973,* itself and thus the Constitutional guarantee given under Article 20 (3) has been circumvented. Sub-sections (2) to (6) provide the following limitations on the protection/immunity of an accused against double jeopardy:

(i) A person acquitted or convicted of any offence may be afterwards tried, with the consent of the State Government for any distinct offence for which a separate charge might have been made against him at the former trial sub-section (1) Section 220.
(ii) A person convicted of any offence constituted by any act causing consequences which, together with such act, constituted a different offence from that of which he was convicted, may be afterwards tried for such last-mentioned offence, if the consequences had not happened, or were not know to the court to have happened, at the time when he was convicted.
(iii) A person acquitted or convicted of any offence constituted by any acts may, notwithstanding such acquittal or conviction, be subsequently charged with, and tried for, any other offence constituted by the same

acts which he may have committed if the court by which he was first tried was not competent to try the offence with which he is subsequently charged.

(iv) A person discharged under Section 258 shall not be tried again for the same offence except with the consent of the court by which he was discharged or of any other court to which the first-mentioned court is subordinate.

(v) Nothing in this section shall affect the provisions of Section 26 of the General Clauses Act, 1897 (10 of 1897) or of Section 188 of this Code.

In addition to the above-stated exceptions, some limitations have also been imposed on this right through judicial interpretation. Article 20 (2) of the Constitution underlines the same principles as has been laid down in Section 300 of the *Cr. P.C., 1973*. The word "and" in the expression "Prosecuted and Punished" has been used not in a "disjunctive" but "conjunctive" sense and thereby giving effect to the meaning of "and' and not "or" and it means both - prosecuted and punished. So, in the case an accused is prosecuted but is discharged for lack of compliance of procedure, there is no punishment; similarly in the case a man is punished departmentally, there is no prosecution—in both the cases benefit of Article 20(3) would not be available due to the strict interpretation of the provision. Procedural technicalities do not weigh with the court in giving an accused the benefit of double jeopardy. Thus, where a fresh trial was ordered after the rectification of an order sanctioning prosecution, it could not be checked on the plea of double jeopardy because Article 20 (2) of the Constitution or Section 300 of the *Cr. P.C., 1973*, do not confer immunity where the trial is a nullity ; and the order of acquittal or conviction is without jurisdiction and can only operate as an order of discharge. Thus, in all these circumstances the prosecution for the same offence on the same facts cannot be said to be barred either by Section 300 of the *Cr.P.C., 1973*, or by Article 20 (2) of the Constitution.

The Calcutta High Court in ***Pulin Krishna v. Shishupati***[95] has held that 'the prosecution and punishment of the accused person must be before a court of law or judicial tribunal.' In other words, in order to bar a fresh trial under Section 300 of *Cr. P.C., 1973*, it is necessary that the accused must have been tried by a court competent to pass a valid order of acquittal or conviction. In this case, the petitioner, a landlord, was fined for his illegal act by the Rent Controller under Section 34 of the West Bengal Premises Rent Control Act 1950 (Temporary Provisions). Subsequently the petitioner was prosecuted in the Court of the Presidency Magistrate under Section 41 of the same Act where he was sentenced to one month's rigorous imprisonment. On revision, the High Court held the petitioner's prosecution and punishment before the Magistrate's court as illegal as the same was in contravention of Article 20(2) of the Constitution. A corollary, an offence tried by a Criminal Court cannot be re-tried by a tribunal without violating the protection guaranteed by Article 20(2).

If an accused has been tried by some other agency/authority other than a competent court or tribunal such prosecution would not be a bar on the launching of a fresh prosecution. For instance, in ***Venkataraman v. Union of India***[96], on the report submitted by the Commissioner, the petitioner was dismissed from his services and thereafter his prosecution was launched under Sections 161 & 165 of the Indian Penal Code and Section 2(2) of the Prevention of Corruption Act, 1947, in the Special Judge, Sessions Court at Delhi. On a petition filed under Article 32 of the Constitution for issuing the writ of *certiorari* and quashing the proceeding started on the ground that it violated the right guaranteed by Article 20(2) of the Constitution, Justice Mukherjee, B.K. of the Calcutta High Court held that 'an order of dismissal of a servant could not be regarded as a punishment for an offence punishable under particular sections of the Penal Code or Prevention of Corruption Act.' Justice Mukherjee, B.K. observed that [97]:

> ". . . in an enquiry under the Public Servants (Inquires) Act of 1850, there is neither any question of investigation of an offence in the sense of an act or omission punishable by any law, for the time being in force, nor is there any question of imposing punishment prescribed by the law which makes that act or omission an offence."

Similarly, in ***Ratilal Bhopilal v. State of Gujarat***,[98] the disciplinary proceeding were not held as prosecution proceedings and, therefore, did not warrant the interference of Article 20(2). The Supreme Court has made it amply clear in ***S.A. Venkataraman v. Union of India***[99] that 'departmental and administrative enquiry instituted against an employee and action consequently taken, upon its report by way of disciplinary action including dismissal does not amount to 'prosecution and punishment' as has been contemplated under Article 20(2) of the Constitution. Thus, it may be said that in order to attract Article 20(2), the proceedings relating to prosecution and punishment of a person must be criminal proceedings before a court of law or judicial tribunal[100]; the departmental or administrative inquiries instituted, even though under statutes, do not attract double jeopardy because such inquiries are generally, not required to be conducted judicially and on strict legal evidence.[101]

There have been conflicting opinions of different High Courts regarding the availability of the protection of double jeopardy in case an accused is discharged. The Allahabad High Court in ***Gurucharan v. State***[102] has held that an accused person who is discharged by a competent Magistrate in respect to a particular cause of action should not be harassed in successive trials before different Magistrates in respect of the same cause of action. The court opined that 'the complainant should go in for revision, rather than launch a second prosecution'. On the other hand, Mysore High Court in ***State v. Mohd. Mirza***[103] has held that 'the order of discharge is not an acquittal and therefore the fresh case is not barred under Section 403 (now Section 300 of Cr.P.C.,1973) of the Code of 1898.'

The Allahabad High Court in ***Ganesh Prasad v. State,***[104] has also held that 'on an appeal, if the conviction is set aside and a re-trial is ordered, the retrial is not hit by Article 20(2), i.e., double jeopardy because it is not a second prosecution but is in continuation of the first prosecution. Similarly, a re-trial has been held to be not barred by Article 20(2) of the Constitution if the trial of the accused is found abortive because of certain irregularities or any other defect or incompetency of jurisdiction of the court.[105] Since Article 20(2) protects an accused only from prosecution and punishment twice for the same offence, it does not protect an accused from prosecution and punishment for an offence under which he was previously prosecuted and was acquitted. It is most unfortunate that in many cases in India the accused (convict) undergoes the punishment and after the completion of a part of the punishment awarded, the appeals are heard and retrial is ordered. In such cases reconsideration of the principle of double jeopardy is needed.

4. Res-Judicata: Issue Estoppel: Autre Fois Acquit and Autre Fois Convict as applicable in India

The principle of 'issue estoppel' in modern India dates back to the Privy Council decision given in ***Sambashivam v. Public Prosecutor, Federation of Malaya.***[106] Sambashivam was charged with two offences : (i) Carrying a firearm, and (ii) being in possession of ammunition. He was acquitted of the second charge. At the second trial a statement alleged to have been made by the appellant (which he denied having made), inter alia, to the effect that he was in possession of ammunition was admitted. The Privy Council opined that the in severability of the statement rendered the whole of the statement inadmissible in the evidence. Since it was admitted without objection, the duty was cast upon the Judge to have told the assessors that the appellant had been acquitted on the second charge at the first trial, and as this had not been done, the conviction was unwarranted and must be quashed. Lord MacDermatt while dealing with the facts of the appeal made the following observations: [107]

> "The effect of a verdict of acquittal pronounced by a competent court on a lawful charge and after a lawful trial is not completely stated by saying that the person acquitted cannot be tried again for the same offence. To that it must be added that the verdict is binding and conclusive in all subsequent proceedings between the parties to the adjudication. The maxim *"Res Judicata pro veritate acciptur"* is not less applicable to criminal than to civil proceedings. Here, the applicant having been acquitted at the first trial on the charge of having ammunition in his possession, the prosecution was bound to accept the correctness of that verdict and was precluded from taking steps to challenge it at the second trial. And the appellant was no less entitled to

> rely on his acquittal in so far as it might be relevant in his defence. That it was not conclusive of his innocence on the firearm charge is plain, but it undoubtedly reduced in some degree the weight of the case against him, for at the first trial the facts proved in support of one charge were clearly relevant to the other having regard to the circumstances in which the ammunition and revolver were found and the fact they fitted each other.

The correctness of the statement of Lord Macdermott made in the ***Sambashivam's Case***[108] was accepted by the Supreme Court in ***Pritam Singh v. State of Punjab***[109] and the Court quoted the passage with approval and applied too in Pritam Singh's case; where it was held that as regards the accused Pritam Singh, his acquittal on a former trial was tantamount to a finding that the prosecution has failed to prove the possession of the said revolver by the appellant could not be proved against him in any further proceeding. The decision given in ***Pritam Singh's case***[110] was subsequently referred to and followed in ***K.B. Ghose v. State of West Bengal***[111] by the Supreme Court. While explaining the rule of "issue estoppel" in a criminal trial, the Supreme Court said in ***Manipur Administration v. Bira Singh***[112] that 'the Rule is that where an issue of fact has been tried by a competent court on a former occasion and a finding has been reached in favour of an accused, such a finding would constitute an estoppel or res-judicata against the prosecution not as a bar to the trial and conviction of the accused for a different or distinct offence, but as precluding the reception of evidence to disturb that finding of fact when the accused is tried subsequently even for a different offence which might be permitted by the terms of Section 403(2) of the *Cr.P.C., 1898* (now Section 300 of the *Cr. P.C., 1973*).

The pleas of *autre fois acquit* and *autre fois convict* as contained under Section 300 of the *Cr. P.C., 1973,* afford larger protection to an accused than is afforded by clause (2) of Article 20(2) of the Constitution because Article 20(2) applies to an accused person who has been prosecuted and punished for any offence whereas Section 300 of the *Cr. P.C., 1973,* applies to an accused who had been prosecuted for an offence and ultimately acquitted. The pleas of *autre fois acquit* and *autre fois convict* have been extended to cover the doctrine of *issue estoppel*.[113] It is pertinent to point that, as had been stated in Part A of this chapter, while discussing the 'Right of an accused to Speedy Trial', the Supreme Court has now finally issued revolutionary directions in a P.L.L. filed by "Common Cause" with regard to long-pending criminal trials.[114] These directions included the fixation of time limit of criminal trials and compulsory closure of trial and thereafter discharging the accused. In case the trial is not completed within the stipulated period, protecting the right of the accused to speedy trial, he shall have to be discharged after the expiry of the stipulated period. However, due to the judicial interpretation of the scope of the Constitutional protection against double jeopardy available under Article 20(2) , i.e., the accused may be retried because he is discharged and not acquitted, the right of the accused to speedy trial would become infructuous, because he is discharged and not acquitted, he might have to face a fresh trial.

The Indian criminal jurisprudence is mainly by and large based upon the basic rules of English law. Under the English system of administration of criminal justice, trials for serious offences are held with the aid of the Jury and it is frequently impossible to determine with certitude the specific issues on which the verdict of the jury is founded. The procedure followed in India is somewhat different particularly trials by Jury have been practically abolished and the cases are tried by judges. Further, several charges arising out of the same transaction/cause of action together at one trial can be tried and specific issues are always raised and determined by the courts. In criminal trials under the Code of Criminal Procedure, there is no uncertainty in the determination of the issues decided.

It may, thus, be concluded that the protection available to an accused against double jeopardy under the Indian law is of two kinds: first, protection available under Article 20(2) of the Constitution, and second, protection available under Section 300(1) of the *Cr. P.C., 1973*. Only the principle of *autre fois convict*, and not the principle of *autre fois acquit*, is contained in the Constitutional guarantee according to which for claiming the constitutional protection against second trial for the same offence previous prosecution as well as conviction - both - are necessary. On the other hand, the provisions of section 300(1) of the *Cr. P.C. 1973*, embody both - *autre fois convict* as well as *autre fois acquit*. In the case where there has been no previous punishment or conviction and the accused is acquitted at the end of a trial, and the accused is tried again for the same offence, he will have to invoke the provisions of Section 300(1) of the *Cr. P.C. 1973*.

It may also be submitted that rigidity in approach of giving a narrowed scope to the plea of double jeopardy either under the constitutional clause of Article 20(2) or under the statutory provision of Section 300(1) of the Code of Criminal Procedure, 1973, is not wholesome. A selective approach would be desirable so as to prevent harassment caused to the accused by the negligent attitude of the State or the complaint in initiating the prosecution. An initiation of a prosecution is a matter of serious concern for the person who is affected by it as an accused and the condonation of such casual behavior of the prosecution amounts to put a premium on their attitude of harassing the individual.

It is pertinent to point that, as had been stated in the preceding chapter while discussing the Right to Speedy Trial, the Supreme Court has recently issued revolutionary directions in a P. I. L. filed by "Common Cause" with regard to long-pending criminal trials.[114] These directions include the fixation of time limit for the completion of criminal trials and compulsory closure of trial and thereafter discharging the accused after the expiry of the stipulated period. The interpretation of the protection against double jeopardy, as stated above that the protection is not available when the accused is not acquitted but is discharged, the benefit given to the accused by the right of speedy trial would become infructuous, because as he is discharged and not acquitted, he might have to face a fresh trial. It is submitted that if the accused is discharged due to the prolonged trial or due to lapses of prosecution, the benefit of the protection of double jeopardy should be made available to an accused.

REFERENCES

1. A I R 1978 S..C.. 597.
2. *Ibid.*
3. Ins. by Act 45 of 1978 , s. 24.
4. · *Ibid.*
5. (1955) SCR 524 : A I R 1955 S.C. 792.
6. (1959) SCR 1211 : A I R 1958 S.C. 1032.
7. 1971 (Suppl) SCR 172 : A I R 1972 S.C. 1367.
8. 1972 3 SCC 504 : A I R 1973 S.C. 494.
9. A I R 1992 S.C. 1701 : (1992) 1 SCC 225.
10. 1988 (Suppl) SCR 477 : AIR 1988 SC 1729.
11. (1990) 2 SCC 340 : A I R 1990 SC 1126.
12. A I R 1979 S.C. 1518 : 1979 Cri L.J. 941.
13. Surya Narayan Singh v. State of Bihar A I R 1987 Pat. 219.
14. (1989) 1 SCC 297 : AIR 1989 SC 542.
15. A I R 1978 S.C. 597.
16. Hussainara Khatoon v. State of Bihar, (1979) 1 SCC 810.
17. *Ibid.*, at p. 814.
18. A I R1979 S.C. 1369 at p. 1376-77.
19. (1979) 3 SCR 393 : A I R 1979 S.C. 1360.
20. (1981) 1 SCC 75 : 1981 SCC (Cri) 108 : (1981) SCR 402.
21. (1979) 1 SCC 810.
22. (1983) 2 SCC 104 : A I R 1982 S.C. 1167.
23. (1983) 2 SCR. 384 : A I R 1983 S.C. 361.
24. A I R 1986 S.C. 1773.
25. *Ibid.*
26. A I R 1992 S.C. 1701.
27. Common Cause v. Union of India, (1996) 6 S.C.C. 775.
28. A I R 1992 SC 1701.
29. (1996) 6 S.C.C. 775.
30. Shiddarth Kumar v. Upper Civil Judge, Senior Division, Ghazipur, AIR 1998 All. 265 (Markandey J.).
31. International Covenant on Civil and Political Rights, 1966, Article 10(2)(a).
32. Vol. II Part 2. A/C N4/SER. A/1993/Add.1, United Nations (1995).
33. Stephen J.F., Sir, 'A History of Criminal Law of England,' Vol. I, London, 1883 p. 354; quoted by A.N. Chaturvedi, at p. 167.
34. Wigmore on Evidence, Vol. IX, 1940, pp. 407-9.
35. S.L. Goswami v. State of M.P., 1972 SCC (Cri.) 258 : (1972) 3 SCC 22.
36. A I.R 1977 S.C. 1936 : 1977 Cri. L.J. 1566.
37. Ajmer Singh v. State of Punjab (1953) SCR 418.

38. 1953 Cr.L.J. 154 (S.C.).
39. Sat Kumar v. State of Haryana, A I R 1974 S.C. 294 : 1974 Cr.L.J. 345: See also Moinuddin v. State of Maharashtra (1971) 3 SCC 338;: Dalbir Kaur v. State of Punjab, A I R 1977 S.C. 172 : 1977 Cr.L.J. 273.
40. Constitution of India, Clause (3) of Art 20,
41. Cr.P.C. 1973, s. 315 (1): Cr.P.C., 1898, 342-A.
42. Cr.P.C. 1973, s. 313 (2); Cr.P.C., 1898, 342 (4).
43. *Ibid.*
44. Cr.P.C., 1973, s. 281.
45. A I R 1960 S.C. 585.
46. A I R 1959 S.C. 436.
47. Tolaram Relumal v. State of Bombay, A I R 1954 S.C. 496.
48. Morgan "The Privilege Against Self-Incrimination", 34 Minn. L.R. 1 (1949).
49. A I R 1957 S.C. 211.
50. (1955) Cri. L.J. 1647 (S.C.).
51. (1963) 2 SCR (405).
52. (1970) Cri L.J. 733 (S.C.).
53. (1973) 2 SCC 793.
54. (1973) 2 SCC 808.
55. Chaturvedi A.N., 'Right of accused under Indian Constitution', Deep & Deep, New Delhi, p. 161.
56. See R. Berger, Congress v. The Supreme Court (1969), p. 16; Wright, "The role of the Supreme Court in a democratic society – Judicial activism or restraint", 54 Cornell L.R. 1 (1968).
57. Per majority judgment in State of Bombay v. Kathi Kalu Oghad, 1961 (2) Cri. L.J. 856 (SC) at 864.
58. *Ibid.*
59. *Ibid.*
60. *Ibid.*
61. M.P. Sharma v. Satish Chandra,1954 SCR 1077 at p. 1088: 195) Cr. L.J. 865(S.C.).
62. *Ibid.*
63. Sec. 119, Evidence Act, 1872 - "A witness who is unable to speak may give his evidence in any other manner in which he can make it intelligible, as by writing or by signs; but such writing must be written and the signs made in open court. Evidence so given shall be deemed to be oral evidence, (1954) SCR 1077 at p. 1088.
64. A I R 1968 S.C. 1479 :1968 Cri L.J. 103.
65. *Ibid.*, at 150.
66. A I R 1973 S.C. 157 : 1973 Cri L.J. 228.
67. A I R 1971 S.C. 1162.

68. A I R 1958 All. 191 : 1958 Cri L.J. 134.
69. A I R 1924 Rangoon 115 (F.B.).
70. 1954 Cri L.J. 865(S.C.).
71. *Ibid.*, at p. 867.
72. A I R 1955 Mad. 685.
73. Krishan Keshvan v. State, 1957 Cr.L.J. 755 at p. 757 (Ker), See also R.C. Gupta v. State, A I R 1954 All. 219. Rahman Kunhappu v. Ali Ahmad, A I R 1957 Ker. 80 (it was held that the legal process to produce the document was in violation of Article 20(3).
74. R.K. Ashere v. Tempton Jahangir, AIR 1961 Guj. 137 : 1961 (2) Cri L.J. 338.
75. Babu Ram v. State 1961 (2) Cri L.J. 55 (All).
76. Mohammad Hussain v. Provident Funds inspector, AIR 1957 M.B. 58: 1957 Cri.L.J. 195 (M.B.).
77. Gurupurb Singh v. Autar Singh,A I R 1960 J.& K. 55, 1960 Cri L.J. 470.
78. A I R 1964 Punj. 325 : 1964 (2) Cri. L.J. 199 (Punj.).
79. A I R 1960 J & K 55.
80. AIR 1965 S.C. 1215 : 1965(2) Cri L.J. 256 (S.C.) But a general search warrant under Sections 96(2) and (3) of Cr.P.C., 1898 (now Section 93 of the Cr.P.C., 1973) could be issued to a police officer for search and the production of a thing if it was not known to be in the possession of the accused.
81. A I R 1960 S.C. 756 : 1960 Cri. L.J. 1159 (S.C.).
82. In re Palani Moogan, A I R 1955 Mad 495 : 1955 Cri.L.J. 1197 (Mad) (Seizure of blood stained cloth from the court room).
83. State v. Gundan Lakhanmal, A I R 1960 Bom. 377.
84. Wills, Constitutional Law, 578; also see American Law Institute Draft, Double Jeopardy (1935) p. 8.
85. Thomas Leon Harris v. State of Oklahoma, 1977-53 L. Ed. 2d. 1054. (held that the double jeopardy clause of the Fifth Amendment was a bar to a prosecution for a lesser crime after conviction for a greater offence).
86. *Ibid.*
87. Per Charles, J., in Reg. v. Miles (1890), 24 QBD. 423; See also, Cooley, 'Constitutional Limitations', 6th Edn., p. 193.
88. Halsbury's Law of England, Hailsham edition, Vol. 9, pp. 152-53, para 212.
89. R. v. Sarne (1887) CCC. Sess. Pap. C. VII 418.
90. Lal, Ratan and Lal, Deeraj, 'The Code of Criminal Procedure', Edn. 13, 1987, Wadhawa & Co., Nagpur, at p. 311.
91. *Ibid.*, at pp. 311-312.

92. A I R 1953 S.C. 131. at p. 132.
93. A I R 1953 S.C. 324, at p. 325.
94. *Ibid.*, at p. 326.
95. 1953 Cri L.J. 294 (Cal.).
96. 1954 Cri L.J. 993 (SC); AIR 1953 S.C. 375.
97. *Ibid.*, at p. 997.
98. A I R 1966 Gujarat. 244.
99. A I R 1954 SC 375.
100. D.A. Kelsikar v. State of Bombay, A I R 1966 Bom. 225.
101. Devi Prasad v. H.N. Vora, 1978 Cri. L.J. 79 (Cal.).
102. 1957 Cri L.J. 918 at p. 919: AIR 1957 All. 557.
103. AIR 1964 Mys. 245; 1964(2) Cri. L.J. 561.
104. AIR 1954 All. 116 : 1954 Cri L.J. 216.
105. Upendra Chandra v. State, 1954 Cri L.J. 851 (Assam).
106. 1950 A.C. 458.
107. *Ibid.*, at p. 479.
108. *Ibid.*
109. A I R 1956 S.C. 451.
110. *Ibid.*
111. A I R 1960 S.C. 239.
112. A I R 1965 S.C. 87 : 1965 Cri, L.J. 120.
113. Chaturvedi A.N., Rights of accused under Indian Constitution, 1984, 1st ed.. Deep & Deep Publications, New Delhi.
114. See, Common Cause v. Union of India, (1996) 6 SCC 775.

Six

Human Rights of "Child Accused" (Delinquent Juvenile/Juvenile in Conflict with Law) and Juvenile Justice in India (Rights Available on and after Arrest, during Inquiry and thereafter Regarding Reformation)

Various human rights of an accused in general and certain specified rights in particular have been examined in the previous chapters and it was found that many rights of an accused are available at global level and many of them are also recommended by the United Nations Declaration of Human Rights or other International Declarations and Conventions. However, as has been pointed out in the beginning, accused persons of certain age (which may vary from country to country) have been treated differently, outside the established framework of criminal law, in reference to the administration of criminal justice not only at National level but also at International level. The first and foremost difference is that if a person of a specified age or below commit any offence or allegations are levelled against him, he is called as "delinquent juvenile" and not as an accused or offender. As the entire approach of handling the cases of juveniles alleged to commit an offence has been different and the traditional criminal procedure adopted in the cases of adults is not applicable, not only in India but in almost all the nations of the world, and thus such persons constitute a separate class of accused having special rights, it becomes necessary to examine in detail the Rights of Juvenile Accused, commonly called as "Delinquent Juvenile", separately. In India, after the passing of the *Juvenile Justice (Care and Protection of Children) Act, 2000,* (referred hereinafter to as *J.J.(C&P of C) Act,2000*), such person is called ***Juvenile in conflict with law***. The subject matter of this Chapter revolves around the Rights of such person, i.e., juvenile in conflict with law.

A. SPECIAL RULES FOR THE PROTECTION OF THE HUMAN RIGHTS OF JUVENILES AT INTERNATIONAL LEVEL

International human rights instruments accord high priority to the issues of juvenile justice. Article 14(4) of the International Covenant on Civil and Political Rights,1966, provides that:

> "In the case of juvenile persons, the procedure (determining a criminal charge) shall be such as will take account of their age and the desirability of promoting their rehabilitation".

It requires the state Parties to take into account for juvenile justice. It imposes duty on the State Parties to treat juveniles in such a way as would maximize their opportunity to mature into responsible citizens rather than to fall into a life of crime. There is now sufficient consensus among States that reformation and rehabilitation and not punishment should be the objective of juvenile justice.[1]

The standards embodied in the Covenant were usefully complemented by the *United Nations Standard Minimum Rules for the Administration of Juvenile Justice* (known as *Beijing Rules*) 1985, which were adopted by the General Assembly, vide its resolution 40/33, on the recommendation of the Seventh Congress. The Rules contribute substantially to the international normative system for the protection of children's rights. They are intended to serve as a model for Member States in the treatment and handing of young persons in conflict with the law, within the framework of a juvenile justice system. The Rules set out a special regime that would safeguard the well-being, status, rights and interests of young persons and ensure their fair treatment by justice systems around the world. They provide for strict limits on the use of juvenile detention, the maximum use of community-based modalities, separate juvenile courts and detention personnel, and the provision of specialized facilities, programmers and services. The Rules also favour according juveniles legal rights comparable to those accorded to adults, with protection based on age and personality and the use of scientific research as a foundation for programme development. The said instrument also recommended raising the lower age limit of criminal responsibility and emphasized the importance of inter-sectoral coordination.[2]

As regards the treatment of pre-trial juvenile accused is

concerned, the relevant principles are set forth in Rules 10.1, 10.2 and 13.2 of the *Beijing Rules,1985*. Rule 13 cautions against under estimation of dangers to juveniles of criminal contamination while detention of pending trial and recommend the widest possible adoption of alternative measures. In particular, the Rules provide as follows:

(1) Detention pending trial shall be used as a measure of last resort and for the shortest possible period of time.[3]

(2) Whenever possible, detention pending trial shall be replaced by alternative measures, such as close supervision, intensive care or placement with a family or in an educational setting or home.[4]

(3) Juvenile under detention pending trial shall be kept separate from adults and shall be detained in a separate institution or in a separate part of an institution also holding adults.[5]

(4) Juveniles under detention pending trial shall be entitled to all rights and guarantees of the *Standard Minimum Rules for the Treatment of Prisoners* adopted by the United Nations.[6]

(5) While in custody, juveniles shall receive such care, protection and all necessary individual assistance as they may require in view of their age, sex and personality.[7]

Further, Rule 13 of the *Beijing Rules* provides that:

(6) Upon the apprehension of a juvenile, his or her parents or guardian shall be immediately notified of such apprehension, and, where such immediate notification is not possible, the parents or guardian shall be notified within the shortest possible time thereafter.[8]

(7) A judge or other competent official or body shall, without delay, consider the issue of release.[9]

The General Assembly resolutions annexed to the Rules[10] bearing on this topic, in the year 1990, the *Rules for the Protection of Juveniles Deprived of Their Liberty*[11] (hereinafter referred to as Rules for the Protection of Juveniles) provided for even more adequate legal safeguards than the *Beijing Rules,1985* by interpreting and elaborating the standards contained in the Covenant and the Rules.

Rule 17 of the *Rules for the Protection of Juveniles* provides, *inter alia*, as follows :

(i) Juveniles who are detained under arrest or awaiting trial ("untried") are presumed innocent and shall be treated as such;

(ii) Detention before trial should be avoided to the extent possible and limited to exceptional circumstances and, therefore, all efforts should be made to apply alternative measures;

(iii) When preventive detention is nevertheless used, juvenile courts and investing bodies shall give the highest priority to the most expeditious processing of such cases to ensure the shortest possible detention; and

(iv) Untried detainees should be separated from convicted juveniles.

The *Rules for the Protection of Juveniles* postulate that the conditions under which an untried juvenile can be detained should be consistent with the provisions of Rule 18 which runs as under:

> The conditions under which an untried juvenile is detained should be consistent with the rules set out below, with additional specific provisions as are necessary and appropriate, given the requirements of the presumption of innocence, the duration of the detention and the legal status and circumstances of the juvenile. These provisions would include, but not necessarily be restricted to the followings :
>
> (a) Juveniles should have the right of legal counsel and be enabled to apply for free legal aid, where such aid is available, and to communicate regularly with their legal advisers. Privacy and confidentiality shall be ensured for such communications;
>
> (b) Juveniles should be provided where possible, with opportunities to pursue work, with remuneration, and continue education or training, but should not be required to do so. Work, education or training should not cause the continuation of the detention;
>
> (c) Juveniles should receive and retain materials for their leisure and recreation as are compatible with the interests of the administration of justice.

Successful implementation of the above discussed standards, rules and principles requires the active cooperation of prosecutors. Accordingly, the *Guidelines on Prosecutors* recommended the following:[12]

> In countries where prosecutors are vested with discretionary functions as to the decision whether or not to prosecute a juvenile, special considerations shall be given to the nature and gravity of the offence, protection of the society, and the personality and background of the juvenile. In making that decision, prosecutors shall particularly consider available alternatives to prosecution under the relevant juvenile justice laws and procedures. Prosecutors shall use their best efforts to take prosecutory action against juveniles only to the extent strictly necessary.

Mention should also be made of the *United Nations Guidelines for the Prevention of Juvenile Delinquency*, known as *Riyadh Guidelines*[13] which sought to provide better safeguards to the juvenile delinquents by interpreting and elaborating the *Beijing Rules*. The provisions of the Beijing Rules, Rules for the Protection of Juveniles and Guidelines on Prosecutors were given the force of International Law by Articles 37 and 40 of the *International Convention on the Rights of child*.[14] Article 37 of the Convention requires the State Parties to ensure the following :

(a) No child[15] shall be subjected to torture or other cruel, inhuman or degrading treatment or punishment. Neither capital punishment nor life imprisonment without possibility of release shall be imposed for offences committed by persons below eighteen years of age;

(b) No child shall be deprived of his or her liberty unlawfully or arbitrarily. The arrest, detention or imprisonment of a child shall be in conformity with the law and shall be used only as a measure of last resort and for the shortest appropriate period of time;

(c) Every child deprived of liberty shall be treated with humanity and respect for the inherent dignity of the human person and in a manner which takes into account the needs of persons of his or her age. In particular every child deprived of liberty shall be separated from adults unless it is considered in the child's best interest not to do so and shall have the right to maintain contract with his or her family through correspondence and visits, save in exceptional circumstances.

(d) Every child deprived of his or her liberty shall have the right to prompt access to legal and other appropriate assistance, as well as the right to challenge the legality of the deprivation of his or her liberty before a court or other competent, independent and impartial authority and to a prompt decision on any such action.

Article 40 of the Convention requires the State Parties to undertake to recognise the right of every child alleged as accused of, or recognized as, having infringed the penal law to be treated in a manner consistent with the promotion of the child's sense of dignity and worth, which reinforces the child's respect for the human rights and fundamental freedoms of others. That takes into account the child's age and the desirability of promoting the child's re-integration and the child's assuming a constructive role in society. This Article also enjoins the State Parties with the responsibility to promote the establishment of laws, procedures, authorities and institutions specifically applicable to juvenile delinquents. In particular, the State parties must establish a minimum age below which children shall be presumed not to have the capacity to infringe the penal law. Whenever appropriate and desirable, measures for dealing with such children other than judicial proceedings must provide that human rights and legal safeguards are fully respected. Besides, a variety of dispositions, such as care, guidance and supervision orders, counseling, probation, foster care, education and vocational training programmes and other alternatives to institutional care must be made available to ensure that children are dealt with in a manner appropriate to their well being and proportionate both to their circumstances and the offence.

It emerges from the proceeding discussion that the objective of the international standards relating to juvenile justice is to provide more 'core-oriented' treatment of juvenile offenders with the goals of reformation and rehabilitation of juveniles on the one hand and the prevention of repetition of offences, on the other hand, in mind. The standards also seek to secure to the juveniles the same guarantees of free and fair process for their protection as are enjoyed by the adults accused of crime. In this context, the recommendation of the sub-commission on Prevention of Discrimination ad Protection of Minorities is relevant which provides that the 'States should examine the bails provisions of their respective laws and as far as practicable do away with the requirement of financial guarantees for the purposes of trial of the pre-trial detainees. They should also take steps to ensure that juveniles are detained only in unavoidable circumstances, and if they are detained, they should be put in special institutions and under the auspices of competent authorities with appropriate judicial supervision. The rehabilitation of the detained juveniles after their release requires meaningful educational and skill-training programmes.'[16]

B. THE STATUTORY FRAMEWORK IN INDIA REGARDING JUVENILE JUSTICE (PARTICULARY TO DELINQUENT JUVENILES)

The Constitution of India has conferred enabling powers on State Governments to make special provisions for children as are found in Article 15 (3), Article 24, Article 39 (e), Article 39(f), Article 39A, Article 41 and Article 45. These provisions stipulate that the tender age of the children should not be abused and they should be given opportunities and facilities to grow in a healthy manner and under conditions of freedom and dignity. The State and the society are legally and morally bound to protect the child and the youth against exploitation and against moral and material abandonment. In order to comply with the mandates of the Constitution, Children's Act were passed by different States in India to deal with juveniles, both neglected and delinquent. However, in the case of ***Sheela Barse v Union of India,***[17] the Supreme Court suggested that instead of each State having its own Children's Act, different in procedure and content, there should be a central legislation on the subject to bring in uniformity in regard to various provisions relating to juveniles in the entire country. Consequently, the *Juvenile Justice Act, 1986* (hereinafter referred to as *J.J. Act,1986*) was enacted to deal with the problems of juvenile neglect and delinquency; the Act came into force on the October 2, 1987. This comprehensive law, although was loaded with highly innovative features, caused numerous constraints which, *inter alia,* could not remove the jail-like conditions in the children's institutions and adult-offender like treatment to the juveniles. Besides almost complete absence of NGOs and civil society's participation in the Juvenile Justice System, there were also serious flaws in the management of the Children's Homes and the Act could not be implemented properly throughout the country in the right spirit during the past 14 years. Finally, the *Juvenile Justice (Care & Protection of Children) Act, 2000* (hereinafter referred to as *J.J. (C&P of C) Act, 2000*) was enacted repealing the *J.J. Act,1986,* and the same was enforced w.e.f. April 1, 2001. As the new Act of 2000, although legally enforced, has not been in real operation in various States due to lack of necessary Rules and infrastructure, and also as most of the provisions of the *J.J. Act,1986* have been retained in the *J.J. (C&P of C) Act, 2000,* it would be appropriate to discuss in brief the salient features of the *J.J. Act,1986.*

1. The Juvenile Justice Act, 1986

(a) Salient Features of the Juvenile Justice Act, 1986 (J.J. Act, 1986)

The *J.J. Act, 1986,* for the first time in the history of Juvenile Justice System of India, conceived a completely independent justice system for the juveniles as is evident from its Preamble, given as under:

> "An Act to provide for the care, protection, treatment, development and rehabilitation of neglected or delinquent juveniles and for the adjudication of certain matters relating to and disposition of, delinquent juveniles".

The *J.J. Act, 1986* which came into force on 2nd October 1987 brought about a uniform statutory framework of juvenile justice system for the whole of India except the state of Jammu and Kashmir.[18] The objective of the Act, as mentioned in the 'statement of objects and reasons', were as under:

(1) to lay down a uniform legal framework for juvenile justice in the country so as to ensure that no child

under any circumstances is lodged in jail or police lock up. This is being ensured by establishing Juvenile Welfare Board and Juvenile Courts;

(2) to provide for a specialized approach towards the prevention and treatment of juvenile delinquency in its full range . . . within the purview of the juvenile justice system. This is proposed to be achieved by establishing observation homes, juvenile homes for neglected juveniles and special homes for delinquent juveniles;

(3) to establish norm and standards for the administration of juvenile justice in terms of investigation and prosecutions, adjudication and disposition, care, treatment and rehabilitation.

(4) to constitute special offences in relation to juveniles and provide for punishment therefor;

(5) to bring the operation of the juvenile justice in the country in conformity with the United Nations Standard Minimum Rules for the Administration of Juvenile Justice.

It is pertinent to mention here that care, protection, treatment, development and rehabilitation of both neglected and delinquent juveniles was the primary object of the Act, in place of the punishment or trial of delinquent juveniles. Even a delinquent child after arrest could not be sent to a police station or jail[19] but the delinquent juvenile must be kept in an observation home[20] in a place of safety or with the parent or with the guardian.[21] It was expected that the observation home, as the name suggests, would have the qualities of a home and its purpose was to observe the attitudes and responses of the juvenile. Even after the finding that he or she had committed an offence, he/she had to be placed in the Special Home,[22] which had to provide to the delinquent juvenile not only care, protection and maintenance but, in addition, also the facilities for his/her reformation. Further, the inclusion of 'neglected juvenile'[23] in the *J.J.Act, 1986,* made the scope of the Act so wider that several million children were put under the object of this Act. Although the *J.J.Act, 1986* has now been repealed by the *J.J.(C&P of C) Act, 2000,* it would be of utility to state some important problems relating to the implementation of the *J.J.Act, 1986* which may be helpful in removing the hurdles in effective implementation of the new *J.J.(C&P of C) Act, 2000.*

(b) Problems Relating to the Implementation of the J.J. Act, 1986

(1) Lack of Resources and Institutions

The *J.J. Act, 1986* set forth a very big target to cover within its ambit even neglected juveniles - who ran into several millions - and the State Governments were required to establish Juvenile Courts, Juvenile Welfare Boards and various Homes under the Act. According to a report of the Ministry of Welfare, in the year 1996-97, there were 271 Juvenile Welfare Boards, 189 Juvenile Courts, 280 Observation Homes, 251 Juvenile Homes, 36 Special Homes and 46 Care Organizations functioning under the *J.J. Act, 1986.*[24] There were at least 13 States who were anyhow managing the payment of the salary bills of their employees; from where they would get the resources to establish the institutions mentioned in the Act, is a very big question. After 14 years in operation of the Act, this figure particularly about the homes etc. is too meager and cannot cater the needs of the millions of juveniles who are covered by the Act. With the existing infrastructural facilities, the total coverage for all categories of children would be just about 36,500. Due to the absence of infrastructure in many parts of the country the children most often land up in jail. The governments constantly had expressed helplessness to create infrastructure on the ground of inadequate funds but, in reality, they also lacked the desired will to create infrastructure.

At this juncture, the observations of the then Chief Justice P.N. Bhagwati, which was made many years back, referring to Article 39(f), and is true even today, is worth quoting:

> "It is matter of regret that despite statutory provisions and frequent exhortations by social scientists there are still large number of children in different jails in the country. Even where children are accused of offences, they must not be kept in jails. It is no answer on the part of the State to say that it has not got enough number of remands homes and observations homes or other places where children can be kept and that is why they are lodged in jails. It is also no

answer on the part of the State to urge the wards in the jail where the children are kept is separate from the ward in which the other prisoners are detained. It is the atmosphere of the jail which has a highly injurious effect on the mind of the child, estranging him from the society and breeding in him aversion, bordering on hatred against the system which keeps him in jail. We would, therefore, like once again to impress upon the State Governments and they must set up necessary remand homes and observation homes where children accused of an offence can be lodged, pending investigations and trial."[25]

(2) Personnel Manning the Juvenile Welfare Boards

Under Section 4 of the *J.J. Act, 1986,* the State Government was empowered to constitute one or more Juvenile Welfare Boards in every district for exercising the powers and discharging the duties conferred or imposed on such board in relation to neglected juveniles. Although the Rules prescribed the qualifications of the 'Chairman and members of the Board' who were entrusted with powers of First Class Magistrate, in actual practice political appointments were made without caring the qualifications prescribed by the rules which had resulted delivery of injustice in place of justice.

(3) Conditions of Home etc. Established Under the Act

Various 'Homes' established and maintained by the State Governments were often referred to as 'Jails', by all within and outside the Juvenile Justice System created by the *J.J. Act, 1986.*[26]

(4) Lack of Awareness Even Among Judges

The judgment of the Allahabad High Court in ***Lal Diwan v. State of U.P.,***[27] brings to light even more distressing facts about the awareness and sensitivity of the judges to law and philosophy relating to delinquent juveniles. A fifteen years of child was found to have committed murder and was sentenced to life imprisonment by the Sessions Judge on 24.7.1980. The child remained in prison for long fifteen years becoming 31 and a half years old. Then on 22.2.1986 the High Court setting him at liberty decided by reference to the *U.P. Children Act* that he could have been sent to prison but not beyond the time when he would have attained the age of 18 years.[28]

(5) Restricted Definition of Delinquent Juvenile

Although the *J.J. Act, 1986,* presented a statutory framework of Juvenile Justice System independent of Criminal Justice System, but the definition of a 'Delinquent Juvenile' given in section 2(e)[29] restricting the scope of operation of the *J.J. Act, 1986* because, unless a juvenile commits an "Offence"[30], the *J.J. Act, 1986* could not intervene. In this way, the definition of Delinquent Juvenile excluded from its ambit such contributory actions which had led to act of offence but those acts were by themselves not an offence. To quote Prof. N.L. Mitra:[31]

> "Exclusion of these acts has a far reaching consequence and may often make the whole Juvenile Justice System as meaningless. As for example, absenteeism, act of defiance to lawful authority, cruelty to animals, alcoholism, drug addiction, violence, disregard to authority, forceful collection of public donations on any pretext all those are symptoms of a child gradually turning into a criminal unless early treated."

2. The Juvenile Justice (Care and Protection of Children) Act, 2000

The *J.J. Act, 1986* which presented a comprehensive statutory framework for Juvenile Justice System in India has now been replaced by the *Juvenile Justice (Care and Protection of Children) Act, 2000 (J.J.(C&P of C) Act,2000)*. The objectives of the *J.J.(C&P of C) Act,2000* as per its 'Preamble' are: "to consolidate and amend the law relating to juveniles in conflict with law and children in need of care and protection, by providing for proper care, protection and treatment, by catering to their development needs, and by adopting a child friendly in the adjudication and disposition of matters in the best interest of children and for their ultimate rehabilitation through various institutions established under this enactment". The new Act is a substantial improvement over the *J.J. Act, 1986* and many changes have been introduced in the *J.J.*

Act, 1986 without changing the Act altogether making the new *J.J.(C&P of C) Act,2000,* child-friendly and more participatory. Some of the changes and salient features of the *J.J.(C&P of C) Act,2000* are highlighted below.

(a) Salient Features of the Juvenile Justice (Care and Protection of Children) Act, 2000

Some of the salient features of the *J.J.(C&P of C) Act,2000* are as under:

(1) The expression 'Delinquent Juvenile' used in the *J.J. Act, 1986* has been replaced by the expression 'Juvenile in conflict with law'.[32] This change signifies the impact of the Convention on the Rights of the Child on this New Act which views that derogatory words should not be attached with the children.

(2) The expression 'Neglected juvenile' used in the *J.J. Act, 1986* has been replaced by the expression 'Child in need of care and protection.'[33]

(3) The scope of the definition of 'Child in need of care and protection' has been widened by including: street child, child without any settled place or abode, child living with persons who is likely to kill or abuse, mentally or physically challenged or ill child or child suffering from terminal diseases or incurable diseases having no one to support or look after, abandoned child and child likely to be tortured or exploited for the purpose of sexual or illegal acts.[34]

(4) "Juvenile Court" established for handling the cases of delinquent juveniles under the *J.J. Act, 1986* has been replaced by the "Juvenile Justice Board" to be constituted under Section 4 of the *J.J.(C&P of C) Act, 2000.*

(5) "Juvenile Welfare Board" established for handling the cases of neglected juveniles under the *J.J. Act, 1986* has been replaced by the "Child Welfare Committee" to be constituted under Section 29 of the *J.J.(C&P of C) Act, 2000.*

(6) The definition of the expression "Juvenile" has been changed by making it in tune with the age of the Juvenile

mentioned under Article 1 of the Convention on the Rights of the Child. In the *J.J. Act, 1986* the expression meant 'a boy who has not attained the age of sixteen years or a girl who has not attained the age of 18 years' but now under the *J.J. (C&P of C) Act, 2000,* the expression 'Juvenile or child' means 'a person who has not completed eighteenth years of age.'[35]

(7) Under Section 66 of the *J.J.(C&P of C) Act, 2000,* the State Government has been empowered to delegate its powers to "local authority" also which has been defined as '*Panchayats* at the Village and *Zila Parishads* at the District level including a Municipal Committee or Corporation or a Cantonment Board or such other body legally entitled to function as local authority by the Government'.[36]

(8) Under *J.J.(C&P of C) Act, 2000,* a concept of "Special Juvenile Police Unit" has been introduced which means 'a unit of the police force of a State designated for handling the cases of juveniles or children under Section 63 of the New Act'; it is a new definition.[37]

(9) A new Chapter - Chapter IV – in conformity with the mandate of the *Convention on the Rights of the Child, 1989,* has been added in the *J.J. (C&P of C) Act, 2000* which is 'devoted to rehabilitation and social reintegration of the child.' The rehabilitation and social reintegration of a child shall begun during the stay of child in the Children's Home or Special Home and it shall be carried out alternatively by (i) adoption (ii) foster care (iii) sponsorship and (iv) sending the child to an After Care Organisation.[38]

(10) Under the *J.J.(C&P of C) Act, 2000,* while individual member of the Committee or Board is empowered to grant permission to place the child in safe custody, the signature of at least two members of the Committee/ Board, as the case may be, has been made mandatory for the final disposition.[39]

(11) Under the *J.J. (C&P of C) Act, 2000,* the Magisterial powers have been vested to the Committee which shall

function as bench of Magistrates and to the individual member of the Committee.[40]

(12) The qualification of the individual to be eligible to be appointed as a members of the Board has been specified as having knowledge and training in child psychology and child welfare or a social worker having seven years experience.[41] The same provisions are likely to be made obligatory for the members of the Committee under the Model Rules to avoid favoured appointments.

(13) A clause for the termination of the appointment of a member of the Board/Committee has also been added to ensure proper functioning.[42]

(14) The use of adversarial or accusatory vocabulary such as "Remand," "Accused", "Trial," "Court," etc. have been avoided in the new Act.

(15) The transitory provision contained in Section 7(2) of the *J.J. Act, 1986* of exercising power by the District Magistrate, or the Sub-divisional Magistrate, or the Metropolitan Magistrate or Judicial Magistrate of the First Class, often used as escape clause by the States, has been deleted.

(16) A speedy disposal of cases within four months has been ensured under the *J.J. (C&P of C) Act, 2000*[43] and the role of legal practitioners in the proceedings of the case has been eliminated.

(17) The charging or the trial of a juvenile for any offence together with a person who is not a juvenile has been prohibited.[44]

(18) Besides Children Homes, Special Homes and Observation Homes, provisions for a new kind of Homes, called the "Shelter Homes", have been made in the *J.J. (C&P of C) Act, 2000*. The Shelter Homes shall also function as "Drop-in Centres for children in need of urgent support."[45]

(19) A provision has been made for constituting Central, State, District and City Level Advisory Boards consisting of members from Panchayat, Zila Parishad, Municipal Corporation, and Social Workers, etc., which is a new dimension for the people's participation.[46]

In addition to the above mentioned statutory changes, the following changes have also been introduced by the *J.J.(C&P of C) Act,2000* in the overall attitude towards the juvenile justice administration.

(1) The Homes for Children in need of care and protection have been converted into comprehensive institution from where the restoration / adoption can take place as is presently done in Observation Home; the children not restored shall continue to live on till they attain the age of 18 (eighteen) years.[47]

(2) The Children's Home meant for the 'Child in need of Care and Protection' established under the *J.J.(C&P of C) Act, 2000,* is now open to media, since there is no stigma attached to these Homes. The prohibition of the publication of photographs and the names of the juvenile under inquiry prescribed under Section 36 of the *J.J. Act, 1986* is now applicable only to such 'juvenile who is in conflict with law' under the *J.J.(C&P of C) Act, 2000.*[48]

(3) Efforts have been made to give the Juvenile Justice Board as much an independent legal status as possible. Further, the role of the State has also been minimized by vesting powers directly to local self-governments, NGOs and social workers and thus has been limited to a facilitator rather than doer.[49]

(4) The provision has been made for the transfer of government run Homes to NGOs.[50] The social voluntary organization, child line, social workers or a child himself have been empowered to receive and produce the children before the Board/Committee, as the case may be, besides by the police.[51]

(5) The definition of the 'child in need of care and protection' replaced by the *J.J.(C&P of C) Act, 2000* is more exhaustive than the definition of 'neglected juvenile used in the *J.J. Act, 1986.* Children vulnerable to drug abuse and trafficking and children victim of armed conflict, civil commotion or natural calamity have also been covered under the *J.J.(C&P of C) Act, 2000.*[52]

(6) Special Juvenile Police Units with a humane approach with provision for sensitization and training has been incorporated in the Act.[53]

Further, certain changes with regard to the dispensation of juvenile justice have been brought by the Model Rules made under the *J.J.(C&P of C) Act, 2000* which, *inter alia,* provide as under:

(1) It has been made mandatory for all Homes to be open to visitors, social workers etc. to maintain transparency in its functioning.
(2) The provision of social auditing to monitor and evaluate the Children's Home through outside person and institution has been made.
(3) A provision has been made for a fresh start/new beginning for the juvenile/child by ensuring erasure of records.
(4) A provision has been made for free legal aid rather than professional in legal attire pleading the juvenile's case before the Board which often leads to lingering the case for years.
(5) Provision has also been made for providing care and protection for foreign children before they are repatriated through procedural arrangements.

(b) Mechanism Provided Under The Juvenile Justice (Care and Protection of Children) Act, 2000, for Dealing with the Juveniles

As had been pointed out earlier, the *J.J.(C&P of C) Act,2000* deals with two types of children: (i) 'Juvenile in conflict with law' (defined as delinquent juvenile in the *J.J. Act, 1986)* and (ii) Child in need of care and protection' (defined as neglected juvenile in the *J.J. Act, 1986)*. Further, provisions have been made to constitute the 'Juvenile Justice Board'[54] (in place of Juvenile Court under *J.J. Act, 1986)* for the 'child in conflict with law', and the 'Child Welfare Committee'[55] (in place of Juvenile Welfare Board under *J.J. Act, 1986)* for the 'child in need of care and protection'. Sections 4, 5, 6, and 7 of the *J.J.(C&P of C) Act, 2000* contain detailed provisions regarding the Juvenile Justice Board which is empowered to deal with the 'Juvenile in conflict with law'.

Section 4 of the *J.J.(C&P of C) Act, 2000* provides with regard to the constitution of the Juvenile Justice Board as under:

(1) Notwithstanding anything contained in the Code of Criminal Procedure, 1973 (2 of 1974), the State Government may, by notification in the Official Gazette, constitute for a district or a group of districts specified in the notification, one or more Juvenile Justice Board for exercising the powers and discharging the duties conferred or imposed on such Board in relation to juveniles in conflict with law under this Act.

(2) A Board shall consist of a Metropolitan Magistrates or Judicial Magistrates of the first class, as the case may be, and two social worker of whom at least one shall be a woman, forming a Bench and every such Bench shall have the powers conferred by the *Code of Criminal Procedure, 1973* (2 of 1974), on a Metropolitan Magistrate or, as the case may be, a Judicial Magistrate of the first class and the Magistrate on the Board shall designated as the Principal Magistrate.

(3) No Magistrate shall be appointed as a member of the Board unless he has special knowledge or training in child psychology or child welfare and no social worker shall be appointed as a member of the Board unless he has been actively involved in health, education, or welfare activities pertaining to children for at east seven years.

(4) The term of office of the members of the Board and the manner in which such member may resign shall be such as may be prescribed.

(5) The appointment of any member of the Board may be terminated after holding inquiry, by the State Government, if—

    (i) he has been found guilty of misuse of power vested under this Act,

    (ii) he has been convicted of an offence involving moral turpitude, and such conviction has not been reversed or he has not been granted full pardon in respect of such offence,

(iii) he fails to attend the proceedings of the Board for consecutive three months without any valid reason or he fails to attend less than three-fourth of the sittings in a year.

Section 5 of the J.J.(C&P of C) Act,2000 makes provisions for the Procedure, etc., in relation to the Juvenile Justice Board as under:

(1) The Board shall meet at such times and shall observe such rules of procedure in regard to the transaction of business at its meetings, as may be prescribed.

(2) A child in conflict with law may be produced before an individual member of the Board, when the Board is not sitting.

(3) A Board may act notwithstanding the absence of any member of the Board, no order made by the Board shall be invalid by reason only of the absence of any member during any stage of the proceeding.
Provided that there shall be at least two members including the Principal Magistrate present at the time of final disposal of the case.

(4) In the event of any difference of opinion among the members of a Board in the interim or final disposition, the opinion of the majority shall prevail, but where there is no such majority, the opinion of the Principal Magistrate shall prevail.

Section 6 of the J.J.(C&P of C) Act,2000, makes provisions for the exercise of the Powers of Juvenile Justice Board, etc. as under:

(1) Where a Board has been constituted for any district or a group of districts, such Board shall, notwithstanding anything contained in any other law for the time being in force but save as otherwise expressly provided in this Act have power to deal exclusively with all proceedings under this Act relating to juvenile in conflict with law.

(2) The powers conferred on the Board by or under this Act may also be exercised by the High Court and the Court of Session, when the proceeding comes before them in appeal, revision or otherwise.

Section 7 of the J.J.(C&P of C) Act, 2000 prescribes the Procedure to be followed by a Magistrate not empowered under the Act as under:

(1) When any Magistrate not empowered to exercise the powers of a Board under this Act is of opinion that a person brought before him under any of the provisions of this Act (otherwise than for the purpose of giving evidence) is a juvenile or a child, he shall without any delay record such opinion and forward the juvenile or the child and the record of the proceeding to the competent authority having jurisdiction over the proceeding.

(2) The competent authority to which the proceeding is forwarded under sub-section (1) shall hold the inquiry as if the juvenile or the child had originally been brought before it.

Detailed provisions have been made in Sections 29 to 39 of Chapter III of the *J.J.(C&P of C) Act, 2000* with regard to 'Child in need of care and protection'. Sections 40 to 45 of Chapter IV of the *J.J.(C&P of C) Act, 2000* contain the provisions with regard to 'rehabilitation and social reintegration' of both types of juveniles and include, *inter alia*, for adoption, foster care, sponsorship, after-care organization and linkages and co-ordination with NGOs etc. The *J.J.(C&P of C) Act, 2000* prescribes separate set of adjudication and disposal mechanism for dealing with the 'Child in Need of Care and Protection' and 'Juvenile in Conflict with Law'. The mechanism may be elaborated briefly in the tabular form for better explanation and understanding.

Power of Competent Authority

Juvenile in conflict with law	*Child in need of Care and Protection*
Juvenile Justice Board	**Child Welfare Committee**
1. Order to send a juvenile to observation home.	1. Order to send a juvenile to children's home.
2. To hold inquiry through probation officers or recognized voluntary organization.	2. All investigation to be done through case worker/child welfare officer
3. Release on bail.	3. Restoration of the child to parents.

Juvenile in conflict with law	*Child in need of Care and Protection*
4. Release after advice or admonition following inquiry and counseling.	4. Placing the child under the care of fit person/fit institution
5. Order the juvenile to perform community services.	5. Issuing of abandonment certificate for the children to be placed in a adoption.
6. Order the parent to pay fine.	6. Complete the inquiry within four months.
7. Release on probation of good conduct.	
8. Send the juvenile to special home.	
9. Release the juvenile on supervision.	
10. No juvenile shall be sentenced to death or life imprisonment.	
11. Place the child in adoption and foster care.	
12. Take action against the exploiter, victimizer, or abuser.	
13. Complete the inquiry within four months.	

Treatment

S. No.	*Treatment*	*Juvenile in Conflict with Law*	*Children in need of Care and Protection*
1.	Apprehension	Police, special juvenile police, voluntary organization	Police officer, or special juvenile police, public servant, children, voluntary organization, social worker, public spirited citizen or the child himself
2.	Precaution by police in apprehension	No handcuff, no lockup, not to be in uniform and production within 24 hours	No handcuff, no lockup, not to be in uniform and production with 24 hours

S. No.	Treatment	Juvenile in Conflict with Law	Children in need of Care and Protection
3.	Disposal	Necessary by the signature of two members	Necessary by the signature of two members
4.	Defence	The probation officer or the child himself	Case worker/child welfare officer or the child himself.
5.	Record	Confidential	Not necessary
6.	Photo publication	Prohibited	Not prohibited
7.	Escape	Explanatory to competent authority and other authority	No cognizance
8.	Transfer	Can order inter-state transfer of juvenile	Can order inter state transfer of child

The above table describes the statutory treatment for the child/juvenile under the new Act. In the *J.J. Act, 1986,* only police was authorized to apprehend and produce the child before the competent authority; however, the new Act empowers social workers and voluntary organizations etc., besides the police in the matter of production. The social worker or voluntary organization which happens to rescue a child/ juvenile, now can directly produce the child before the competent authority. In the matter of 'disposal, now signatures of two members of competent authority are necessary'. Matters relating to special offences have gone under the jurisdiction of the Juvenile Justice Board since it has a regular Magistrate on the Board and for the same reason, jurisdiction of giving the child in 'adoption and foster care' has also been vested with the Juvenile Justice Board.[56]

The creation of 'Special Juvenile Police Unit' is also a new concept introduced by Section 63 of the *J.J.(C&P of C) Act, 2000* which provides thus:

(a) In order to enable the police officers who frequently deal with juveniles or are primarily engaged in the prevention of juvenile crime or handling of the juveniles or children under this Act to perform their function more effectively, they shall be specially instructed and trained.[57]

(b) In every police station at least one officer with aptitude and appropriate training and orientation may be designated as the 'Juvenile or Child Welfare Officer' who will handle the juvenile or the child in coordination with the police.[58]

(c) Special juvenile police unit, of which all police officers designated above, to handle juvenile or children will be members, may be created in every district and city to upgrade treatment of the juveniles and the children.[59]

When police personnel happens to apprehend any child / juvenile, it is expected that he should immediately get in touch with the nearest juvenile police unit or a voluntary organization, which, in turn can produce the child before the competent authority. Such juvenile police unit or the voluntary organisation are also required to simultaneously inform the parent/ guardian and the probation officer of the area. The police play a very crucial role in the prevention of juvenile delinquency as was observed by James J. Brennan:[60]

> "Intelligent crime prevention must begin with delinquency prevention. Prevention of delinquency and crime is not to be confused with crime suppression. Prevention is of different character. Here the concern is with the causative factors and contributing factors. Prevention is concerned with motivation for behaviours". Therefore, police can play very important role if they are concerned with prevention of delinquency rather than suppression of the crime."

Although the existing police had failed to play its expected role with regard to the juvenile delinquents, it is hoped that the Special Juvenile Police Unit would play the desired role in the times to come.

C. MEANING AND DEFINITION OF THE EXPRESSIONS "DELINQUENCY", "JUVENILE" AND "JUVENILE IN CONFLICT WITH LAW"

Before the examination of the various rights of juvenile accused in detail is made, it would be appropriate to discuss in brief the meaning and definition of the expressions "Delinquency",

"Juveniles", used generally, and the expression "juvenile in conflict with law" used in India.

1. Extra Legal Definition

The extra legal definition of the expression 'Juvenile Delinquency' has been advanced by the socio-psychological thinkers. Reformist argue that the legal definitions of these terms are of no help in understanding the true nature of delinquency; because they assert that the legal definitions vary from time to time and place to place. It is also argued that by a legal definition one is said to be a delinquent only if his behaviour comes within the jurisdiction of a court and the court holds him to be a delinquent. Sociologists have defined juvenile delinquency in the terms of the violations of the moral of the society to which a child belongs.[5] It has also been regarded as an 'anti-social' tendency to subject of an official action.[61] Others have defined a juvenile delinquent as 'any child or youth whose conduct deviates sufficiently from normal social usage, which warrant him to be considered a menace to himself.[62] The sociological definitions connote the standards of behaviour of a particular society and if the conduct of a youth does not conform to those standards they say that the youth is a delinquent. Thus, the measuring yardstick of delinquency is according to them, the approved social norms or behaviours of the society to which the child belongs. Some socio-psychological thinkers have called it as a 'behavioural disease'[63] also and they believe that this disease is curable also. The psychologists say that juvenile delinquency is the reflection of psychosis. They insist that it is an expression of the individual's need. It may be called as the mental hygiene approach.[64] By way of conclusion, a definition can be given here that- "Juvenile Delinquency" is the violation of an accepted social behaviour by a youth of a prescribed age limit; whether or not the youth is brought before the "juvenile court".

2. Legal Definition

Legal definitions are mostly concerned with the doing of an act by a child under a prescribed age limit; the act being prohibited by law. As it is accepted view that if there were no law there would be no crime (*nullum crimen sine lege*). So the lawyers are concerned only with the officially acknowledged and labelled delinquents which means that the juveniles who come within the jurisdiction of the juvenile court are delinquents. Codes of the different nations have enumerated different kinds of behaviour which determine delinquency.[65] Some of the behaviours which are determinants of juvenile delinquency may not be 'crime' if done by an adult member. Those behaviours are either social or moral. But some of the Codes have left it to be determined by the juvenile courts as to what kind of behaviour falls under "Delinquency".[66] The factor of age limit with the juvenile courts jurisdiction varies considerably across different nations of the world.[67] Because 'adult-hood mark' varies from society to society, so the statutes have different age limit for determining the jurisdiction of the juvenile courts. In some statutes, there are different age limits for boys and girls but some statutes have a general classification. Moreover, some statutes have expanded the jurisdiction of the juvenile courts to try the delinquents as well as the children who are in 'need of care and protection'.[68]

In this context, a reference to Section 82 of the *Indian Penal Code, 1860* needs to be made which lays down that: 'Nothing is an offence which is done by a child under 7 years of age'. This immunity has been further extended by Section 83 of the *Penal Code, 1860* 'in case an offence is done by a child above 7 years of age and under 12 if he has not attained sufficient maturity of understanding to judge the nature and consequences of his conduct on that occasion'. Further Section 27 of *Cr. P.C., 1973,* provides for trial of a juvenile committing an offence by 'special court' provided the offence is not punishable, with death or imprisonment for life and without making any distinction between a boy and a girl, prescribes a uniform age for both - as sixteen years. At this juncture, however, a reference need be made to Section 5 of the *Cr. P.C., 1973,* which provides that 'the provisions of Criminal Procedure Code 1973 shall not effect any special or local law for the time being in force, or any special jurisdiction or power conferred, or any special form of procedure prescribed, by any other law for the time being in force.' In view of this provision, the laws and procedures applicable to adult accused had been applicable to juvenile accused in India only subject to Children Acts of various States earlier and *J.J. Act,1986,* later; now such accused are primarily governed with the provisions of the *JJ(C&P) C Act, 2000.* Thus, the definitions given in the *J.J. Act,1986* and *J.J. (C&P of C) Act, 2000,* are required to be examined.

The expression 'juvenile' as defined by Section 2(h) of the *J.J.Act,1986,* means 'a boy who has not attained the age of sixteen years or a girl who has not attained the age of eighteen years.' Similarly, the expression offence has been defined by Section 2(n) of the *J.J.Act,1986,* as 'an offence punishable under any law for the time being in force'. In other words, the *J.J.Act,1986,* covered a juvenile if he committed an offence punishable under the Indian Penal Code, 1860 or any other law and he was treated as "delinquent juvenile" as per definition given in Section 2(e) of the *J.J.Act,1986* which provided that 'delinquent juveniles' means a 'juvenile who has been found to have committed an offence.' It should be noted that the *J.J.Act,1986,* made a change with regard to the power of court in the cases of juveniles as contained in Section 27 of the *Cr. P.C.,1973,* and covered all offences irrespective of the punishment. Further, deviating from the provision of the *Cr. P.C., 1973,* of providing uniform age for boys and girls to be called juveniles, the *J.J.Act,1986,* provided different age, i.e., below 16 years age for a boy and below 18 years for a girl - to be called delinquent juvenile. Thus, the *J.J.Act,1986,* provided a wider jurisdiction to the courts (known as 'Juvenile Courts') established under the *J.J.Act,1986,* in comparison to the traditional 'criminal courts' established under the *Cr. P.C., 1973.* The *JJ(C&P)C Act,2000,* while retaining the definition of "offence" changed the definition of "juvenile" by Section 2(k) which provides that:

> "juvenile" or "child" means a person who has not completed eighteen years of age.

The expression "delinquent juvenile" has been dropped by the *J.J. (C&P of C) Act,2000* and in its place a new expression "Juvenile in conflict with law" has been introduced which has been defined in Section 2(l) as:

> "juvenile in conflict with law" means a juvenile who is alleged to have committed an offence.

In other words, it may be concluded that according to the existing Indian law, the expression 'juvenile accused' or 'delinquent juvenile' means: "A 'juvenile in conflict with law' who has not completed the age of eighteen years and is alleged to have committed an offence punishable under any law for the time being in force." For the purposes of the present study the discussion is confined to only such juvenile, i.e., a 'juvenile in conflict with law'.

It may be pointed out that in an attempt to treat a 'delinquent juvenile (juvenile in conflict with law)', it is necessary to include the social definitions along with the legal ones; further, any complete system of treatment of juveniles must also take note of psychological concept of juvenile delinquency and it should not delimit itself to legal definitions only. Such approach would provide a wide field to treatment technique. At this juncture, the views expressed by the Supreme Court in ***Sheela Barse v. Union of India***[69] that 'no child under any circumstances is lodged in jail or police lock up' and also expressed in ***Gaurav Jain v. Union of India***[70], that 'the convicted and neglected juvenile should be refrained to fall in crime and the necessity of their development and circumstances leading to anti-social feelings should be completely banished' should be kept in mind. The adoption of such approach would also help in fulfilling in reality the objectives of the *J.J.(C&P of C) Act,2000* as stated in its "Preamble", i.e., to 'provide proper care, protection and treatment by catering to the development needs (of such juveniles) and to provide a child friendly approach in the adjudication and disposition of matters in the best interests and for ultimate rehabilitation of such juveniles through various institutions'. As the *J.J.(C&P of C) Act, 2000* (enacted in place of *J.J.Act,1986*) is a special law, it shall prevail over the general criminal laws applicable to adult accused, i.e., *Cr.P.C.,1973* and *I.P.C.,1860*; it shall apply in the cases with regard to the offences committed by a juvenile unless any specific provision to the contrary is made in the *J.J.(C&P of C) Act, 2000* itself.

The discussion hereinafter is confined to the rights of 'delinquent juvenile (juvenile in conflict with law)' keeping in view the parameters stated above and the provisions of the *J.J.(C&P of C) Act,2000*. While discussing the rights of an accused who are excluded from the definition of juvenile, the various rights were divided mainly in three broad categories; viz., rights available at all stages, rights available at the time of arrest and after arrest during police custody and rights available during trial. In the case of juvenile the expression 'trial' has been substituted by the expression 'inquiry'. Therefore, the rights of a 'delinquent juvenile

(juvenile in conflict with law)'are proposed to be discussed by classifying them into the broad headings: (i) Rights of such juveniles at the time of arrest and (ii) Rights of such juveniles after arrest and during inquiry. It may be mentioned that the expressions – "delinquent juvenile" and "juvenile in conflict with law" are hereinafter used interchangeably as per context.

D. RIGHTS OF THE 'JUVENILE IN CONFLICT WITH LAW' (DELINQUENT JUVENILE) AT THE TIME OF ARREST

1. Right of the 'Juvenile in conflict with Law' (Delinquent Juvenile) to be Released on Bail

Special provisions, different to the provisions contained in the Criminal Procedure Code 1973 applicable to adult accused, were made with regard to the arrest, bail and custody of juveniles after arrest in Section 18 of the *J.J.Act,1986*, which were later on replaced by Section 12 of the *J.J.(C&P of C) Act,2000.* Section 12 of the *J.J.(C&P of C) Act, 2000,* provides that:

(1) When any person accused of a bailable or non-bailable offence and apparently a juvenile is arrested or detained or appears or is brought before a Juvenile Board, such person shall, notwithstanding anything contained in the Code of Criminal Procedure, 1973 (2 of 1974), or in any other law for the time being in force, be released on bail with or without surety but he shall not be so released if there appear reasonable grounds for believing that the release is likely to bring him into association with any known criminal or expose him to moral, physical or psychological danger or that his release would defeat the ends of justice.

(2) When such person having been arrested is not released on bail under sub-section (1) by the officer-in-charge of the police station, such officer shall cause him to be kept only in an observation home in the prescribed manner until he can be brought before a Board.

The provisions of Section 12 of the *J.J.(C&P of C) Act,2000* (Section 18 of the *J.J.Act,1986*) make it obligatory that the officer-in-charge of the police station arresting a juvenile must first see whether his release on bail with or without surety is likely to bring him into association with any known criminal or expose him to moral, physical or psychological danger or that his release would defeat the ends of justice, and if no such fact is found he must release the juvenile on bail with or without surety. In case the juvenile is not released, the officer-in-charge of the police station arresting a juvenile shall keep the said juvenile in an observation home before he is brought before the Board who shall decide the matter regarding the release of the juvenile on bail. Section 12(3) of *J.J.(C&P of C) Act, 2000,* makes an additional provision if the said juvenile is not released on bail even by the Juvenile Justice Board, as under:

> When such person is not released on bail under sub-section (1) by the Board it shall, instead of committing him to prison, make an order sending him to an observation home or a place of safety for such period during the pendency of the inquiry regarding him as may be specified in the order.

The Supreme Court in ***Sarita Nayak Sawant v. State***[71] has stated that 'there is no theory of punishment imported into the Act. Juvenile cannot be sent to prison and bail cannot be refused.' In the words of Justice Kamath :

> "The sweep is that even in the matters of non-bailable offences the juvenile has to be released on bail except when court come to hold that the release is likely to bring such juvenile into association with any known criminal or expose him to moral danger or that his release would defeat the ends of justice. When a police officer arrests and in the event of refusal of the bail the mandate is that such officer-in-charge of the police station has to forward the delinquent to an observation home but not at a police station or jail. Similar is a duty cast on a juvenile court when it rejects the bail application with the result that at every stage - pre-trial and post-trial - there is no detention in custody or in jail."

Similar view was earlier expressed in the case of ***Gopinath Ghosh v. State of West Bengal,***[72] prior to the enactment of the *J.J. Act, 1986*. In ***Laxmi v. Sub-inspector of Police Nagamali Pukukottai Police Station,***[73] the Division Bench of the Madras High Court pointed out that the Judicial Magistrates in the State shall exercise their judicial discretion strictly in accordance with law and see that the accused before making any order of remand to police custody and or judicial custody. They shall be acting in accordance with law by asking for the production of the accused before any remand order is made and in each case the accused appears to be juvenile, to follow the procedure prescribed in Juvenile Justice Act and in case any doubt is created as to the age of accused, inquire as prescribed under the juvenile justice act to find out whether the accused is a juvenile or not. The Magistrate shall record that age of the accused in the order of the remand and say under which law the accused is being dealt with. It has been held further in ***Antaryami Patra v. State of Orissa,***[74] that the juvenile should be kept in a separate place so that he would not come in association with hardened criminals, which would serve the objective and purpose of Section 18(2) of the *J.J. Act, 1986.*

The Criminal Rules of Practice and Circular Orders, 1958, provide that: 'children or young persons under arrest or remand or committal for trial shall be ordered to be detained as far as possible, in-charge of their parents or guardians and if that is not possible in the custody of respectable persons, philanthropic societies, or institutions or in remand houses. Under no circumstances they should be detained in jail with other persons. No girl arrested, remanded or committed for trial shall be detained in police custody. The magistrate shall place such a girl in the custody of such persons, who in his opinion will produce her at the next hearing.'[75]

It is a well known fact that the system of 'Bail' as it exists today operates in India very harshly against the poor. The poor find it difficult to furnish bail even without sureties and consequently remain in jail until such time as the court is able to take up their cases for trial leading to grave consequences.[76] Section 12 of the *J.J.(C&P of C) Act, 2000* provide for bailing out a Juvenile even for non- bailable offences. It is clear that release on bail, even in non-bailable offences, is conditioned by the consideration that the juvenile is kept away out of the association of reputed criminals and be saved from being exposed to moral dangers. This position of law was fortified by the Supreme Court's Judgement in ***Gopi Nath Ghosh v. The State of West Bengal***[77] which provided that:

> Where a Juvenile Delinquent is arrested he/she has to be produced before a Juvenile Court and if no Juvenile Court

is established for the area, the Court of Sessions will have powers of a Juvenile Court. Such a Juvenile Delinquent ordinarily has to be released on bail irrespective of the nature of the crime alleged to have been committed unless it is shown that there appears to be reasonable grounds for believing that the release is likely to bring him under the influence of any criminal or expose him to moral danger or defeat the ends of Justice.[78]

A minor girl cannot be allowed to live without a home. A court of law is duty bound to insure that she is kept in a place of safety meaning any place or institution, not being a police station or a jail, the person in charge of which is willing to receive and take care of the juvenile girl child until she attains majority[79]. A problem had arisen in connection with the *J.J. Act, 1986,* that a juvenile arrested for committing an offence under the *Narcotic Drugs and Psychotropic Substances Act, 1989* (referred hereinafter to as *N D Act, 1989),* would be dealt with under the *J.J. Act, 1986,* or would be governed by the *N D Act, 1989.* It had been argued that although the *J.J. Act, 1986,* made a general provision with regard to the right of a juvenile delinquent to be released on bail irrespective of the offence committed by him, the *ND Act, 1989,* was also a special statute and in that special statute a further special provision had been made with regard to the pre-conditions to be satisfied for an accused being released on bail. Therefore, the special provision of the special statute, namely Section 87 of the *ND Act, 1989,* would override S. 18 of the *J.J. Act, 1986,* and, therefore, even in case of a juvenile delinquent involved in commission of an offence under the said Act, no bail could be granted until and unless the provisions of S. 37 of the *ND Act, 1989,* are complied with. No doubt *ND Act, 1989,* was enacted earlier in point of time than the *J.J. Act, 1986,* but the special provision in relation to the bail by way of insertion of S. 37 in the *ND Act, 1989,* came on the statute book by the Amending Act 2 of 1989 (two years after the enactment of *J.J. Act, 1986*) and the 'Statement of Objects and Reasons' of the said amendment indicates that the Parliament thought it appropriate to make stringent provisions in respect of an accused being released on bail to meet the challenge arising from drug trafficking. However, this problem would not exist now because the provisions of *J.J.(C&P of C) Act, 2000* would supersede the provisions of the *N D Act, 1989,* being the legislation.

2. Duty of the Police Officer to inform regarding Arrest of Delinquent Juvenile

As has been observed earlier, an adult accused has been guaranteed by the Constitution a right to know the grounds of arrest. However, a juvenile is treated to be a person in the eyes of law possessing not that degree of maturity which an adult is supposed to possess. Therefore, a special provision has been made in Section 13 of the *J.J. (C&P of C) Act, 2000* (Section 19 of the *J.J. Act, 1986*), to inform about the arrest of the juvenile to his parent or guardian and also direct such parent or guardian to be present at the Board before which the juvenile will appear. Many times it is not possible to know the details of parent or guardian and, therefore, a duty has also been imposed upon the arresting person to inform the Probation Officer who is expected to take necessary steps for finding out the whereabouts of parent or guardian, antecedents and family background of the juvenile and other material circumstances likely to be of assistance to the Board for making the inquiry. Section 13 of the *J.J. (C&P of C) Act, 2000,* provides thus:

> Where a juvenile is arrested, the officer-in-charge of the police station or the special juvenile police unit to which the juvenile is brought shall, as soon as may be after the arrest, inform—
>
> (a) The parent or guardian of the juvenile, if he can be found, of such arrest and direct him to be present at the Board before which the juvenile will appear; and
>
> (b) The probation officer of such arrest to enable him to obtain information regarding the antecedents and family background of the juvenile and other material circumstances likely to be of assistance to the Board for making the inquiry.

It may be mentioned in this connection that under Section 19 of the *J.J. Act, 1986,* also, the police was under an obligation to inform the probation officer in all cases after the arrest of the juveniles; however, the police regularly forgot to do this and the

Court also did not insist on it. As Section 13 of the *J.J.(C&P of C) Act, 2000* is a verbatim reproduction of Section 19 of the *J.J. Act, 1986*, the compliance of this provision is also uncertain.

E. RIGHTS OF DELINQUENT JUVENILE AFTER ARREST AND DURING INQUIRY

1. Procedure to be followed by the Juvenile Justice Board in Inquiry and by the Higher Courts in Appeals and Revision Proceedings

(a) Apprehension of Juvenile in Conflict with Law

Section 10 of the *J.J.(C&P of C) Act, 2000* (no analogous provision in the *J.J.Act,1986*) provides that :

(1) As soon as a juvenile in conflict with law is apprehended by police, he shall be placed under the charge of special juvenile police unit or the designated police officer who shall immediately report the matter to a member of a Board.

(2) The State Government may make rules consistent with this Act,—

(i) to provide for persons through whom (including registered voluntary organisations) any juvenile in conflict with law may be produced before the Board;

(ii) to provide the manner in which such juvenile may be sent to an observation home.

Section 11 of the *J.J.(C&P of C) Act,2000,* makes the provision regarding the 'control of custodian over such juvenile' which runs as under:

> Any person in whose charge a juvenile is placed in pursuance of this Act shall, while the order is in force have the control over the juvenile as he would have if he were his parents, and shall be responsible for his maintenance, and the juvenile shall continue in his charge for the period stated by competent authority, notwithstanding that he is claimed by his parents or any other person.

(b) Procedure to be Followed by the Juvenile Justice Board

In contrast with the provisions of trial of an adult accused, given under *Cr. P.C., 1973*, special provision has been made with regard to delinquent juveniles and there is no provision for holding a trial in case of a delinquent juvenile; in place of 'trial', an 'inquiry' is to be held. Section 14 of the *J.J. (C&P of C) Act, 2000* (Section 20 of the *J.J. Act, 1986*) provides thus:

> Where a juvenile having been charged with an offence is produced before a Board, the Board shall hold the inquiry in accordance with the provisions of this Act and may make such order in relation to the juvenile as it deems fit:
>
> *Provided* that an inquiry under this section shall be completed within a period of four months from the date of its commencement, unless the period is extended by the Board having regard to the circumstances of the case and in special cases after recording the reasons in writing for such extensions.

One of the purposes behind promulgating the *J.J. Act, 1986,* and also the *J.J. (C&P of C) Act, 2000,* was to bring the entire country under one legal system to be applicable to juveniles. More important purposes were to establish norms and standards for the administration of juvenile justice in terms of investigation and prosecution, and to bring the operation of the juvenile justice system in the country in conformity with the *United Nations Standard Minimum Rules for the Administration of Juvenile Justice, 1985*, known as "Beijing Rules".

Section 54 of the *J.J. (C&P of C) Act, 2000* (Section 30 of the *J.J. Act, 1986*) provides for the 'Procedure in inquiries, appeals and revision proceedings' as under:

> (1) Save as otherwise expressly provided by this Act, a competent authority while holding any inquiry under any of the provisions of this Act, shall follow such procedure as may be prescribed and subject thereto, shall follow, as far as may be, the procedure laid down in the *Code of Criminal Procedure, 1973 (2 of 1974),* for trials in summons cases.
>
> (2) Save as otherwise expressly provided by or under this Act, the procedure to be followed in hearing appeals or revision proceedings under this Act shall be, as far as practicable, in accordance with the provisions of the *Code of Criminal Procedure, 1973* (2 of 1974).

Section 46 of the *J.J.(C&P of C) Act, 2000* (Section 29 of the *J.J. Act, 1986*) empowers the competent authority to 'require any parent or guardian having the actual charge of or control over the juvenile or the child to be present at any proceeding in respect of the juvenile or the child.' Further, under Section 47 of the *J.J.(C&P of C) Act,2000* (Section 30 of the *J.J.Act,1986*) the competent authority is 'empowered to dispense with the attendance of juvenile or child during the course of an enquiry and proceed with the inquiry in the absence of the juvenile if it is satisfied that the attendance of the juvenile is not essential.'

As the procedure to be followed by the Juvenile Justice Board is the procedure prescribed for the trial of summons case, which primarily aims at speedier disposal, it would be advantageous to state the same in brief.

(i) When the accused appears or is brought before the Magistrate, the particulars of the offence is stated to him and he is asked whether he pleads guilty or has any defense to make. It is not necessary to frame a formal charge.

(ii) If the accused pleads guilty, the Magistrate records the plea. If he accepts the plea, he may convict the accused on such plea.[80]

(iii) But if the Magistrate does not so convict the accused under S. 252 *Cr. P.C., 1973*, or if the accused pleads 'not-guilty', the Magistrate hears the prosecution and takes all such evidence as may be produced by the prosecution.[81]

(iv) Under S. 313 of *Cr. P.C., 1973*, the court may at any stage of trial, without previous warning, question the accused on the case. Such questioning or examination by the Magistrate is compulsory after the witnesses for the prosecution have been examined and before the accused is asked to put forward his defence.

(v) During such examination, the Magistrate should warn the accused that although he is not bound to answer that he may give may be used as evidence. Refusal of the accused to answer such questions is not an offence.

(vi) As the accused cannot be administered oath at this

stage, any answer found to be false cannot be used to frame a charge of perjury against him. If he later comes as a witness and takes oath, a false evidence given by him may be used to charge him for perjury. Thereafter the Magistrate hears the accused and takes such evidence as may be produced by the defence.[82]

(vii) The Magistrate may of his own motion examine such witness as he may think fit. After hearing the arguments of the parties, the Magistrate may order acquittal if he finds the accused not guilty.[83]

(viii) If, however, he finds the accused guilty, he may pass any of the following orders under Section 255(2) of *Cr.P.C. 1973.*)

 (a) release the accused after admonition, or on probation of good conduct under Section 360 of *Cr.P.C.,1973;* or

 (b) sentence the accused according to law under Section 255(2) *Cr.P.C., 1973;* or

 (c) if the Magistrate is of the opinion that the accused ought to receive a punishment different in kind from, or more severe than the Magistrate is empowered to inflict, he may forward the accused to the Chief Judicial Magistrate.

(ix) Ordinarily, the complainant also has to remain present on the dates of hearing. Otherwise, the Magistrate may acquit the accused only on that ground. Of course, the Magistrate may dispense with the personal attendance of the complainant.[84]

(x) For any sufficient ground the Magistrate may permit the complainant to withdraw the complaint against the accused persons or some of them and in that event acquit such accused person or persons as the case may be.

(xi) The Magistrate may stop the proceedings for any sufficient reason at any stage without pronouncing any judgement and release the accused, which would mean that the accused has been discharged. If such stoppage order is made after the evidence of the principal witnesses has been recorded, the accused would be acquitted.

The observations made in the western countries that – (i) Making of probation order is not passing of sentence,[85] (ii) Where a court makes a probation order under Criminal Justice, Act, 1948 (English law, since repealed), it has no power at the same time to impose a fine[86] and (iii) a probation order should not be made concurrently with a sentence the serving of which will postpone the effective commencement of the probation[87] - may be of some relevance in inquiries made by the Juvenile Justice Board under the *J.J.(C&P of C) Act,2000*:

(c) Prohibition of Certain Proceedings Against Juveniles

Section 17 of the *J.J.(C&P of C) Act, 2000* (Section 29 of the J.J.Act,1986) provides that:

> Notwithstanding anything to the contrary contained in the Code of Criminal Procedure, 1973 (2 of 1974), no proceeding shall be instituted and no order shall be passed against a juvenile under Chapter VIII of the said Code.

Further, Section 18 of the *J.J.(C&P of C) Act,2000* (Section 24 of the *J.J.Act,1986*) prohibits the joint trial of juvenile and person not a juvenile and provides thus:

> (1) Notwithstanding anything contained in Section 223 of the Code of Criminal Procedure, 1973 (2 of 1974), or in any other law for the time being in force, no juvenile shall be charged with or tried for, any offence together with a person who is not a juvenile.
>
> (2) If a juvenile is accused of an offence for which under Section 223 of the *Code of Criminal Procedure, 1973* (2 of 1974), or any other law for the time being in force, such juvenile and any person who is not a juvenile would, but for the prohibition contained in sub-section (1), have been charged and tried together, the Board taking cognizance of that offence shall direct separate trials of the juvenile and the other person.

Special provision has been made with regard to pending cases under Section 20 of the *J.J.(C&P of C) Act, 2000* (Section 26 of the *J.J.Act, 1986*) which is as under:

Notwithstanding anything contained in this Act, all proceedings in respect of a juvenile pending in any Court in any area on the date on which this Act comes into force in that area, shall be continued in that Court as if this Act had not been passed and if the Court finds that the juvenile has committed an offence, it shall record such finding and instead of passing any sentence in respect of the juvenile, forward the juvenile to the Board which shall pass orders in respect of that juvenile in accordance with the provisions of this Act as if it had been satisfied on inquiry under this Act that the juvenile has committed the offence.

(d) Committal to Approved Place of Juvenile or Child Suffering from Dangerous Disease and His Future Disposal

When a juvenile brought before the Juvenile Justice Board is suffering from dangerous diseases special provision has been made in Section 48 of the *J.J. (C&P of C) Act, 2000* (Section 31 of the *J.J. Act, 1986*), viz.:

(1) When a juvenile or the child who has been brought before a competent authority under this Act, is found to be suffering from a disease requiring prolonged medical treatment or physical or mental complaint that will respond to treatment, the competent authority may send the juvenile or the child to any place recognised to be an approved place in accordance with the rules made under this Act for such period as it may think necessary for the required treatment.

(2) Where a juvenile or the child is found to be suffering from leprosy, sexually transmitted disease, hepatitis-B, open cases of tuberculosis and such other diseases or is of unsound mind, he shall be dealt with separately through various specialised referral services or under the relevant laws as such.

(e) Other Protections Available to Juvenile During or After Inquiry

(1) Removal of disqualification attaching to conviction: Section 19 of the *J.J.(C&P of C) Act,2000* (Section 28 of the *J.J.Act,1986*) provides for the removal of disqualification attaching to conviction of a juvenile who has committed an offence and has been dealt with under the provisions of the *J.J.(C&P of C) Act,2000.* It has also been provided that the Juvenile Justice Board 'shall make an order directing that the relevant records of such conviction shall be removed after the expiry of the period of appeal or a reasonable period as prescribed under the rules, as the case may be.'

(2) Prohibition of publication of names, etc.: Further, the publication of names, etc., of juveniles involved in any proceeding under the Act has been prohibited. Section 21 of the *J.J.(C&P of C) Act,2000* (Section 36 of the *J.J.Act,1986*) provides that:

(1) No report in any newspaper, magazine or news-sheet or visual media of any inquiry regarding a juvenile in conflict with law under this Act shall disclose the name, address or school or any other particulars calculated to lead to the identification of the juvenile nor shall any picture of any such juvenile be published:

Provided that for reasons to be recorded in writing, the authority holding the inquiry may permit such disclosure, if in its opinion such disclosure is in the interest of the juvenile.

Contravention of the above provisions has been made punishable with fine which may extend to one thousand rupees. The spirit of the above stated provision is to clothe the juveniles in cloaks of special protection so that they may turn out to be useful members of the society and the nation. It, therefore, follows that the juveniles in conflict with law will not be treated *at par* with adult offenders and the provisions of Section 298 of the Cr. P.C., 1973 (proof of previous conviction) or Section 106 Cr. P.C. 1973 (security for keeping the peace on conviction) have no application against such juveniles dealt with under this Act.

(3) Reports to be Treated Confidential: In order to safeguard the interest of the juvenile facing an inquiry, Section 51 of the *J.J.(C&P of C) Act, 2000* (Section 35 of the *J.J.Act, 1986*) provides that:

> The report of the probation officer or social worker considered by the competent authority shall be treated as confidential:

Provided that the competent authority may, if it so thinks fit, communicate the substance thereof to the juvenile or the child or his parent or guardian and may give such juvenile or the child, parent or guardian an opportunity of producing such evidence as may be relevant to the matter stated in the report.

(4) Provision regarding the Escaped Juvenile: Special provision has been made with regard to the escaped juvenile under Section 22 of the *J.J.(C&P of C) Act, 2000* (Section 50 of the *J.J.Act, 1986*) as under:

> Notwithstanding anything to the contrary contained any other law for the time being in force, any police officer may take charge without warrant of a juvenile in conflict with law who has escaped special home or an observation home or from the care of a person under whom he was placed under this Act, and shall be sent back to the special home or observation home or that person, as the case may be; and no proceeding shall be instituted in respect of the juvenile by the reason of such escape, but the special home or observation home or the person may, after giving the information to the Board which passed the order in respect of the juvenile, take such steps in respect of the juvenile as may be deemed necessary under the provision of this Act.

(f) Procedure Regarding Appeal and Revision

The following provisions have been made with regard to appeal and revision against the order of the Juvenile Justice Board or other Competent Authority made under the *J.J.(C&P of C) Act, 2000.* Section 52 of the *J.J.(C&P of C) Act,2000* (Section 37 of the *J.J.Act, 1986*) provides for **Appeals** as under:

(1) Subject to the provisions of this section, any person aggrieved by an order made by a competent authority under this Act may, within thirty days from the date of such order, prefer an appeal to the Court of Session:

Provided that the Court of Session may entertain the appeal after the expiry of the said period of thirty days if it is satisfied that the appellant was prevented by sufficient cause from filing the appeal in time.

(2) No appeal shall lie from—

(a) Any order of acquittal made by the Board in respect of a juvenile alleged to have committed an offence; or

(b) Any order made by a Committee in respect of a finding that a person is not a neglected juvenile.

(3) No second appeal shall lie from any order of the Court of Session passed in appeal under this section.

Similarly, provisions regarding **Revision** have been made in Section 53 of the *J.J.(C&P of C) Act, 2000* (Section 38 of the *J.J.Act,1986*) as under:

> The High Court may, at any time, either of its own motion or on an application received in this behalf, call for the record of any proceeding in which any competent authority or Court of Session has passed an order for the purpose of satisfying itself as to the legality or propriety of any such order and may pass such order in relation thereto as it thinks fit:
>
> *Provided* that the High Court shall not pass an order under this section prejudicial to any person without giving him a reasonable opportunity of being heard.

(g) Special Protections Available to Juveniles in Cases of Special Offences Committed Against Them

(1) Punishment for Cruelty to juvenile or child: Section 23 of the *J.J. (C&P of C) Act, 2000* (Section 41 of the *J.J. Act, 1986*) provides that :

> Whoever, having the actual charge of, or control over, a juvenile or child, assaults, abandons, exposes or willfully neglects the juvenile or causes or procures him to be assaulted, abandoned, exposed or neglected in a manner likely to cause such juvenile or the child unnecessary mental or physical suffering shall be punishment with imprisonment for a term which may extend to six months, or fine, or both.

(2) Punishment for the Employment of Juvenile or Child for Begging: Section 24 of the *J.J.(C&P of C) Act, 2000* (Section 42 of the *J.J.Act, 1986*) provides that:

(1) Whoever employs or uses any juvenile or the child for the purpose or causes any juvenile to beg shall be punishable with imprisonment for a term which may extend to three years and shall also be liable to fine.

(2) Whoever, having the actual charge of, or control over, a juvenile or the child abets the commission of the offence punishable with imprisonment for a term which may extend to one year and shall also be liable to fine.

(3) Punishment for Exploitation of Juvenile or Child Employees: Section 26 of the *J.J.(C&P of C) Act, 2000* (Section 44 of the *J.J.Act,1986*) provides that:

> Whoever ostensibly procures a juvenile or child for the purpose of any hazardous employment, keeps him in bondage and withholds his earnings or uses such earnings for his own purposes shall be punishable with imprisonment for a term which may extend to three years and shall also be liable to fine.

(4) Penalty for giving intoxicating liquor or narcotic drug or psychotropic substance to a juvenile: Section 25 of the *J.J.(C&P of C) Act, 2000* (Section 43 of the *J.J.Act,1986*) provides that:

> Whoever gives, or causes to be given, to any juvenile or the child any intoxicating liquor in a public place or any narcotic drug or psychotropic substance except upon the order of a duly qualified medical practitioner or in case of sickness shall be punishable with imprisonment for a term which may extend to three years and shall also be liable to fine.

(5) Declaration of these offences as Cognizable and Alternative Punishments: Section 26 of the *J.J.(C&P of C) Act, 2000* makes the offences punishable under Sections 23, 23, 25 and 26 as 'cognizable'. It is also provided by section 28 of the *JJ(C&P)C Act, 2000* (Section 45 of the *J.J.Act,1986*) that 'Where an act or omission constitutes an offence punishable under this Act and also under any other Central or State Act, then, notwithstanding anything contained in any law for the time being in force, the offender found guilty of such offence shall be liable to punishment only under such Act as provides for punishment which is greater in degree.

2. Powers of the Juvenile Justice Board regarding Delinquent Juveniles

The *J.J.(C&P of C) Act, 2000,* specifically makes provisions with regard to the powers of the competent authority in reference to the orders which may be passed regarding Delinquent Juvenile after completing the inquiry. It also contains provisions prohibiting the court from passing certain orders.

(a) Orders that may be Passed by the Juvenile Justice Board Regarding Delinquent Juveniles

Section 15 of the *J.J.(C&P of C) Act, 2000* (Section 21 of the *J.J.Act,1986*) provides as under:

(1) Where a Board is satisfied on inquiry that a juvenile has committed an offence, then, notwithstanding anything to the contrary contained in any other law for the time being in force, the Board may, if it thinks so fit,—

- (a) ***allow*** the juvenile to go home after advice or admonition following appropriate inquiry against and counseling to the parent or guardian and the juvenile;
- (b) ***direct*** the juvenile to participate in group counseling and similar activities;
- (c) ***order*** the juvenile to perform community service;
- (d) ***order*** the parent of the juvenile or the juvenile himself to pay a fine, if he is over fourteen years of age and earns money;
- (e) ***direct*** the juvenile to be released on probation of good conduct and placed under the care of any parent, guardian or other fit person, on such parent, guardian or other fit person executing a bond, with or without surety as that Board may require, for the good behavior and well-being of the juvenile for any period not exceeding three years;
- (f) ***direct*** the juvenile to be released on probation of good conduct and placed under the care of any fit institution for the good behavior and well-being

of the juvenile for any period not exceeding three years;

(g) *make* an order directing the juvenile to be sent to a special home,—

(i) in the case of juvenile, over seventeen years but less than eighteen years of age for a period of not less than two years;

(ii) in case of any other juvenile, for the period until he ceases to be a juvenile:

Provided that the Board may, if it is satisfied that having regard to the nature of the offence and the circumstances of the case it is expedient so to do, for reasons to be recorded, reduce the period of stay to such period as it thinks fit;

(2) The Board shall obtain the social investigation report on juvenile either through a probation officer or a recognised voluntary organisation or otherwise, and shall take into consideration the finding of such report before passing an order;

(3) Where an order under clause (d), clause (e) or clause (f) of sub-section (1) is made, the Board may, if it is of opinion that in the interests of the juvenile and of the public it is expedient so to do, in addition make an order that the juvenile in conflict with law shall remain under the supervision of a probation officer named in the order during such period, not exceeding three years, as may be specified therein, and may in such supervision order impose such conditions as it deems necessary for the due supervision of the juvenile in conflict with law :

Provided that if at any time afterwards it appears to the Board on receiving a report from the probation officer or otherwise, that the juvenile in conflict with law has not been of good behavior during the period of supervision or that the fit institution under whose care the juvenile was placed is no longer able or willing to ensure the good behavior and well-being of the juvenile it may, after making such inquiry as it deems fit, order the juvenile in conflict with law to be sent to a special home;

(4) The Board shall while making a supervision order under sub-section (3), explain to the juvenile and the parent, guardian or other fit person or fit institution, as the case may be, under whose care the juvenile has been placed the terms and conditions of the order and shall forthwith furnish one copy of the supervision order to the juvenile, the parent, guardian or fit institution, as the case may be, the sureties, if any, and the probation officer.

(b) Orders that may not be Passed by the Juvenile Justice Board Against Delinquent Juveniles

Section 16(1) of the *J.J.(C&P of C) Act, 2000* (Section 22 of the *J.J.Act,1986*) prohibits the Juvenile Justice Board from passing certain orders by providing that 'no juvenile in conflict with law shall be sentenced to death or imprisonment, or committed to prison in default of payment of fine or in default of furnishing security'. Special provisions have, however, been made where the juvenile has attained the age of sixteen years and committed an offence of serious nature. It is provided that :

> Where a juvenile who has attained the age of sixteen years has committed an offence and the Board is satisfied that the offence committed is of so serious in nature or that his conduct and behavior have been such that it would not be in his interest or in the interest of other juvenile in a special home to send him to such special home and that none of the other measures provided under this Act is suitable or sufficient, the Board may order the juvenile in conflict with law to be kept in such place of safety and in such manner as it thinks fit and shall report the case for the orders of the State Government.

Section 16(2) of the *J.J.(C&P of C) Act,2000* also provides that:

> On receipt of a report from a Board under sub-section (1), the State Government may make such arrangement in respect of the juvenile as it deems proper and may order

such juvenile to be kept under protective custody at such place and on such conditions as it thinks fit:

Provided that the period of detention so ordered shall not exceed the maximum period of imprisonment to which juvenile could have been sentenced for the offence committed.

(c) *Powers Regarding the Age Determination of Juvenile and Sending Him Outside Jurisdiction*

(1) Presumption and Determination of the Age of Juvenile

Section 49 of the *J.J. (C&P of C) Act, 2000* (Section 32 of the *J.J.Act,1986*) makes provision for 'presumption and determination of age of a juvenile'. Sub-section (1) provides that 'Where it appears to a competent authority that a person brought before it under any of the provisions of this Act (otherwise than for the purpose of giving evidence) is a juvenile or the child, the competent authority (a) shall make due inquiry as to the age of that person, (b) for that purpose shall take such evidence as may be necessary (but not an affidavit), and (c) shall record a finding whether the person is a juvenile or the child or not, stating his age as nearly as may be.' According to Sub-section (2), 'No order of a competent authority shall be deemed to have become invalid merely by any subsequent proof that the person in respect of whom the order has been made is not a juvenile or the child'. It is also provided that the presumption of law shall be that 'the age recorded by the competent authority to be the age of the person so brought before it shall, for the purposes of this Act, be deemed to be the true age of that person.'

(2) Sending a Juvenile or Child outside Jurisdiction

Section 50 of the *J.J.(C&P of C) Act, 2000* (Section 34 of the *J.J.Act,1986*) makes provision for sending a juvenile outside jurisdiction of the Juvenile Justice Board when the ordinary place of residence of the juvenile lies outside the jurisdiction. It provides thus:

> In the case of a juvenile or the child, whose ordinary place of residence lies outside the jurisdiction of the competent authority before which he is brought, the competent

> authority may, if satisfied after due inquiry that it is expedient so to do, send the juvenile or the child back to a relative or other person who is fit and willing to receive him at his ordinary place of residence and exercise proper care and control over him, notwithstanding that such place of residence is outside the jurisdiction of the competent authority; and the competent authority exercising jurisdiction over the place to which the juvenile or the child is sent shall in respect of any matter arising subsequently have the same powers in relation to the juvenile or the child as if the original order had been passed by itself.

(d) Power of the Juvenile Justice Board to Discharge and Transfer Juvenile from One Children's Home or Special Home to the Other

Section 56 of the *J.J.(C&P of C) Act, 2000* (Section 46 of the *J.J.Act,1986*) empowers the Juvenile Justice Board to discharge and transfer a Juvenile in Conflict with Law. It provides thus:

> The competent authority or the local authority may, notwithstanding anything contained in this Act, at any time, order a child in need of care and protection or a juvenile in conflict with law to be discharged or transferred from one children's home or special home to another, as the case may be, keeping in view the best interest of the child or the juvenile, and his natural place of stay, either absolutely or on such conditions as it may think fit to impose:
>
> *Provided* that the total period of stay of the juvenile or the child in a children's home or special home a fit institution or under a fit person shall not be increased by such transfer.

(e) Power of the Juvenile Justice Board to Transfer Juvenile of Unsound Mind or Suffering from Leprosy or Addicted to Drugs

Section 58 of the *J.J.(C&P of C) Act, 2000* (Section 48 of the *J.J.Act,1986*) empowers the Juvenile Justice Board to transfer juveniles of unsound mind or suffering from leprosy or addicted to drugs to the appropriate places of safety. It provides thus:

> Where it appears to the competent authority that any juvenile or the child kept in a special home or children's home or shelter home or in an institution in pursuance of

this Act, is suffering from leprosy or is of unsound mind or is addicted to any narcotic drug or psychotropic substance, the competent authority may order his removal to a leper asylum or mental hospital or treatment centre for drug addicts or other place of safety for being kept there for such period not exceeding the period for which he is required to be kept under the order of the competent authority or for such further period as may be certified by the medical officer necessary for the proper treatment of the juvenile or the child.

(f) Power of the Juvenile Justice Board to Release or Grant Leave of Absence or Placing Out on License

Section 59 of the *J.J.(C&P of C) Act, 2000* (Section 49 of the *J.J.Act,1986*) empowers the Juvenile Justice Board to release or permit leave of absence to any juvenile in certain circumstances. It provides thus:

(1) When juvenile a or the child is kept in a children's home or a special home and on report of probation officer or social worker or of government or a voluntary organisation, as the case may be, the competent authority may consider, the release of such juvenile or the child permitting him to live with his parent or his guardian or under the supervision of any authorised person named in the order, willing to receive and take charge of the juvenile or the child to educate and train him for some useful trade or calling or to look after him for rehabilitation.

(2) The competent authority may also permit leave of absence to any juvenile or the child, to allow him, on special occasions like examination, marriage of relatives, death of kith and kin or the accident or serious illness of parent or an emergency or like nature, to go on leave under supervision, for maximum seven days, excluding the time taking journey.

(3) Where a permission has been revoked or forfeited and the juvenile or the child refuses or fails to return to the home concerned or the juvenile to which he was directed so to return, the Board may, if necessary, cause him to

be taken charge of and to be taken back to the concerned home.

(4) The time during which a juvenile or the child is absent from a concerned home in pursuance of such permission granted under this section shall be deemed to be part of the time for which he is liable to be kept in the special home:

Provided that when a juvenile has failed to return to the special home on the permission being revoked or forfeited, the time which elapses after his failure so to return shall be excluded in computing the time during which he is liable to be kept in the institution.

(g) Power of the Juvenile Justice Board to make an Order for Contribution by Parents

Section 60 of the *J.J.(C&P of C) Act, 2000* (Section 51 of the *J.J.Act,1986*) empowers the Juvenile Justice Board to make orders for contribution by parents in the event the juvenile is sent to home or placed under the care of a fit person. It provides thus:

(1) The competent authority which makes an order for sending a juvenile or the child to a children's home or to a special home or placing the juvenile under the care of a fit person or fit institution may make an order requiring the parent or other person liable to maintain the juvenile or the child to contribute to his maintenance, if able to do so, in the prescribed manner according to income.

(2) The competent authority may direct, if necessary, the payment to be made to the poor parent or guardian by the Superintendent or the Project Manager of the home to pay such expenses for the journey of the inmate or parent or guardian or both, from the home to his ordinary place of residence at the time of sending the juvenile as may be prescribed.

(h) Powers of the Juvenile Justice Board to amend its Own Orders

Section 55 of the *J.J.(C&P of C) Act, 2000* (no analogous provision in the *J.J.Act,1986*) empowers the Juvenile Justice Board to amend its own orders. It provides that :

(1) Without prejudice to the provisions for appeal and revision under this Act, any competent authority may, on an application received in this behalf, amend any order as to the institution to which a juvenile or the child is to be sent or as to the person under whose care or supervision a juvenile or the child is to be placed under this Act:

Provided that there shall be at least two members and the parties or its defence present during the course of hearing for passing an amendment in relation to any of its order.

(2) Clerical mistakes in orders passed by a competent authority or errors arising therein from any accidental slip or omission may, at any time, be corrected by the competent authority either on its own motion or on an application received in this behalf.

(i) Continuation of Inquiry in Respect of Juvenile who has Ceased to be a Juvenile

Section 3 of the *J.J.(C&P of C) Act, 2000* (Section 3 of the *J.J. Act, 1986*) provides for continuation of an inquiry with regard to a juvenile who ceases to be such as under:

> Where an inquiry has been initiated against a juvenile in conflict with law . . . and during the course of such inquiry the juvenile or the child ceases to be such, then, notwithstanding anything contained in this Act or in any other law for the time being in force, the inquiry may be continued and orders may be made in respect of such person if such person had continued to be a juvenile or a child.

(j) Provisions with Regard to Bonds

According to Section 66 of the *J.J.(C&P of C) Act, 2000* (Section 69 of the *J.J.Act,1986*), 'Provisions of Chapter XXXIII of the Cr. P.C., 1973, shall as far as may be, apply to bonds taken under this Act'.

3. Powers of the State Government regarding Delinquent Juveniles

Various powers have been given to the State Governments with regard to juveniles – Juvenile in conflict with law and child in need of care and protection. They are enumerated as under.

(a) Transfer of Juveniles Between Children's Homes, Juvenile Homes of Like Nature in Different Parts of India

Section 57 of the *J.J.(C&P of C) Act, 2000* (Section 47 of the *J.J.Act,1986*) provides for the transfer of juveniles from one children's home to another in different parts of India; such power has been given to the State Government or the local authority. It is provided by Section 57 that:

> The State Government or the local authority may direct any child or the juvenile to be transferred from any children's home or special home outside the State to any other children's home, special home or institution of a like nature with the prior intimation to the local committee or the Board, as the case may be, and such order shall be deemed to be operative for the competent authority of the area to which the child or the juvenile is sent.

(b) Establishment of Different Types of Homes for Juveniles

The *J.J.(C&P of C) Act, 2000* imposes an obligation upon every State Government to establish different types of institutions for juveniles, namely, observation homes, special homes, children's homes, shelter homes and after care institutions in each district or group of districts in the country. Such homes may be established and maintained either by the State Government itself or under an agreement with voluntary organizations; association of voluntary organizations was not envisaged under the *J.J.Act,1986.* The State Government may also certify other institutions other than a home established or maintained by the State Government itself or under an agreement with voluntary organizations as 'fit institutions'. Section 8 of the *J.J.(C&P of C) Act, 2000* (Section 11 of the *J.J.Act,1986*), provides with regard to the "Observation Homes" as under:

> (1) Any State Government may establish and maintain either by itself or under an agreement with voluntary

organisations, observation homes in every district or a group of districts, as may be required for the temporary reception of any juvenile in conflict with law during the pendency of any inquiry regarding them under this Act.

(2) Where the State Government is of the opinion that any institution other than a home established or maintained under sub-section (1) is fit for the temporary reception of juvenile in conflict with law during the pendency of any inquiry regarding them under this Act it may certify such institution as an observation home for the purposes of this Act.

(3) The State Government may, by rules made under this Act provide for the management of observation homes, including the standards and various types of services to be provided by them for rehabilitation and social integration of a juvenile, and the circumstances under which, and the manner in which, the certification of an observation home may be granted or withdrawn.

(4) Every juvenile who is not placed under the charge of parent or guardian and is sent to an observation home shall be initially kept in a reception until the observation home for preliminary inquiries, care and classification for juveniles according to his age group, such as seven to twelve years, twelve to sixteen years and sixteen to eighteen years, giving due considerations to physical and mental status and degree of the offence committed, for further induction into observation home.

Regarding "Special Homes", provisions have been made under section 9 of the *J.J.(C&P of C) Act,2000* (Section 10 of the *J.J.Act,1986*) as under:

(1) The State Government may establish and maintain either by itself or under an agreement with voluntary organisations, special homes in every district or a group of districts as may be required for reception and rehabilitation of juvenile in conflict with law under this Act.

(2) Where the State Government is of the opinion that any

institution other than a home established or maintained under Sub-section (1), is fit for the reception of juvenile in conflict with law to be sent there under this Act, it may certify such institution as a special home for the purposes of this Act.

(3) The State Government may, by rules made under this Act, provide for the management of special homes, including the standards and various types of services to be provided by them which are necessary for re-socialisation of a juvenile, and the circumstances under which, and the manner in which, the certification of a special home may be granted or withdrawn.

(4) The rules made under sub-section (3) may also provide for the classification and separation of juvenile in conflict with law on the basis of age and nature of offences committed by them and his mental and physical status.

Section 44 of the *J.J.(C&P of C) Act, 2000* (Section 12 of the *J.J.Act,1986*) makes provisions with regard to the establishment and maintenance of "After-care Organisations" as under:

The State government may, by rules made under this Act, provide—

(a) for the establishment or recognition of after-care organisations and the functions that may be performed by them under this Act;

(b) for a scheme of after-care programme to be followed by such after-care organisations for the purpose of taking care of juveniles or the children after they leave special homes, children homes and for the purpose of enabling them to lead an honest, industrious and useful life;

(c) for the preparation or submission of a report by the probation officer or any other officer appointed by that Government in respect of each juvenile or the child prior to his discharge from a special home, children's home, regarding the necessity and the nature of after-care of such juvenile or of a child, the period of such after-care, supervision thereof and for the submission of report by the probation officer or any other officer appointed for the purpose, on the progress of each juvenile or the child;

(d) for the standards and the nature of services to be maintained by such after-care organisations;

(e) for such other matters as may be necessary for the purpose of carrying out the scheme of after-care programme for the Juvenile or the child;

Provided that any rule made under this section shall not provide for such juvenile or child to stay in the after-care organisation for more than three years;

Provided further that a juvenile or child over seventeen years of age would stay in the after-care organisation till he attains the age of twenty years.

The *J.J.(C&P of C) Act, 2000* has introduced a new concept of establishment of "Shelter Homes" for functioning as 'drop-in-centres' for the children in the need of urgent support. Section 37 of the *J.J.(C&P of C) Act, 2000,* provides thus:

(1) the State government may recognise reputed and capable voluntary organisations and provide them assistance to set up and administer as many shelter home for juveniles or children as may be required.

(2) The shelter homes referred to in Sub-section (1) shall function as drop-in-centres for the children in the need of urgent support who have been brought to such homes through such persons as are referred to in sub-section (1) of Section 32.

(3) As far as possible the shelter homes shall have such facilities as may be prescribed by the rules.

As had been observed earlier, the *J.J.(C&P of C) Act, 2000* also deals with the 'children in need of care and protection' who were termed as 'neglected juveniles' under the *J.J. Act, 1986,* and for them provisions have been made for the establishment of "Children's Homes" under Section 34 of the *J.J.(C&P of C) Act, 2000.*[88] It is to be noted that under the *J.J. Act, 1986,* for such children , "Juvenile Homes" were established under Section 9 of the *J.J. Act, 1986.*

The 'juveniles in conflict with law' are initially kept in Observation Home for a maximum period of 4 months for completion of the enquiry. At the disposal stage some juveniles may, after giving admonition and counseling, be released on bail and supervision, etc. Those who in the opinion of the Juvenile Justice Board may require further stay in the institution, will be shifted to Special Home from the Observation Home. It is expected that in the Special Home, there shall be elaborate provisions for formal education and training. The juvenile may also, from the Special Home, join separate after care institution for completion of their education and training.

(c) Transfer of Juvenile in conflict with law undergoing sentence at the commencement of the J.J.(C&P of C) Act, 2000

With regard to a juvenile in conflict with law who is undergoing any sentence of imprisonment at the commencement of this Act, the State Government or the local authority has been empowered under Section 64 of the *J.J.(C&P of C) Act, 2000,* to direct that such juvenile :

> "shall, in lieu of undergoing such sentence, be sent to a special home or be kept in fit institution in such manner as the State Government or the local authority thinks fit for the reminder of the period of the sentence; and the provisions of this Act shall apply to the juvenile as if he had been ordered by the Board to be sent to such special home or institution or, as the case may be, ordered to be kept under protective care under sub-section (2) of Section 16 of this Act."

(d) Constitution of Central, State, District and City Advisory Boards

The Central Government or the State Government have been empowered to "Central Advisory Board" or "State Advisory Board", as the case may be. Section 64 of the *J.J.(C&P of C) Act,2000* provides thus:

(1) The Central Government or a State Government may constitute a Central or a State Advisory Board, as the case may be, to advise that Government on matter relating to the establishment and maintenance of the homes, mobilisation of resources, provision of facilities for education, training and rehabilitation of child in

need of care and protection and juvenile in conflict with law and co-ordination among the various official and non-official agencies concerned.

(2) The Central or State Advisory Board shall consist of such persons as the Central Government or the State Government, as the case may be, think fit and shall include eminent social workers, representatives of voluntary organisations in the field of child welfare corporate sector, academician, medical professionals and the concerned department of the State Government.

It has been further provided under Sub-section (3) that 'The district or city level Inspection Committee constituted under Section 35 of this Act shall also function as the district or city advisory board.

(e) Creation of Fund for the welfare and rehabilitation of juveniles

The State Government or local authority has been empowered to create a Fund under such name as it thinks fit for the welfare and rehabilitation of the juveniles or the child dealt with under the *J.J.(C&P of C) Act, 2000*. All voluntary donations, contributions or subscriptions made by any individual or organization shall be credited to such Fund and the same shall be administered by State Advisory Board in such manner and for such purposes as may be prescribed.[89]

F. SOME REFLECTIONS OF JUDICIARY TOWARDS JUVENILE JUSTICE

The *J.J.(C&P of C) Act, 2000* has not been fully operative as yet and, therefore, judicial response to it is not available. However, a review of cases decided with regard to the *J.J.Act, 1986*, reveals that judicial response is available on the aspects related to : (i) Overriding effect of TADA(P);[90] (ii) Overriding effect of NDPS Act 1985;[91] (iii) Neglected Juvenile;[92] (iv) Determination of Age;[93] (v) Bail;[94] (vi) Offence Against Juvenile;[95] (vii) Juvenile Justice Act is complete code in itself;[96] (viii) Separate Trial for Juvenile & Non–Juvenile;[97] (ix) Remand to Juvenile home;[98] (x) Juvenile delinquent entitled for compensation for his unlawful detention;[99] (xi) Supreme Court's Direction for proper running of Remand

Home and observation home;[100] (xii) Supreme Court's Direction to Magistrate or trial judge to specify the age of the person to be detained;[101] (xiii) Supreme Court's Direction to Implement the Juvenile Justice Act, 1986;[102] (xiv) Applicability of the *J.J. Act, 1986* or Jurisdictional Dilemma;[103] and (xv) Jail sentence to Juvenile or His Detention in Jail.[104] Time and space does not permit us to deliberate in detail on all the judicial decisions. However, as majority of the cases are related to the applicability of the *J.J.Act, 1986,* or Jurisdictional Dilemma, Jail sentence to juvenile or his detention in jail, determination of age, granting of bail and detention of juvenile in jails, the judicial response with regard to these aspects may be examined in brief.

1. Applicability of the Juvenile Justice Act, 1986 or Jurisdictional Dilemma

The question of applicability of the Juvenile Justice Act, 1986 has arisen in many cases in spite of the fact that the accused was a juvenile on the date of offence.[105] Despite of the explicit definition given in the J.J. Act, 1986,[106] in ***Sangeeta R Jain v. S.A Dwivedi***[107] by making the reference of section 27 of *Cr.P.C.,1973,* it was argued that a Juvenile Court had no jurisdiction to deal with children committing offences punishable with death or life imprisonment or with children over the age of 16 years. It is unfortunate that despite of the decisions of the Supreme Court in ***Rohtas v. State of Haryana***[108] and ***Raghubir v. State of Haryana***[109], the Punjab and Haryana High Court in ***Daljit Singh's case***[110] and Bombay High Court and ***Sarita's case***[111] held that the Juvenile Court had no jurisdiction. In ***Rohtas v. State of Haryana***[112] the Supreme Court observed as under :

> "Section 5 [of the Code of 1973][113] carves out a clear exception to the provisions of the trial of an offence under any special or local law for the time being in force... It is not disputed that the Haryana Act was in force when the code of 1973 was passed and, therefore, the Haryana Act far from being inconsistent with Section 5 of the Code of 1973 appears to be fully protected by the provisions of Section 5 of the Code of 1973".

In ***Raghubir v. State of Haryana,***[114] the Supreme Court referred to ***Rohtas's case***[115] in which it had held that the trial of a child under the provisions of the Act was not barred. In that case, however, it appears that Section 27 of the Code of 1973 [116] was not brought to the notice of the Court. In the opinion of the Court, Section 27 was not a specific provision to the contrary within the meaning of Section 5 of the Code; the intention of the Parliament was not to exclude the trial of delinquent children for offences punishable with death or imprisonment for life, as Section 27 does not contain any expression to the effect "notwithstanding anything contained in the Children Act passed by an State Legislature". Parliament certainly was not unaware of the existence of the *Haryana Children Act, 1974,* coming into force a month earlier of the Central Children Act coming into force nearly fourteen years earlier. What Section 27 contemplates is that a child under the age of 16 years may be tried by a Chief Judicial Magistrate or any Court specially empowered under the *Children Act, 1960*. It is an enabling provision and has not affected Haryana Act in the trial of delinquent children for offences punishable with death or imprisonment for life.[117] Thus, the Supreme Court has restored the very object of having special law, procedure and separate personnel for dealing with children. It is unfortunate that sometimes even Judges lack the desired awareness of the applicability of the Juvenile Justice Act. The Judgement of the Allahabad High Court in ***Lal Diwan v. State of U.P.***[118] presents a very sorry state of affairs about the awareness and sensitivity of the judges concerning juvenile jurisprudence. In this case, a 15 years old child was found to have committed murder and was sentenced to life imprisonment by the Sessions Judge on 24.7.80. The child remained in prison for long 15 years becoming 31 and half years old. There on 22.2.85 the High Court setting him at liberty decided by reference to the *U.P. Children Act* that he could have been sent to prison best not beyond the time when he would have attained the age of 18 years. In ***Pradeep Kumar v. State of U.P.***[119], a child below 16 years of age was convicted for murder and sentenced to life imprisonment by the sessions courts dispute the because of which he should have been sent to an approved school till the age of 18 years.

2. Jail Sentence to Juvenile or his Detention in Jail

The main objective of the Juvenile Justice is 'to reform and rehabilitate the delinquent juvenile' and, thus, the usual and ordinary penal sanctions are completely excluded from the Juvenile Justice system. Section 22 of the *J.J. Act, 1986*, lays down that: "notwithstanding anything to the contrary contained in any other law for the time being in force, no delinquent juvenile shall be sentenced to death or imprisonment or committed to prison in default of payment of fine or in default of furnishing security"; the same language is used in Section 16 of the *J. J.(C & P of C) Act, 2000*. By this provision it is clear that the law is very much concerned to see that juveniles do not come into contact with hardened criminals and their chances of reformation are not blighted by contact with criminal offenders. It is the duty of the State to look after the child with a view to ensure full development of the personality of the child. In this regard it is to be noted that statutes dealing with children provide that Jail for Juvenile should be averted.

In ***Munna v. State of U.P.***[120] three writ petitions came before the Supreme Court to seek relief in respect of certain juvenile under trial prisoners in the Kanpur Central Jail. It was alleged that though there was a Children's Home in Kanpur, these juveniles were lodged in the Kanpur Central Jail and they were being sexually exploited by the adult prisoners. In this case, Mr. Justice Bhagwati and Mr. Justice Pathak highlighted the pathetic conditions of under trial juvenile prisoners in the following words:

> "Juvenile delinquency is, by and large, a product of social and economic maladjustment. Even if it is found that these juveniles have committed any offences, they cannot be allowed to be maltreated. They do not shed their fundamental rights when they enter the Jail."[121]

The learned justices further observed that :

> "The law is very much concerned to see that juveniles do not come into contact with hardened criminals and their chances of reformation are not blighted by contact with criminal offenders. The law throws a cloak of protection round juveniles and seeks to isolate them from criminal offenders, because the emphasis placed by law is not on incarceration but on reformation".[122]

In this regard the following observations of Mr. Justice Bhagwati and Mr. Justice Mishra in ***Sheela Barse v. Union of India*** [123] are relevant:

> "Everywhere children are accused of offences, they must not be kept in jails. It is the atmosphere of the jail which has a highly injurious effect on the mind of the child, estranging him from the society and breeding in him aversion, bordering on hatred against a system which kept him in jail; on no account should the children be kept in jail.[124]

The Supreme Court directed the States which had Children Acts to bring the Acts into force.[125] Further, Justice Bhagwati and Justice Pathak got anguished by the repeated practice of sending the juvenile delinquents to the jails in the State of U.P.[126] and gave judicial warning to the judicial officers, in charge of the Administration of Juvenile Justice, in the following words:

> "The Magistrates in the State of U.P. and what we say here must apply *mutatis mutandis* to the magistrates in the other parts of the country where the Children Acts are in force, that they must be extremely careful to see that no person apparently under the age of 16 years is sent to jail but he must be detained in a Children's Home or other place of safety;....no words we can use would be strong enough to convey our feeling in this regard".[127]

Thereafter, the Supreme Court in the case of ***Sanjay Suri v. Delhi Administration***[128] ultimately directed the Jail Superintendents that 'no child shall be sent to jail' and observed that 'no warrant of detention should be treated as a valid one unless the age of the detenu is shown therein' and that 'it shall be open to the jail authorities to refuse to honour a warrant if age of the person remanded to jail custody is not indicated.' It would therefore be lawful for such officers to refer back the warrant to the issuing court for rectifying the defect before it is honoured. Despite the law and the Supreme Court directions, instances are still found of sending Juveniles to Jails.[129]

The *J.J.Act, 1986* provided for separate trial of delinquents and non-delinquent and also provide for separate committal institutions. The delinquent children were required to be committed to the care of Special Homes[130] and neglected juvenile to the Juvenile

Homes.[131] In the J.J. (C&P of C) Act, 2000, 'Juveniles in conflict of law' are committed to Observation Homes[132] for temporary reception and to Special Homes [133] for reception and rehabilitation and children's homes[134] (to be newly established) are meant for the reception of 'Child in need of care and protection'. All these institutions are not penal but correctional homes aiming at the rehabilitation and reform of the juvenile. The stay or detention in these institutions may not be equated to punishment. In ***Sunil Kumar v. State***[135] the Kerala High Court has laid down that in the scheme of Children Acts there is no scope for conviction of the child. In ***Public Prosecutor, A.P. v. Shaik Valli,*** [136] the Andhra Pradesh High Court has observed that detention in a Certified School is not to be considered as or equated to punishment in the sense in which the word is used in Section 53 of the Indian Penal Code, 1860; though, of course, it is punishment in a narrow sense because there is restraint on personal liberty. The object of detention in certified schools is to reclaim erring young persons lost or likely to be lost to society by reason of environment or bad upbringing, or companionship and to make good citizens of them. Although a certified schools are correctional institutions and not a prisons,[137] in actual practice these 'Institutions' or "Homes" established and maintained by the State governments are often referred to as "Jails – *bachcha jails*" by all within and outside the Juvenile Justice System created by the Juvenile Justice Act[138]. If the delinquent is not released on bail, he cannot be detained in jail or in the custody. The court may consider his stay at a place of safety or fit institution or with fit person. Mr. Justice V.R. Krishna Iyer observed in ***Sunil Batra v. Delhi Administration***[139] thus:

> The slurring over the rule in Ss. 27(2) and (3) of the *Prison Act, 1894,* and its violation must be visited with judicial correction and punishment of the Jail staff. Sex excesses and exploitative labour are vices adolescents are subjected to by the adults. The young inmates must be separated and freed from exploitation by adults. It is inhuman and unreasonable to throw young boys to the sex-starved adult prisoners or to run menial jobs for the affluent or tough prisoners. Article 19 of the Constitution then intervenes and shields.[140]

3. Bail of Juveniles

It is a matter of common knowledge that the system of 'Bail' as it exists today operates very harshly against the poor. The poor find it difficult to furnish bail even without sureties and consequently remain in jail until such time as the court is able up their cases for trial leading to grave consequences.[141] The *J.J. Act,1986,* under Section 18 and the *J. J.(C & P of C) Act, 2000,* under Section 12 (the provisions of both the Acts are similar) provide for bailing out a juvenile even for non-bailable offences.[142] It is clear that release on bail, even in non-bailable offences, is conditioned by the consideration that the juvenile is kept away out of the association of the reputed criminals and be saved from being exposed to moral dangers and sexual abuse. The above stated position of law was fortified by the Supreme Court's judgement in ***Gopi Nath Ghosh v. The State of West Bengal***[143] in which it was stated that 'where a Juvenile delinquent is arrested, he/she has to be produced before a Juvenile Court and if no Juvenile Court is established for the area, the Court of Sessions will have powers of a Juvenile Court. Such a juvenile delinquent ordinarily has to be released on bail irrespective of the nature of the crime alleged to have been committed unless it is shown that there appears to be reasonable grounds for believing that the release is likely to bring him under the influence of any criminal or expose him to moral danger or defeat the ends of justice.[144] In a comparatively recent case decided by the Madhya Pradesh High Court , Rahul Mishra v. State of MP,[145] Mr. Justice S.C.Pandey, while deliberating upon in detail the various grounds on which the bail can be refused to juvenile offender, has held that 'the existence of a prima facie case against juvenile cannot be the sole ground to reject the bail.' It was observed by the learned justice that:

> "In the instant case, it was only third ground which appears to have prohibited the court below because it held that it was not proper to release the applicant on bail on the ground that there was a prima facie case against him. This interpretation of statute under Section 18 of the Act is not exactly in consonance with the intention of the legislature. The words "notwithstanding anything contained in the *Code of Criminal Procedure, 1973*" would indicate that the

consideration which are germane for granting or refusing bail to persons who are not juvenile delinquent shall not come into play for granting or refusing bail to them. Here the words "ends of justice" should be confined to those facts which show that grant of bail itself is likely to result in injustice. For example, there is likelihood of juvenile delinquent, to whom the bail is granted, interfering the course of justice or he is likely to abscond from the jurisdiction of the court. The aforesaid categories are only by way of illustrative and not exhaustive. The juvenile delinquent may appear to be guilty prima facie but he is especially protected by the Act and is favourably considered for grant of bail under Section 18 of the Act for the reasons of his age."

Other cases on this aspect has already been dealt with in detail earlier in this chapter.[146]

4. Age Determination of a Juvenile Accused

With regard to the age determination of a juvenile accused, mainly two issues have arisen before the courts: (a) What should be the relevant date for the applicability of the Juvenile Justice legislation, and (b) What should be the criteria for age determination?

(a) The Relevant Date for the Applicability of the Juvenile Justice Legislation

As has been pointed out earlier,[147] Sub-section (1) of Section 32 of the *J.J.Act,1986*, makes provision for 'presumption and determination of age of a juvenile' and provides that:

'Where it appears to a competent authority that a person brought before it under any of the provisions of this Act (otherwise than for the purpose of giving evidence) is a juvenile or the child, the competent authority (a) shall make due inquiry as to the age of that person, (b) for that purpose shall take such evidence as may be necessary (but not an affidavit), and (c) shall record a finding whether the person is a juvenile or the child or not, stating his age as nearly as may be.'

A similar provision has been made under Section 49 of the *J.J.(C&P of C Act), 2000*. Two conflicting views have been given by the apex court on the issue if the relevant date for the application of the Juvenile Justice legislation to a juvenile accused. The first view is represented by ***Umesh Chandra v. State of Rajasthan***[148] in which the Supreme Court while dealing with a *pari materia* statute, the *Rajasthan Children Act*, observed that ' The relevant date for applicability of the Act so far as the age of the accused, who claims to be a child, is concerned, is the date of the occurrence of the offence and not the date of the trial.'[149] On the other hand, the second view to the second view is represented by ***Arnit Das v. State of Bihar*** [150] in which the Supreme Court held that in order 'to determine the question whether a person is juvenile, the crucial date is the date when he is brought before the competent authority and not the date of commission of the offence.' In this judgment no mention was made of the view taken in the ***Umesh Chandra's case***,[151] although a contrary view different from the earlier one was taken by the Supreme Court. The relevant extracts of the judgement are given as under:

> The date of the commission of the offence is irrelevant for finding out whether a person is a juvenile within the meaning of Clause (h) of Section 2 of the Act. If that would have been the intendment of the Parliament, nothing had prevented it from saying so specifically. Therefore a police officer or a Magistrate who is not empowered to act or cannot act as a competent authority has to merely form an opinion guided by the apparent age of the person and ... has to forward him to the competent authority at the earliest.... The competent authority shall proceed to hold inquiry as to the age of that person for determining the same by reference to the date of appearance of the person before it or by reference to the date when person was brought before it under any of the provisions of the Act. It is irrelevant what was the age of the person on the date of commission of the offence. Any other interpretation would not fit in the scheme and phraseology employed by the Parliament in drafting the Act. Moreover, the use of the word "is" at two places in Sub-section (1) of Section 32 of

the Act read in conjunction with "a person brought before it" also suggests that the competent authority is required to record the finding by reference to an event in praesenti before it, i.e. by reference to date when the person is brought before it and not by reference to a remote event, i.e., the date on which the offence was committed. The scheme of the Act contemplates its applicability coming into play only when the person may appear or brought before the competent authority. . .

The term "juvenile justice" before the onset of the delinquency may refer to social justice; after the onset of the delinquency; it refers to justice in its normal juridical sense. The Juvenile Justice Act provides for justice after the onset of delinquency. The societal factor leading to the birth of delinquency and the preventive measures which would check juvenile delinquency fall within the scope of social justice. Once a boy or a girl has assumed delinquency, his or her treatment and trial at the hands of justice delivery system is taken care of by the provisions of the Juvenile Justice Act. The Act aims at laying down a uniform juvenile justice system in the country avoiding lodging in jails or police lock-up of the child; and providing for the prevention and treatment of juvenile delinquency, for care, protection etc. in post-juvenility. In short, the field covered by the Act is not one which had led to juvenile delinquency but the field when a juvenile having committed a delinquency is placed for being taken care of post-delinquency. Thus, the legislative aims and objectives go to show that this legislation has been made for taking care of the care and custody of a juvenile during investigation, inquiry or trial, i.e., from the point of time when the juvenile is available to the law administration and justice delivery system; it does not make any provision for a person involved in an offence by reference to the date of its commission by him. The long title of the Act too suggests that the content of the Act is the justice aspect relating to juveniles.

Generally speaking *Santenu Mitra, Bhola Bhagat and Gopinath Ghose* cases are authorities for the proposition that:

(i) The technicality of the accused having not claimed the benefit of the provisions of then juvenile justice Act at the earliest opportunity or before any of the courts below should not, keeping in view the intendment of the legislation, come in the way of the benefit being extended to the accused – appellant even if the plea was raised for the first time before the Supreme Court.

(ii) A hyper-technical approach should not be adopted while appreciating the evidence adduced on behalf of the accused in support of the plea that he was a juvenile and if two views are possible on the same evidence, the court should lean in favour of holding the accused to be a juvenile in borderline cases; and

(iii) The provisions of the Act are mandatory and while implementing the provisions of the Act, those charged with the responsibilities of implementation should show sensitivity and concern for the juvenile.

However, in none of the cases the specific issue – by reference to which date, the date of commission of offence or the date of production of the person before the competent authority, the court shall determine whether the person was a juvenile or not, was either raised or decided.[152]

The main reasons given by the Supreme Court for its decision. contrary to the one given earlier, may be summarized as under:

(1) Section 32 of the *J.J.A.,1986*, uses the expression "Where it appears that a person is brought before it (court)... is a juvenile..." This expression indicates that the jurisdiction to record the finding of age commences when the person is brought before the court and he should be a juvenile on that date.

(2) Section 8 of the *J.J.A.,1986,* directs the Magistrate not empowered to deal with juveniles under the *J.J.A.,1986,* to transfer them if such Magistrate is of the opinion that the person brought before it is a juvenile.

(3) Sections 18 and 20 of the *J.J.A.,1986*, also indicate that inquiry into age has to be made only by the competent authority. Other Magistrates or the police have to reach a tentative finding of age for sending those cases to the competent authority.

(4) There was no need to have Section 3 of the *J.J.A.,1986,* if age at the date of commission of the offence was conclusive of its applicability.

(5) The decisions of the Supreme Court in ***Santenu Mitra v. State of West Bengal,***[153] ***Bhola Bhagat v. State of Bihar***[154] and ***Gopinath Ghosh v. State of West Bengal,***[155] were authorities on issues other than the one under consideration.

(6) The decision of the Calcutta High Court in ***Dilip Saha's case***[156] proceeded on an erroneous understanding of Article 20(1) of the Constitution. The Patna High Court in ***Krishna Bhagwan's case***[157] was faced with questions that were different from those before it.

(7) The long title of the *JJA* also suggests that it deals with juveniles.

Dr. Ved Kumari[158] is of the opinion that each one of these reasons is subject to question by reference to the provisions, their intent and the scheme of the *J.J.A.,1986,* apart from the philosophy behind juvenile justice. It is submitted that Juvenile Justice has its origin in the twin concepts of *mens rea* and *parens patriae*. Children found in difficult circumstances, including those committing offences, are treated differentially because they are less culpable and less capable of looking after themselves. This less culpability and less capability relates to the time when the act is being committed as well as the period while the person continues to be so. The scheme of the Act clearly shows that it is geared to deal with persons who were below the specified age at the time of occurrence but ceased to be so during the inquiry. Section 32 which has been relied upon by the Supreme Court, itself provides that an order of the competent authority shall not become invalid merely because of any subsequent proof that the person before it was not a juvenile. The age as determined by the competent authority shall be deemed to be the true age of the person for the purpose of the Act. The section is apparently inclusive in its approach.The same inclusiveness has been incorporated in Section 3 of the *J.J.Act, 1986,* which clarifies that even if the juvenile cases to be so during the inquiry, the *J.J.Act, 1986,* will continue to be applied as if the person continues to be so. The section was intended to clarify any doubts that may arise regarding continued applicability of the *J.J.Act, 1986,* rather to create doubts on the age at the date of occurrence being conclusive of its applicability. Juvenile Justice looks backwards at the time of commission of the offence as well as forward to what can be done to ensure care and protection to the child. Absence of such a section may have given rise to the question whether the Act will continue to apply if the juvenile cases to be so by the time of final order in the matter.[159] The scheme of residential care too extends the protection of the *J.J.Act, 1986,* to children beyond the age of a juvenile. A juvenile sent to a Juvenile Home or a Special Home may be kept there till the age of 18 in case of a boy and till the age of 20 in case of a girl-two years later than they cease to be juveniles according to the definition of juvenile in the *J.J.Act, 1986.*

There seems to be no logical explanation for differential application of the *J.J.Act, 1986,* to persons who were juveniles on the date of commission of the offence and the persons who were juveniles on the date of production before the Court. It also makes no difference whether such a juvenile cases to be juvenile during an inquiry or before being brought before the competent authority. In both cases the twin concepts of *mens rea* and *parens patriae* apply similarly. However, the Supreme Court posed to the counsel for the appellant in the ***Arnit Das's case,***[160] the following question:

> "What happens if a boy or a girl of just less than 18 or 18 years of age commits an offence and then leaves the country or for any reasons neither appears nor is brought before the competent authority until he or she attains the age of say 50 years ? If the interpretation suggested by the learned Senior Counsel for the appellant were to be accepted, he shall have to be sent to a juvenile home, special home or an observation home or entrusted to an aftercare organisation where there would all be boys and girls of less than 16 or 18 years of age. Would he be required to be dealt by a Juvenile Welfare Board or a Juvenile Court ?[161]

The learned counsel could not answer this question to the satisfaction of the Court. It is submitted that the question posed by the Supreme Court reflects the focus of the Court being on the offence rather than on the person. The object of the *J.J.Act, 1986,* is to ensure care, protection, etc., to children. It does not concern itself with punishing such children for committing offences. If for some reasons the opportunity to provide that care and protection is lost, there is not much that can be done to salvage the situation and the matter ought to be dropped.

The same question arises in those cases also where the "child" becomes too old to be dealt with under the provisions of the Act after the competent authority has ceased of the matter. There is already a precedent of the Supreme Court on the matter. In ***Jayendra v. State of U.P.,***[162] by the time the Court finally determined that the accused was a child on the date of the offence, the accused had become 25 years of age. The Supreme Court ordered the proceedings to be closed as no useful purpose would be served to send the matter back to the Juvenile Court for disposal under the Act. It may be mentioned, however, that the Supreme Court has not dealt with the subject consistently. In the ***Umesh Chandra's case***[163] which was decided by the Supreme Court a month and a half later than the ***Jayendra's case***[164], although the "Child" had become 26-and-a-half years old by the time the Supreme Court decided that he was a child of the date of the offence, the matter was referred to the Juvenile Court for final disposal in accordance with the Children Act.[165] It is further submitted that even if Sections 18 and 20 of the *J.J.Act, 1986,* indicate that the competent authority is the body that has to determine the age of the child, it does not mean that the age at the time of production determines applicability of the *J.J.Act, 1986.* The Supreme Court in the ***cases of Santenu Mitra***[166], ***Bhola Bhagat***[167] and ***Gopinath Ghosh***[168] has extended the benefits of this social legislation (*J.J.Act, 1986)* to children and not restricted its operation by taking resource to technicalities of law. ***Arnit Das's***[169] judgement takes a technical interpretation of Section 32 of the *J.J.Act, 1986,* by focusing on the use of "is" twice in the section. It ignores that sub-section (2) of the same section extends the benefits of the legislation even when in fact the person was not a child as determined by the competent authority. By technically interpreting the definitions of delinquent juvenile and juvenile, it is possible to argue that the date of decision in fact determines the applicability of the Act, Juvenile is a person who has not attained the specified age[170] and delinquent juvenile is the juvenile found to have committed an offence.[171] As the word used is "juvenile found to have committed an offence" it is possible to argue that the person must be a juvenile when the finding of delinquency is reached. Such an approach to interpretation is not constructive to the aims and objects of the *J.J.Act, 1986,* to extend uniform care to all children in need of care and protection. Similarly, in Section 32 the substantive approach rather than the formalistic language incorporated in it should determine the meaning to be given to this section.

Further, the Supreme Court in ***Arnit Das's case*** [172] has pointed out that the *J.J.Act, 1986* :

> "(the Act). . .has been made for taking care of the care and custody of a juvenile during investigation, inquiry and trial, i.e., from the point of time when the juvenile is available to the law administration and justice delivery system; it does not make any provision for a person involved in an offence by reference to the date of its commission by him".

This statement itself points out the contradictory positions in the judgment. On the one hand, the Court has held that the applicability of the JJA comes to be decided from the point the juvenile is produced before the competent authority, but on the other hand, it has incorporated investigation as being within the ambit of the *J.J.Act, 1986,* which is a stage prior to production of juvenile before the competent authority. It is submitted that the decision in ***Arnit Das's case*** [173] is *per incurrium* and it is against the philosophy of Juvenile Justice System in India – and therefore requires to be reviewed.

(b) The Criteria for Age Determination of a Juvenile Accused

An analysis of different cases decided by the High Courts and the Supreme Court , the following rules may be outlined for the age determination of a juvenile accused:

(1) Entry as to date of birth in the Register of Births and Deaths can be taken as basis for determining age and holding accused juvenile; such entry is admissible in evidence and Opinion of Radiologist cannot be preferred over entry made in register of births and deaths.[174]

(2) Inquiries can be made by the High Court, Court of Sessions, and, magistrate if empowered to exercise powers of Juvenile Welfare Board or Juvenile Court. Regarding the determination of age.[175] In case a plea of minority is taken in the Sessions Court, it is empowered to make inquiries and determine age of accused and it need not refer the case back to magistrate or to juvenile court to determine the age.[176]

(3) Authority determining the age should make inquiry by giving opportunities to parties to adduce oral and documentary evidence and also right to cross examine to opposite party.[177]

(4) Entries in electoral roll or age mentioned therein cannot be treated as conclusive piece of evidence and cannot be relied upon to determine age of juvenile.[178]

(5) Entry made in high school certificate or School Leaving Certificate is presumed to be correct and burden lies on either side to prove it otherwise by producing either scholar register or initial application by which the scholar was admitted in the register to disbelieve the date of birth mentioned in the High School Certificate.[179]

(6) In case of different age in School Leaving Certificate and the horoscope, the reliance would be given to School Leaving Certificate.[180]

(7) Medical Evidence and primary school register showing accused below 16 years at the time of commission of offence is sufficient; Presumption of authenticity cannot be raised as to admission form submitted by accused in private school.[181]

(8) Entry in register of births and deaths recorded by an official in performance of his duties – Cannot be doubted merely on ground that it was not contemporaneous with date of the suggested date of birth of offender – More so, when LIC policy and matriculation certificate also mentioned the same date of birth as mentioned in the register of births and deaths.[182]

(9) Where medical evidence including age estimation report of medical board based on radiological examination

and other physical characteristics available, conflicting evidence regarding date of birth entered in records of two schools in which accused studied is unsafe to rely on and the medical opinion shall be preferable to school records in case of conflict between the two.[183]

(10) In the age estimation report of the medical board it was shown that 'All the epiphyses at the wrist, elbow, shoulder and iliac crest had united while four pieces of the body of sternum and the medial end of clavicle had fused recently – In the space behind the second molar indication of eruption of tooth found and in the left lower jaw, third molar found to be just visible – Regular beard shaved cleanly.' – Accused being a Punjabi, even reducing the age by 2-3 years from the table given in *Modi's book for males of Bengal*, it was held that he was at least 19 years of age.[184]

(11) Where an application for bail taking plea that applicants were juvenile delinquents was made but the evidence for determining true age of applicant was not recorded and the enquiries for the same were not made, an order determining the age of applicant on the basis of classification test only is not proper.[185]

(12) Even if the plea of minority was neither taken before committal court nor taken before Sessions Court – prior to stage of examination of accused, it may be entertained if it is taken thereafter at belated stage but before conclusion of trial. Sessions Court should decide the issue and remitting the case to juvenile court is not improper.[186]

In this context, it is relevant to mention that Section 33 of the *J.J. Act, 1986*, provided the guidelines to the Juvenile Courts and the Juvenile Welfare Boards for making orders under the Act according to which the factors to be considered while determining the age of the juvenile accuse were the age of the child, the circumstances in which the child was living, the report made by the Probation Officer and the religious persuasion of the child. In order to ensure that such factors do not bias the court regarding the issue of guilt of the child, it was also provided that in case of a delinquent child the above considerations are to be made only after the issue of guilt has been decided. However, for the reasons unexplained, this useful provision has not been included in the new *J.J. (C & P of C) Act, 2000*. Perhaps, this aspect might have been left to be regulated by the Rules but is such case there would be no uniformity in the country as the Rules of different States might vary. The object might have been also to leave the matter to the entire discretion of the court as the objective of the *J.J. (C & P of C) Act, 2000*, is to adopt liberal approach.

To conclude, it may be said that the new *J.J. (C & P of C) Act, 2000*, is comprehensive enough to suit the best interest of the children. Besides protecting the rights and interests of the juvenile accused, the Act contains exclusive chapter on adoption, foster care and sponsorship for their social integration[187] and the power of giving such children in adoption has been vested with the Juvenile Justice Board.[188] This will ensure the adoptions to be made easy, popular and will also be monitored and facilitated objectively by the probation officer/child welfare officer/social worker, i.e., professionals, under Juvenile Justice System. Besides the existing adoption agencies, the children's homes have also been recognized to place the children in adoption and foster care. Earlier, the children were just lodged in the institutions for no purposeful rehabilitation. The role of the social workers, voluntary organizations and local bodies has been strengthened. The Act provides a major opportunity to the voluntary organizations to take up the responsibility to run and manage the defunct or ill-managed government-run children's institutions. Qualification, mode of selection and grounds for termination of the members of the Juvenile Welfare Committees, Juvenile Justice Boards have been prescribed in the Act/Rules to engage only committed persons with genuine background to administer the Juvenile Justice System. The role of the State has been changed from a doer to a facilitator. In conformity with the *United Nation's Resolution*, the Act provides the uniform age of 18 years for both boys and girls. Setting up of special Juvenile police unit and juvenile/child welfare officer in each police station and mode of treatment to the juvenile like admonition, community services etc. are now on statute. The *J.J. (C & P of C) Act, 2000*, has done away with many of the deficiencies existed in the *J.J.Act, 1986* and tried to provide effective solutions to the difficulties faced in the implementation of the *J.J.Act, 1986*.

From the above brief description made in the preceding pages of this Chapter, it emerges that a different procedure and treatment has to be applied and adopted in cases of a child accused – commonly known as 'delinquent juvenile' in general and a 'juvenile in conflict with law' in India in particular, and the procedure adopted in the case of adult accused is not applicable. Such Juveniles have been given special rights and most of the provisions of the *J.J.(C&P of C) Act, 2000* (earlier *J.J. Act, 1986*) satisfy the 'Standard Minimum rules for the Administration of Juvenile Justice' - known as the "Beijing Rules" adopted by the United Nations Congress and U.N. General Assembly in the year 1985. Past experience has shown that in spite of being in operation for 14 years, all the benefits given to 'delinquent juveniles' stated under *J.J. Act, 1986* were not made a reality and for this reason a new approach had to be adopted by enacting the *J.J.(C&P of C) Act, 2000*. However, the success of even this new *J.J.(C&P of C) Act, 2000*, also much depends upon the attitude of the 'Juvenile Justice Boards' and the commitment of the State Governments to implement and follow the provisions of the Act in order to deliver real justice to 'delinquent juveniles – juveniles in conflict with law' as has been promised by the *J.J.(C&P of C) Act, 2000*. The conditions so far are not very satisfactory as evidenced from the fact that in majority of the States, necessary Rules have not been framed so far due to which the Juvenile Justice Boards have not been constituted for disposing of the cases of 'juveniles in conflict with law' and the juvenile accused are even deprived of getting various relief available to them under the old *J.J.Act, 1986*, because the same has been repealed and bodies functioning under the said Act have become dysfunctional. Therefore, number of cases of such juveniles alleged to have committed offences are pending for disposal and in many cases the juveniles are languishing in Homes without any hearing. The Children Act was enacted in 1960; thereafter in 1986, the Juvenile Justice Act was enacted and ultimately in the year 2000, the Juvenile Justice (Care and Protection of Children) Act was enacted. Between 1960 and 1986, several State Legislations dealing with delinquent and neglected juveniles were enacted. In spite of lapse of more than 43 years, it is found that still the attitude of police and other agencies involved in handling such juveniles has not changed which is evidenced from some instances reported in the *Times of India* — Delhi Police put three boys in Tihar Jail on flimsy theft charge – the boys had no record of crime but still the police made no attempt to contact their families;[189] about 88 juveniles were moved out in phased process – said Jail spokesperson Sunil Gupta;[190] experts debate on juvenile justice;[191] 'we said we were 17 years of age, the police wrote 18' – said detained juveniles;[192] Police knows the Juvenile Justice Act, 'haul up the erring officials, boys can claim damages';[193] another boy is out of Tihar Jail after 28 days;[194]—these are some of the disturbing news items and show the working of the police of no other place but of the Capital of India; the situation at other places cannot be better. *The Juvenile Justice Act, 1986* , was enacted at the initiative of Prime Minister Rajiv Gandhi and after 14 years, the *Juvenile Justice (Care and Protection of Children) Act, 2000,* was enacted at the initiatives of *Mrs. Maneka Gandhi* – the then *Social Welfare Minister*. However, in spite of lapse of more than four decades, much has not been done with regard to the implementation of these statutes in letters and spirit. The responsibility for the implementation of these Acts lies upon mainly on the State Government but many State Governments have not taken the desired interest in the implementation – this job was entrusted to the Ministry of *Harijan and Samaj Kalyan Vighag* and the governments had during the past years paid its total attention towards *harijan kalyan* to build up their voting bank and had neglected the *samaj kalyan involving juvenile welfare* because these juveniles do not constitute their voting bank. The recommendation of the Supreme Court made in the year 1986 that 'only persons of maturity, wisdom and those well versed in law and science of human behaviour and child psychology should be made juvenile judges,' is yet to be implemented. The social workers appointed on the Juvenile Court (under *J. J. Act, 1986*) had been very often political nominees who are not conversant with the law, child psychology and philosophy of juvenile justice – this unethical practice is inimical to whole system of juvenile justice. Most of the State Governments showed their inability to provide adequate facilities for the required care and protection of the neglected and delinquent juvenile due to inadequate financial resources and number of qualified personnel for the purpose. Further, the implementation of these Juvenile Acts demands the active support and participation of the different segments of general public and community and non-governmental social organisations, however, the same had not been made available. The effective coordination among the three principal and interdependent power-centres functioning under the juvenile justice system - Police , Magistracy and Social Welfare services is found lacking – they in effect pool their resources in an *ad hoc* system of cooperation and sometimes work for cross purposes. Law is considered as an instrument of justice and it has been said that 'the Criminal Justice System rests on three pillars, each of which contributes to the strength and performance of the system as a whole. The three pillars are: (a) Criminal Laws - Penal Code, Procedure Code, Evidence Act, etc;. (b) The Structures and Institutions — Police, Prosecution, Courts, Prisons, Homes, etc. (c) The Personnel - Policemen, lawyers prosecutors, probation officers, judges etc. Weakness in any one pillar reflects on the productivity of the whole system. There is a view often asserted that even if the laws are outdated and the institutions archaic, if the personnel are well motivated and trained, the system will be able to perform at a reasonable level.'[195] These observations are more true and appropriate with regard to criminal justice system relating to juveniles; unfortunately, it is here the juvenile justice system, as it operates at present in India, suffers serious setback.

Due to the above reasons, the *Juvenile Justice Act, 1986,* in most of the States has remained more or less an ornamental piece of legislation. What would be the fate of the *Juvenile Justice (Care and Protection of Children) Act, 2000,* only the future will tell; at present the future does not seem very bright because in spite of lapse of 3 years since its operation, so far even the necessary Rules have not been made in most of the States and the various agencies and institutions contemplated in the Act have not been established. In case sincere efforts are not made towards the implementation of the *Juvenile Justice (Care and Protection of Children) Act, 2000* in letters and spirit, the special rights recognized for the juvenile accused and the various protections recommended for them at international and national level would remain only on paper – rather the legal position has become worse because, on the one hand, whatever special protection was available to such juveniles under the *Juvenile Justice Act, 1986,* is also not available to them because the *Juvenile Justice Act, 1986,* has been repealed and made inoperative and, on the other hand, although the *Juvenile Justice (Care and Protection of Children) Act, 2000* has been made operative, it is only on paper but not in practice. In order to make the various human rights of juvenile accused effective in reality and practice, necessary suggestions and recommendations are proposed to be given in the Chapter to follow for consideration and appropriate action.[196]

REFERENCES

1. For details see, Seventh United Nations Congress on the Prevention of Crime and the Treatment of Offenders, Milan, 26 Aug. – 6 Sep. 1985.United Nations, New York, 1986 at pp. 89-91; see also, Compendium of United Nations Standards and Forms in Crime Prevention and Criminal Justice, United Nations Publication (Special 50th Anniversary Issue) (Sales No. E. 92. IV.1).
2. See, "Juvenile Justice and the Implementation of the United Nations Standard Minimum Rules for the Administration of Juvenile Justice", International review of Criminal Policy, No.43-44 (1994) United Nations Publication (Sales No. E. 94. IV.5).
3. The Beijing Rules,1985, Rule 13.1.
4. *Ibid.*, Rule 13.2.
5. *Ibid.*, Rule 13.4.
6. *Ibid.*, Rule 13.3.
7. *Ibid.*, Rule 13.5.
8. *Ibid.*, Rule 10.1.
9. *Ibid.*, Rule 10.2.
10. First, The United Nations Guidelines for the Prevention of Juvenile Delinquency (Riyadh Guidelines) and second, the United Nations Rules for the Protection of Juveniles Deprived of Their Liberty, 1990.
11. United Nations Rules for the Protection of Juveniles Deprived of Their Liberty, 1990, adopted by General Assembly resolution no. 45/113 of 14th December, 1990.
12. Guideline 18 of the Guidelines on Prosecutors.

13. Adopted by General Assembly resolution no. 45/112 of 14th December, 1990 (referred to as the 'Riyadh Guidelines).
14. Adopted and opened for signature, ratification and accession by General Assembly Resolution no. 44/25 of 20th November,1989.
15. *Ibid.* A "child" is defined in Article 1 of the Convention as " every human being below the age of eighteen years unless under the law applicable to the child, majority is attained earlier."
16. "Application of International Standards Concerning the Human Rights of Detained Juveniles", Report prepared by the Sub-Commission on Prevention of Discrimination and Protection of Minorities (E/CN.4/sub.2/1991/24), Para 82. See also, Arab-African Seminar on Criminal Justice and Penal Reform (Tunis, 2nd Dec, 1991), Recommendations, p. 4; quoted from United Nations, Human Rights and Pre-trial Detentions : 4 Handbook of International Standards relating to Pre-trial Detention, Geneva, 1994, at p. 45.
17. A I R 1986 S.C. 1773.
18. Juvenile Justice Act, 1986, S. 1(2).
19. *Ibid.*, Ss. 18(2) and (3).
20. *Ibid.*, S. 11.
21. *Ibid.*, S. 21.
22. *Ibid.*, Ss.10 and 21.
23. *Ibid.*, S. 2(1) which defines 'neglected juvenile' in a very exhaustive manner.
24. *The Times of India* (Daily News Paper) New Delhi, June 30, 2000 at p.8.
25. Sheela Barse v. Union of India, A I R 1986 S.C. 1773.
26. Susan Mathews, "A Report of the National Consultation on Juvenile Justice" Centre for Child and Law, National Law School of India University, Bangalore, India, as quoted in Ved Kumari Current Issues. in Juvenile Justice in India". J.I.L.I .1999 Vol. 41 at p. 393.
27. 1995 *Cr. L.J.* 389 (All.).
28. See, *supra*, note 26, at p. 395.
29. Juvenile Justice Act, 1986, S. 2(e) - "delinquent juvenile" means a juvenile who has been found to have committed an offence.
30. *Ibid.*, S. 2(n) - "Offence" means an offence punishable under any law for the time being in force.
31. N.L. Mitra, "Offence Factor in Delinquency Behaviour in Juvenile Justice" in N.K. Chakrabarty (ed.) *Juvenile Justice in the Administration of Criminal Justice* (Deep & Deep Publication New Delhi, 199) at 24.
32. Juvenile Justice (Care and Protection of Children) Act, 2000, s. 2(l).
33. *Ibid.*, S. 2(d).
34. *Ibid.*

35. *Ibid.*, s. 2(k).
36. *Ibid.*, s. 2(m).
37. *Ibid.*, s. 2(w).
38. *Ibid.*, s. 40.
39. *Ibid.*, ss. 5 and 30.
40. *Ibid.*, s. 29.
41. *Ibid.*, s. 4(3).
42. *Ibid.*, ss. 4(4) and 29(3).
43. *Ibid.*, s. 14.
44. *Ibid.*, s, 18.
45. *Ibid.*, Section 37.
46. *Ibid.*, Section 63.
47. *Ibid.*, ss. 30, 37 and 39.
48. *Ibid.*, s. 21.
49. *Ibid.*, s. 60.
50. *Ibid.*, ss. 34, 36 and 44.
51. *Ibid.*, s. 32.
52. *Ibid.*, s. 2(d).
53. *Ibid.*, s. 63.
54. *Ibid.*, s. 4.
55. *Ibid.*, s. 29.
56. *Ibid.*, s. 41.
57. *Ibid.*, s. 63(1).
58. *Ibid.*, s. 63(2).
59. *Ibid.*, s. 63(3).
60. James J. Bernnar, "Police and Delinquent Youth", Journal of Criminal Law, Criminology and Police Science, Vol. 46 at p. 886.
61. Cyril Burt, 'The Young Delinquent', 1969, p. 15.
62. Parmeshwar P. Srivastava, "Juvenile Delinquent" Cri. L.J. (1981), p. 9.
63. S.M. Anwarul Haque, "Delinquency - Disease but not Crime" Cri. L.J. (1978), p. 71. See also , Justice P. Chennakesar Reddi, "Pathology of Crime and its control" Cri. L.J. (1982), p. 41. See also Mohd. Giasuddin v. State of A.P., (1977), 3 SCC, p. 289-90; A I R 1977 SC 1928-29; Cri L.J. (1977), p. 1659-60.
64. Sophia M. Robinson, Juvenile Delinquency, 1961, p. 9.
65. Law of New Mexico has enumerated the behaviours of habitually refusing to obey the commands of their parents or of other lawful authority; habitually way ward; habitually truant; habitually insures the morals, health and welfare of himself or others etc. (Quoted by Rught Cavans, Concept of Tolerance and contra culture as applied to delinquency" Sociological Quarterly (1961) p. 243).

Most of the American states have prohibited the following behaviours by their statutes: violation of any law or ordinance; immoral or indecent conduct; enjoying in illegal occupation; associating with vicious or immoral or person; growing up in crime; entering or visiting house of ill-repute; visiting policy shop liquor is sold; wandering in night without a lawful business in railway yards and tracks; jumping into trains; truancy; incorrigible; habitually using vilel, obscene or vulgar language in public place;

66. In Japan it is the court which determines whether the behaviour of a child is delinquency or not.
67. In U.S.A. it is generally 16, 17 and 18 years. In England it is 16 years for boys and 18 years for girls. In Italy and Germany it is 18 years. In Jápan it is 20 years. In India, it is 16 years for boys and 18 years for girls whereas in the state of Uttar Pradesh it is 16 years[1].
68. In England, (Nigel Walker : Crime and punishment in Britain p. 180).
69. Sheela Barse v. Union of India A I R 1986 S.C. 1773.
70. J.T. 1997 S.C. 305.
71. SC. Cr. R. 1990, p. 86.
72. (1984) SCC 228; 1984 SCC (Cri) 478.
73. 1991 L.W. (Cri) 417.
74. Antaryami Patra v. State of Orrisa, 1993 Cr. L.J. 1908.
75. Sambandham s. "The Juvenile Justice Act, 1986", Prints Edn. Malathi Publications, Madras, 1994, p. 27.
76. Gopi Nath Ghosh v. State of West Bengal, A I R 1984 S.C. 237 at p. 241,
77. A I R 1984 S.C. 237.
78. *Ibid.*, at p. 238.
79. Rathinam v. Kamala Vaiduriam and another, 1991 L.W.(Cri.) 433 (DB).
80. Criminal Procedure Code,1973, s. 252.
81. *Ibid.*, s. 254.
82. *Ibid.*
83. *Ibid.*, s. 255(1).
84. *Ibid.*, s. 256.
85. R. Sherman, (1974) 60 Cr. RPP. Rep. 143 CA.
86. R. v. Parry, (1951) 1 T.L.R. 187.
87. R. Evans, 1958 All E.R. 673.
88. Section 34 of the J. J.(C & P of C) Act, 2000, provides as under: **Children's Homes**— (1) The State Government may establish and maintain either by itself or in association with the voluntary organisations, children's homes, in every district or group of

districts, as the case may be for the reception of child in need of care and protection during the pendency of any inquiry and subsequently for their care, treatment, education, training, development and rehabilitation.

(2) The State Government may, by rules made under this Act, provide for the management of children's home including the standards and the nature of services to be provided by them, and the circumstances under which, and the manner in which, the certification of a children's home or recognition to a voluntary organisation may be granted or withdrawn.

Section 35 of the said Act, *inter alia*, makes the provision as under for **Inspection of such Homes**:

(1) The State Government may appoint inspection committees for the children's home (hereinafter referred to as the inspection committees) for the State, a district and city, as the case may be, for such period and for such purposes as may be prescribed.

(2) The inspection committee of a State, district or of a city shall consist of such number of representative from the State Government, local authority, committee, voluntary organisations and such other medical experts and social workers as may be prescribed.

For **Social Auditing of such Homes** it has been provided under section 36 that: "the Central Government or State Government may monitor or evaluate the functioning of the Children's home at such period and through such persons and institutions as may be specified by that Government."

89. J. J.(C & P of C) Act, 2000, section 61.
90. Jagdish Bhuyan, Shri v. State of Assam (1992) 3 Cri.LJ 3194 (Gauhati) (Manisana and Smt. M. Sarma, JJ.).
91. Antaryami Patra v. State of Orissa (1993) 2 Cri. LJ 1908 (Orissa) (GB Patnaik, J.).
92. Amrita Ahluwalia v. Union of India 1992 Cri.LJ 1906 (Del.) *(B.N.Krirpal and Arun Kumar, JJ.)*; Gaurav Jain v. Union of India (1997) 8 SCC 114 (K. Ramaswamy and D.P. Wadhwa, JJ.).
93. Km. Anita v. Atal Bihari (1993) Cri.LJ 549 (MP)*(S.K.Dubey,J.)*;Arjun Ram v. State of Rajasthan (1998) 4 Cri.LJ 4375 (Raj.)*(Amaresh Kumar Singh, J.)*;Aquil Alvi v. State of U.P. (1996) Cri.LJ 103 (All.)*(C.A. Rahim, J.)*;Arnit Das v. State of Bihar (2000) Cri.LJ 2971 (SC); A I R 2000 SC 2264; (2000) 5 SCC 488*(K.T.Thomas and R.C. Lahoti,JJ.)*;Bandela Ailaiah v. State of A.P. (1995) Cri.LJ 1083 (AP)*(M.N.Rao and R.K. Somsekhara,JJ.)*;Balbir Singh v. State of Rajasthan 1994 Cri. LJ 2750(Raj.)*(N.L. Tibrewal,J.)*;Bhola Bhagat v. State of Bihar A I R 1998 SC 23 : (1998) 1 Cri.LJ 390 (SC) *(Dr. A.S.*

Anand and K. Venkataswami, JJ.);Bhupinder Singh v. State of Himachal Pradesh (1997) 1 Cri.LJ 339 (HP)(*R. L. Khurana,J.)*;Bijoy Singh v. State 1986 Cri. LJ 2016(Cal.)*(N.G.Chaudhuri and G.C.Chatterjee, JJ.)*; Dayachand v. Sahib Singh (1991) 2 SCC 379*(B.C. Ray and J.S. Verma JJ.)*; Devendra Singh v. State of MP, *(1998)4 Cri.LJ 3654 (M.P.)(Dipak Mishra, J.)*;Fanu v. State of UP (1997)1 Cri.L J 275 (All.)*(G.S.N. Tripathi, J.)*;Jyoti Shankar Tripathy v. State (1995) Cri.LJ 3048 (Orissa) *(R.K. Patra, J.)*;Karuppayee v. State (1997) 2 Cri.LJ 1627 (Mad.) *(Kanakaraj and Ramasamy,JJ.)*;Krishna Bhagwan v. State of Bihar 1991 Cri.LJ 1283 (Pat.): A I R 1989 Pat.217*(N.P.Singh, Prabha Shanker Mishra and Bimalendu Narayan Sinha,JJ.)*;Mayank Rajput v. State of U.P. (1998) 3 Cri.LJ 2797 (All.)*(J.C. Mishra, J.)*; Milap Singh v. State of U.P. (2000) Cri.LJ 3059 (All.)*(S.K.Agrawal, J.)*; Mukhwinder Singh v. State of Punjab 1992 Cri.LJ 1897;Nazir Hossain Haldar v. State (1998) 2 Cri.LJ 1720 (Cal.)*(Dibyendu Bhusan Dutta, J.)*;Om Prakash Sharma v. State of UP (1997) 3 Cri.LJ 2710 (All.)*(D.C. Srivastava, J.)*;Om Prakash v. State of Rajasthan 2001 Cri.LJ 230(*Sunil Kumar Garg, J.)*;Onkar Tiwari v. State of UP (2000) Cri.LJ 4723 (All.)*(B.K. Rathi, J.)*;Raj Singh v. State of Haryana (2000) 6 SCC 759 *(S.Rajendra Babu and Syed Mohammed Quadri, JJ.)*;Raja Singh v. State of Bihar (2000) Cri.LJ 3388 (Pat.)*(D.N. Prasad, J.)*;Rama Kant v. State of UP (2000) Cri.LJ 4682 (All.)*(B.K. Rathi, J.)*;Rinkoo Khatri v. State of M.P. (1998) 1 Cri.LJ 775 (Madhya Pradesh, Gwalior Bench)*(S. S. Jha, J.)*;Sahib Singh v. State 1991 Cri.LJ 687 (Del.) *(M.K. Chawla,J.)*;Santenu Mitra v. State of WB, A I R 1999 S.C. 1587;Sheo Mangal Singh v. State of U.P., 1990 Cri.LJ 1698 (All.) *(Rajeshwar Singh, J.)*;State of Haryana v. Balwant Singh, (1993) 1 SCC 409 *(S. Ratnavel Pandian and M.M. Punchhi JJ.)*; State of M.P. v. Ashok Kumar (1995) 4 Cri. LJ 3955 (MP) *(S.K. Dubey and T.S. Doabia, JJ.)*; Sultan Singh v. State of M.P. (1997) 1 Cri. LJ 657 (M.P.High Court, Gwalior Bench) *(T.S. Doabia, J.)*; Sunil v. State of MP 2001 Cri.LJ 1862 (MP) *(S.C. Pandey,J.)*; Sunil Kumar v. State of U.P. 2000 Cr.LJ (All.) *(B.K.Rathi, J.)*; Suresh Prasad v. State of Bihar 2001 Cri.L.J. 1088 (Pat.) *(S.N. Pathak, J.)*.

94. Amit v. State of UP, (1999) 2 Cri.LJ 1878*(P.K. Jain, J.)*;Mata v. State of Rajasthan, (1996) Cri.L.J. 743 (Raj.) Jaipur Bench *(N.L. Tibrewal, J.)*;Rahul Mishra v. State of M.P. 2001 Cri.LJ 214 (MP)*(S.C. Pandey,J.)*;Shokat Ali v. State of Rajasthan, 1992 Cri.LJ 1335 (Raj.)*(N.L. Tibrewal, J.)*;State of MP v. Ashok Kumar (1995) 4 Cri. LJ 3955 (MP)*(S.K. Dubey and T.S. Doabia, JJ.)*;Sunil v. State of M.P., 2001 Cri.LJ 1862 (MP)*(S.C. Pandey,J.)*;Tajuddin s/o Mohd. Yunus v. State of UP, 2001 Cri.LJ 350(All.)(*U.S. Tripathi,J.)*.
95. Shyam Narayan Singh v. State of Bihar, (1993) 1 Cri. LJ 772 (Pat.)

(S. Haider Shaukat Abidi and Shashank Kumar Singh, JJ.);Sunita v. State (U.T. Chandigarh), (1998) 4 Cri.LJ 4249*(V.S. Aggarwal,J.)*.

96. Daljit Singh v. State of Punjab, (1992) Cri.LJ 1051 (P&H)(*S.S. Rathore,J.)*;In re Sessions Judge Kalpetta, (1995) Cri. LJ330 (Ker.).
97. Guddu v. State of U.P., 1996 ALJ 390*(Mathur V.P., J.)*.
98. Harold Hamre & Elin Aasland Hamre, Norwegian National, AIR 1999 Bom.325 *(F.I. Rebello,J.)*.
99. Lakshmi v. Sub Inspector, N.P. Police Station, 1991 Cri.LJ 226.
100. Sheela Barse v. Secretary Children Aid Society A I R 1987 SC 656.
101. Sanjay Suri v. Delhi Administration AIR 1988 SC 414 *(Ranganath Misra and M.M. Dutt)*.
102. Supreme Court Legal Aid Committee v. Union of India 1989 Cri.LJ 1126: A I R 1989 SC 1278*(Ranganath Misra and M. N. Venkatachaliah, JJ.)*.
103. Pradeep Kumar v. State of U.P, A I R 1994 S.C. 104; Lal Diwan v. State of U.P., 1995 *Cr. L.J.* 389 (All.). Sarita's case, 1990 Cri. L.J. 351 (Bom.);. Daljit Singh's Case, 1992 Cri.L.J. 1051 (P&H); Ragubir v. State of Haryana, A I R 1981 SC 2037; Rohtas v. State of Haryana, A I R 1979 SC 1839 Sangeeta R Jain v. S.A Dwivedi, (1996) Cri. L.J. 24. (Bom.)
104. Sunil Batra v. Delhi Administration, A I R 1980 S.C. 1579: 1980 Cr.L.J. 1099; Public Prosecutor, A.P. v. Shaik Valli, (1971) Cr.L.J. 1229; Sunil Kumar v. State, (1983) Cr.L.J. 99; Sanjay Suri v. Delhi Administration, AIR 1988 SC414; Sheela Barse v. Union of India, AIR 1986 S.C. 1773;Munna v. State of U.P., (1982) 1 SCC 545; Gopi Nath Ghosh v. State of West Bengal, A I R 1984 S.C. 237.
105. Daljit Singh v. State, 1992 Cri.L.J. 1051 (P&H) and Sarita v. State, 1990 Cri. L.J. 351 (Bom.).
106. The Juvenile Justice Act, 1986, s. 2(h).
107. (1996) Cri. L.J. 24. (Bom.).
108. AIR 1979 SC 1839.
109. AIR 1981 SC 2037.
110. 1992 Cri.L.J. 1051 (P&H).
111. 1990 Cri. L.J. 351 (Bom.).
112. *Supra*, note 108 at 1840.
113. "Nothing contained in this code shall, in the absence of a specific provisions to the contrary, affect any special or local law for the time being in force, or any special jurisdiction or power conferred, or any special form of procedural prescribed, by any other law for the time being force".
114. A I R 1981 SC 2037.
115. A I R 1979 SC 1839.

116. Section 27 reads: "any offence not punishable with death or imprisonment for life, committed by any person who at the date of when he appears or is brought before the Court is under the age of 16 years may be tired by the Court of Chief judicial Magistrate or by any court special empowered under the Children Act, 1960 or any of the law for the time being in force providing for the treatment training and rehabilitation of youthful offenders".
117. *Supra,* note 109 at 2040.
118. (1995) Cri. L.J. 1899 (All).
119. A I R 1994 S.C. 104.
120. (1982) I SCC 545.
121. *Ibid.,* at 548.
122. *Ibid.,* at 551
123. A I R 1986 S.C. 1778.
124. *Ibid.*
125. *Ibid.,* at 1776.
126. Munna v. State of U.P.(1982) 1 SCC 545.
127. *Ibid.,* at 551.
128. A I R 1988 S.C. 414.
129. Police put three boys in Tihar on flimsy theft charge The Sunday Times of India, New Delhi, March 31, 2002 at 3. See also, Times of India, New Delhi, April 10, 2002 at 3.
130. J.J.Act, 1986, s. 10.
131. *Ibid.,* s. 9.
132. J.J. (C & P of C) Act,2000, s. 8.
133. *Ibid.,* s. 9.
134. *Ibid.,* s. 34.
135. 1983 Cr.L.J. 99.
136. 1971 Cr.L.J. 1229.
137. *Ibid.,* at p.1231.
138. Susan Mathews, "A Report of the National Consultation on juvenile Justice" , Centre for Child and the Law, National Law School of India University ,Bangalore, 1999, p. 41.
139. A I R 1980 S.C. 1579: 1980 Cr.L.J. 1099.
140. Also see, J.J.Act,1986, s. 22.
141. Gopi Nath Ghosh v. State of West Bengal, A I R 1984 S.C. 237 at 241.
142. See, *supra,* at p. 217.
143. A I R 1984 S.C. 237.
144. *Ibid.,* at p. 238.
145. 2001 Cr.L.J. 214(M.P.)
146. For detailed discussion, see, *supra,* pp. 216-221.
147. See, *supra,* at pp. 237-238.

148. (1982) 2 SCC 202.
149. *Ibid.*, at p. 210.
For the applicability of the Act on the basis of the date of occurrence of the offence see also, Bandela Ailaiah v. State of A.P., (1995) Cri.LJ 1083 (AP) -*(M.N.Rao and R.K. Somsekhara,JJ.* Held that the 'Burden of proving age – Is not on Delinquent Juvenile; It is for the court to hold inquiry and the Crucial date for determination whether accused is juvenile is the date of commission of offence – trial of juvenile delinquent without holding inquiry as to his age vitiates the trial.); Fanu v. State of U.P., (1997)1 Cri.L J 275 (All.) - *(G.S.N. Tripathi, J.)*; Jyoti Shankar Tripathy v. State of Orissa, (1995) Cri.LJ 3048 (Orissa) -*(R.K. Patra, J.)*; Mayank Rajput v. State of U.P., (1998) 3 Cri.LJ 2797 (All.) -*(J.C. Mishra, J.)*.
150. (2000)5 SCC 488.
151. (1982) 2 SCC 202.
152. (2000)5 SCC 488.
153. (1998) 5 SCC 697 : 1998 SCC (Cri) 1381.
154. (1997) 8 SCC 720 : 1998 SCC (Cri) 125: AIR 1998 SC 23. In this case, Justices Dr. A. S. Anand and K. Venkataswami held that 'when a plea is raised by accused in court that he was a child at the time of commission of offence, it is obligatory for the court to examine the plea and hold inquiry if necessary to determine the age and give a finding in that regard ; Court cannot overlook beneficial provisions of Acts on technical grounds and deny the benefit of the provisions to an accused. The court must hold an inquiry and return a finding regarding the age, one way or the other.
155. (1984) Supp. SCC 228 : 1984 SCC (cri) 478.
156. Dilip Saha v. State of West Bengal, A I R 1978 Cal. 529.
157. Krishna Bhagwan v. State of Bihar, A I R 1989 Pat. 217. In this case, Justices N.P.Singh, Prabha Shanker Mishra and Bimalendu Narayan Sinha, held that 'an accused though a child at the commencement of inquiry, ceasing to be so during pendency of inquiry, is still entitled to benefit of the Act. If the appellate court is prima facie satisfied as to the accused being child on date of commission of offence, the court should call for finding that accused was child / juvenile under relevant Act on date of commission of offence. Even those charges are established, a very liberal approach has been provided in respect of punishment for such offences. Different sections put a strict bar on the child/juvenile being sent to jail custody either before an enquiry or after the conclusion of the inquiry in respect of the offence alleged or prove to have been committed. Even if such a child has committed a murder or rape,

in view of Section 22, neither he can be sentenced to death nor to imprisonment. It is true that in many cases the offence committed by such delinquent children may be shocking to the conscience and their conduct and behaviour may be abhoring but Section 22 is quite conscious of such situations. Still it provides for keeping the children/juveniles accused of such serious offences, in safe custody at a place ordered by the State government. This benefit is to be extended not only to an accused who is a child/juvenile at the time of the commencement of the inquiry and has continued as such till the conclusion of the inquiry, but even to an accused who has ceased to be a child/juvenile during the pendency of the inquiry.... If the plea that the accused was a child or juvenile on the date of commission of offence is taken for the first time in the appellate court, then that court should proceed with the hearing of the appeal, as required by Section 26 of the Juvenile Justice Act and should record finding in respect of the charge which has been levelled against such an accused. If such an accused is acquitted, there is no question of holding any inquiry in respect of the accused being a child on the relevant date but, if the finding of the guilt recorded by the court below is affirmed and the appellate court on the basis of materials on record is prima facie satisfied that the accused may be child or juvenile within the meaning of the relevant Act on the date of commission of offence, it should call for a finding from a children court/juvenile court in accordance with S. 32. If the finding so received is accepted by the appellate court, then that court in terms of Section 26 of the Juvenile Act should pass an order directing the juvenile court to pass orders in accordance with Ss. 21 and 22. As the applicability of provisions of two Acts, i.e., Juvenile Act and Children Act are dependent on the age of the accused on the date of the commission of the offence, the appellate court as well as the juvenile court have to be cautious while recording finding on that question, so that the person found guilty of committing offence which are shocking to the conscience of the court do not escape punishment by getting themselves declared as children/juveniles on the basis of certificates. The determination should not be based merely on written opinion of the doctors produced before the appellate court. Prosecution has right to cross examine such medical or forensic experts who have given their opinion about the age of the accused in order to demonstrate that the accused was not a juvenile on the date of commission of offence. This is necessary because by the time plea is taken before the appellate court in almost all the cases the accused concerned must have ceased to be a juvenile due to lapse of time making it more difficult for the appellate court as well as the juvenile court to determine as to what was his age at the time of commission of offence. In such a situation, the courts including juvenile court should get the accused guilty of serious offences, examined by the medical board and should determine the age of such accused on the basis of the material on the record including the opinion of the medical board. Once the legislature has enacted a law to extend special treatment in respect of trial and conviction to juveniles, the court should be jealous while administering such law so that delinquent juveniles derive full benefit of the provisions of such Act but, at the same time, it is the duty of the courts that the benefits of the provisions meant for juveniles are not derived by unscrupulous persons, who have been convicted and sentenced to imprisonment for having committed heinous and serious offences, by getting themselves declared as children or juvenile on the basis of procured certificates.

158. Dr. Ved Kumari, "Relevant Date For Applying The Juvenile Justice Act", (2000)SCC Vol. 6.
159. Krishna Bhagwan v. State of Bihar, A I R 1989 Pat 217. — See, *supra*, note 157 for detailed findings.
160. (2000) 5 SCC 488.
161. *Ibid.*, at p. 497.
162. (1981) 4 SCC 149 : 1989 SCC (Cri) 809.
163. (1982) 2 SCC 202.
164. (1981) 4 SCC 149 : 1989 SCC (Cri) 809.
165. While the Allahabad High Court considered such a case fit to be sent to the State Government for appropriate orders - Ghanshyam v. State, 1982 Cri. L.J. 138 (All). Overruled in Ghanshyam v. State of U.P., (1982) 2 SCC 400: 1982 SCC (Cri) 449. — the High Court of Punjab ordered that such child be released on probation of good conduct —.Bhudha Singh v. State of Punjab, 1979 Chandigarh L R (Cri)114.
166. (1998) 5 SCC 697 : 1998 SCC (Cri) 1381.
167. (1997) 8 SCC 720 : 1998 SCC (Cri) 125: A I R 1998 SC 23.
168. (1984) Supp. SCC 228 : 1984 SCC (Cri) 478.
169. (2000)5 SCC 488.
170. J.J.Act,1986, s. 2(h).
171. *Ibid.*, s. 2(e).
172. (2000)5 SCC 488.
173. *Ibid.*
174. Km. Anita v. Atal Bihari (1993) Cri.LJ 549 (MP) -(*S.K.Dubey,J.*).

175. Arjun Ram v. State of Rajasthan (1998) 4 Cri.LJ 4375 (Raj.)(*Amaresh Kumar Singh, J.*); Balbir Singh v. State of Rajasthan 1994 Cri. LJ 2750(Raj.) -(*N.L. Tibrewal,J.*); Aquil Alvi v. State of UP (1996) Cri.LJ 103 (All.) -(*C.A. Rahim; J.*).
176. Aquil Alvi v. State of UP (1996) Cri.LJ 103 (All.)-(*C.A. Rahim, J.*).
177. Balbir Singh v. State of Rajasthan 1994 Cri. LJ 2750 (Raj.)-(*N.L. Tibrewal,J.*); Krishna Bhagwan v. State of Bihar 1991 Cri.LJ 1283 (Pat.): A I R 1989 Pat.217 (*N.P.Singh, Prabha Shanker Mishra and Bimalendu Narayan Sinha,JJ.*).
178. Mayank Rajput v. State of UP (1998) 3 Cri.LJ 2797 (All.)-(*J.C. Mishra, J.*); Bhupinder Singh v. State of Himachal Pradesh (1997) 1 Cri.LJ 339 (HP)-(*R. L. Khurana,J.*); Fanu v. State of UP (1997)1 Cri.L J 275 (All.)-(*G.S.N. Tripathi, J.*).
179. Mayank Rajput v. State of UP (1998) 3 Cri.LJ 2797 (All.).
180. Bhupinder Singh v. State of Himachal Pradesh (1997) 1 Cri.LJ 339 (HP)- (*R. L. Khurana,J.*).
181. Sahib Singh v. State 1991 Cri.LJ 687 (Del.)-(*M.K. Chawla,J.*).
182. Santenu Mitra v. State of W.B., A I R 1999 S.C. 1587.
183. Dayachand v. Sahib Singh (1991) 2 SCC 379-(*B.C. Ray and J.S.. Verma JJ.*); Sunil Kumar v. State of U.P., 2000 Cr.LJ (All.)-(*B.K.Rathi, J.*) –"Juvenile Justice Act, 1986, section 32 – juvenile – age – proof – entry in school register not appearing to be genuine – Medical evidence would prevail over entry in school register."
184. Dayachand v. Sahib Singh, (1991) 2 SCC 379. See also, Arnit Das v. State of Bihar, (2000) Cri.LJ 2971 (S.C.); A I R 2000 S.C. 2264; (2000) 5 SCC 488-(*K.T. Thomas and R.C. Lahoti, JJ.*) .
185. Sunil v. State of MP 2001 Cri.LJ 1862 (MP)-(*S.C. Pandey, J.*).
186. Suresh Prasad v. State of Bihar 2001 Cri.LJ 1088 (Pat.) -(*S.N. Pathak, J.*).
187. J.J. (C & P. of C) Act, 2000, Chapter IV.
188. *Ibid.*, s. 41.
189. Times of India (Daily Newspaper) New Delhi, March 31,2002, at p.3.
190. *Ibid.*, April 2, 2002, at p. 3.
191. *Ibid.*, April 6, 2002, at p. 3.
192. *Ibid.*, April 7, 2002, at p. 3.
193. *Ibid.*, April 9, 2002, at p. 3.
194. *Ibid.*, April 10, 2002, at p. 3.
195. N. R. Madhav Menon, "Criminal Justice : Radical reforms Needed", The Statesman, (Daily Newspaper), New Delhi, October 9, 2000, at p. 6.
196. See, *infra*, Chapter 7.

Seven

Conclusion and Suggestions

A. CONCLUDING OBSERVATIONS

It has been observed in the present study that the subject relating the Rights of accused which is an integral part of criminal justice administration has assumed great importance not only in India but also at international level. In ancient India, *Vedas* and religious scriptures provided the basis for Hindu jurisprudence and criminal justice administration. Village Assemblies and the King with assistance of select villagers and townsfolk administered justice. People directly participated in adjudicating guild and awarding punishment. The emphasis was on the good of the society, and the impact of punishment on the individual was of no relevance. Punishment served the purpose of retribution and as an example to deter and prevent others to take to crime. On some occasions punishment served the purpose of compensating the victim. During Muslim Rule, Islamic Law formed the basis for jurisprudence and criminal justice administration. The offender was viewed as a sinner against the society, who observed to be socially deprived. Punishment was severe and cruel and was meant to serve as a warning to others.

British rule in India, for the first time, introduced egalitarian principles of Anglo-Saxon jurisprudence and the criminal justice system assumed the modern day role of reformist character. Though British adopted double standard in the administration of criminal justice - 'whites" always had many special privileges - it should be said to their credit, The justice was administered with even hardness. World War II saw human behavior at worst and what were considered as Natural Rights of people came to be fine tuned into Human Rights. United Nations took upon itself the role of the ladder for Human Rights. As the preamble of. United Nations Charter declared, "it was determined to reaffirm faith in

Fundamental Human Rights, in the dignity and worth of human person, in equal rights of men and women and of the Nations large and small". : Universal Declaration of Human Rights was adopted in 1948 followed by Covenants on Political and Civil Rights and Social, Economic and Cultural Rights in 1966. India adopted its Republican Constitution in 1950 and included a special part on Fundamental Rights in the Constitution. During the past two decades, in a number of cases, the Supreme Court of India had elaborated the dimensions of constitutional rights available to an accused.

The moment a formal accusation is levelled against a person he becomes an accused although he may not have been arrested and he continues to be called an accused even after he is arrested, released on bail or detained in police custody or judicial custody, and is facing trial in the court. Generally, he ceases to be an accused when he is finally convicted and punished or acquitted by the competent court. However, if he files an appeal against the conviction order or the State files an appeal against the order of acquittal and the order of the trial court is suspended, he again continues to remain an accused till he is finally convicted and punished or acquitted by the highest appellate court. On the basis of the present study, the various rights of an accused which are available to him under statutory law (i.e., *Code of Criminal Procedure, 1973, Indian Evidence Act, 1872*) and the *Constitution of India*, can be broadly classified into three main heads:

A. Rights of an accused before arrest
B. Rights of an accused after arrest
C. Rights of an accused after conviction but conviction is stayed.

Rights of an accused after arrest may be further sub-classified into the following two heads :

(1) Rights of an accused after arrest detained during police custody, and
(2) Rights of an accused after arrest detained during judicial custody.

The rights enjoyed by an accused detained under judicial custody by an order of the competent court may be further sub-classified into three parts:

(i) Prior to Trial,
(ii) During Trial, and
(iii) Post Trial

In addition to the above rights, an accused also enjoys certain additional rights when he is detained in the judicial custody and kept in jail. These rights are based on the provisions of the Jail Manual. The various rights which are available to an accused at different stages may be enumerated in summarised form as under:

1. Rights of an Accused before Arrest

Various rights enjoyed by an accused before arrest are as under:

1. Right to know the grounds of arrest;[1]
2. Right to know the power of arrest;[2]
3. Right to be released on bail;[3]
4. Right to seek the services of a counsel of his own choice;[4]
5. Right to be protected against arbitrary or unlawful arrest;[5]
6. Right to be protected against arbitrary or unlawful searches;[6]
7. Right to surrender;[7] and
8. Right to know certain informations.[8]

2. Rights of an Accused after Arrest

(a) During Police Custody

The rights enjoyed by an accused during police custody are as under:

(1) Right to be produced before the Magistrate within 24 hours of his arrest;[9]
(2) Right to be released on bail;[10]
(3) Right to seek services of a counsel of his choice;[11]
(4) Right to be released, when evidence is deficient;[12]
(5) Right against unnecessary restraint;[13]
(6) Rights relating to search of body and seizure of the articles;[14]
(7) Right to be examined by medical practitioner to disprove the commission of the offence;[15] and
(8) Right to be protected from any kind of torture in police custody.[16]

(b) During Judicial Custody

The rights enjoyed by an accused during judicial custody, i.e., detained in jails, are as under:

(1) Pre-trial: Rights enjoyed by an accused, detained in judicial custody, prior to the commencement of the trial are given below:

(1) Right to have speedy investigation;[17]
(2) Right to be defended by counsel of his choice;[18]
(3) Right to be released on bail;[19]
(4) Rights in the reference of handcuffing and fetters;[20]
(5) Right to get copies of statements of prosecution witnesses and other documents on which prosecution wants to build up its case against the accused;[21]
(6) Right with regard to period of limitation for taking cognizance of an offence;[22] and
(7) Right to have notice of charges.[23]

(2) During Trial: Rights enjoyed by an accused, detained in judicial custody, during trial are given below:

1. Right to be presumed innocent;[24]
2. Right to have open and fair trial;[25]
3. Right to have speedy trial or accelerated hearing;[26]
4. Right to seek protection against self-incrimination;[27]
5. Right to ensure examination of witness in his presence;[28]
6. Right to test the evidence of the prosecution by means of cross examination;[29]
7. Right to seek protection against Double Jeopardy;[30]
8. Right to be heard on the question of sentence before the sentence is passed ;[31]
9. Right to apply for and get free legal aid ;[32]
10. Right to be released on bail ;[33]
11. Right to enter upon defence or to examine witness ;[34]
12. Rights with regard to handcuffing and fetters ;[35]
13. Right to receive a copy of judgement ;[36]
14. Right to be protected against conviction or enhanced punishment under *ex post facto law* ;[37]
15. Right to get opportunity for explaining away evidence in court;[38]

16. Right to submit written arguments at conclusion of the trial in addition to oral submission;[39]
17. Right to restrain police form intrusion on his privacy ;[40] and
18. Right to be tried by an independent and impartial judge.[41]

(3) Post-trial: Rights enjoyed by an accused, detained in judicial custody, during post-trial period are mainly two :

1. Right to get compensation;[42] and
2. Right to be released on bail pending appeal.[43]

3. Rights of Accused after Conviction but the Conviction is stayed

In case an accused is convicted but his conviction is stayed, he has a 'Right to file an Appeal/Revision' under Articles 132 and 136 of the Constitution and Section 363 of *Cr.P.C.,1973*, which provides a substantive Right of Appeal.

4. Rights of an Accused Detained in Jail under Judicial Custody, i.e., Under-trial Prisoners (based on Jail Manual of U.P.)

Various rights and privileges may be enjoyed by an accused detained in jail under judicial custody based on the provisions of Jail Manuals of States. Here below, some of these rights have been enumerated under three heads: (a) Rights Available to All (Male And Female) Under Trial Prisoners , (b) Rights Available to Only Female Under Trial Prisoners and (c)) Rights Available to Only Juvenile Youthful Offenders (Of The Age of 16 or Above But Below 21). Sections mentioned with regard to various rights of an accused detained in jails are of *U. P. Jail Manual.*

(a) Rights Available To All (Male and Female) Under Trial Prisoners

The following rights have been recognised by U.P. Jail Manual to all — male and female — under trial prisoners:

(1) Right to be informed of the date fixed for the production in Session's case;[44]

(2) Right of not to be detained for more than fifteen days without a fresh remand;[45]

(3) Right to be examined by Medical Officer;[46]
(4) Right to be kept separate from convicted prisoners;[47]
(5) Right against unnecessary restraint;[48]
(6) Right against handcuffing, link-fetters and bar fetters;[49]
(7) Right against belchains;[50]
(8) Right to receive food, clothing and bedding from private sources;[51]
(9) Right to receive the non-labouring diet of the jail;[52]
(10) Right to cook his own food;[53]
(11) Right to wear his own clothes;[54]
(12) Right of superior class under trial prisoners to be allowed to sleep in the open during summer;[55]
(13) Right of not to be compelled to work or labour;[56]
(14) Right against undue detention;[57]
(15) Right to receive food before the convicts;[58]
(16) Right to write letters at government expense;[59] and
(17) Right to be informed of the rules, regarding the jail.[60]

(b) Rights Available to Only Female Under Trial Prisoners

Special privileges in the form of rights have been granted to female under trial prisoners by the *U.P. Jail Manual* - some of which are as under:

(1) Right of the female under trial prisoners under forty years to be accompanied by a female warder ;[61]
(2) Right of female under trial prisoners to interview and communicate with their relative, fired or legal advisors;[62]
(3) Right to be kept in separate enclosures and also to be kept separate from convicted female prisoners;[63]
(4) Right of female adolescent and juvenile under trial prisoner to be kept separate from adult prisoners;[64]
(5) Right of superior class female under trial prisoners to be kept apart from ordinary female prisoners;[65]
(6) Right of the female under trial prisoners, in the circumstances, when she is alone in the jail, to live with a female warder;[66]
(7) Right against handcuffing, fetters, or whipping;[67]
(8) Right to receive comb, soap, mirror at the expense of jail authority;[68]

(9) Right to get replaced her *churi,* nose-ring etc. at her own expense;[69]

(10) Right to receive food, inside the compartment only by female warder;[70]

(11) Right to have all the medial and other necessary facilities in the case of delivery;[71]

(12) Right to be allowed to keep her child below the age of 6 years, with her;[72] and

(13) Right to receive diet and clothing for her children who live with her.[73]

(c) Rights Available to Only Juvenile Youthful Offenders (of the Age of 18 or Above But Below 21)

The U. P. Jail Manual also recognises certain special rights of youthful offenders who are of the age of 16 or above but below 21. It is to be mentioned here in this connection that all jails have separate rooms (barracks) known as children jail for such offenders. Now after passing of the *Juvenile Justice Act, 1986,* and also due to several decisions of the Supreme Court, keeping a boy of below 16 years of age and a girl of below 18 years of age in jail was made unlawful; they had to be kept in the observation homes. Later on, after the enactment of the *Juvenile Justice (Care and Protection of Children) Act, 2000,* now the age of boy has been raised from 16 years to 18 years. Thus, the special rights recognized in the U.P. Jail Manual given below are only applicable to such youthful offenders who are of the age of above 18 but below 21.

(1) Right to be kept in reformatory school;[74]

(2) Right of Juvenile delinquents to be kept in separate enclosures from adult convicts; [75]

(3) Protection to delinquent juveniles against daily labour;[76]

(4) Right of delinquent juveniles to get education and training;[77]

(5) Right of delinquent juveniles to receive games facility;[78]

(6) Right to be treated as a juvenile when the delinquent is below the age of 21 years;[79]

(7) Right of the under-trial prisoners below the age of 21 years to be kept separate from other prisoners;[80] and

(8) Female juvenile can entertain all those rights whatever a female under trial prisoner has, as stated above.[81]

B. RECOMMENDATIONS AND SUGGESTIONS

1. General Recommendations and Suggestions

On perusal of the various rights enumerated above and also in the preceding chapters of this dissertation, one may be tempted to conclude that position of an accused seems to be very sound as he has been given so many rights. However, the reality is otherwise because in most of the cases the laws relating to the rights of accused are not followed by the persons involved in the criminal proceedings at different stages. Further, the accused, particularly the under trials detained in the jails or in police custody are still subjected to torture and other human rights violations. In order to make effective the various human rights protections declared at national and international level some suggestions are put forward for consideration. These suggestions would be helpful in halting the practice of torture by the police and creating an effective institutional framework for the prevention of torture and other human rights violations[82]:

1. The government should strengthen its International commitment and should now, like an increasing number of other countries throughout the world, accede to the U.N. Convention against Torture and Other Cruel, Inhuman or Degrading Treatment or Punishment. It will be a step in the right direction and affirmation of the country's determination to do away with torture. It will also send correct signals to the public servants, particularly members of the police and security forces not to transgress laws and rules of international conventions.[83]
2. India should ratify or accede to the (first) Optional Protocol to the ICCPR, which allows individuals to complain to the Human Rights Committee for effective remedies after they have exhausted all domestic avenues for redress. The government should remove the reservations it made when acceding to the ICCPR withholding from Indian citizens the right to compensation in case of wrongful arrest or detention. This is all the more necessary because the Supreme Court has already recognized the right to get compensation in such cases.

3. The government should launch an intensive programme of human rights education as a standard part of the training curriculum for all police and security forces personnel involved in the arrest, detention and interrogation of suspects.
4. Actual practices amounting to torture should be clearly spelled out under the Indian Police Act,1861, and other legal instruments relating to treatment and the training courses meant for the police personnel and members of the security forces should be restructured with the focus on human rights of the accused prisoners.[84]
5. The obligations undertaken by India with regard to promotion and protection of human rights and the abolition of torture and cruel, degrading inhuman treatment should be focused in the training programmes for the police personnel and a system of incentives should be introduced for those who show care to protect the rights of detainees and prisoners in their custody while the errant police personnel and the members of the security force should be sternly dealt with.
6. Recommendations for police reforms such as those proposed by the Second Report of the National Police Commission, 1979, and other expert bodies to free the force from political influence and patronage and also constitute a statutory body such as State Security Commission in each State to help the State Government 'to discharge its superintending responsibility in an open manner, under the frameworks of law', should be implemented [85]
7. At the time of arrest, the accused should necessarily be examined medically at the instance of the police. Failure of the accused to make the request for such medical examination under Section 54 of the *Cr. P.C.,1973,* should not exonerate the police from such liability.
8. Judicial inquiries should be conducted mandatory into all allegations of torture, including rape and deaths in police or judicial custody by an independent and impartial body, particularly made in the reports

published by the news media and by civil liberties groups are promptly and effectively investigated. The Supreme Court and the High Court should conduct their own inquiries whenever a victim alleges tortures or illegal detention in a *habeas corpus* petition.[86]

9. Right to compensation to the victims of torture and custodial deaths should be statutorily recognised and an effective machinery for providing redress to such victims should be established. The view taken by the National Human Rights Commission in its continuing effort to end custodial violence that the compensation due to the next of kin of those who have died in custody should be the liability not just of the State Government, but of the offending police officials themselves should be statutorily recognised. This would provide a further, powerful deterrent to aberrant behaviour by elements of the law enforcement machinery.[87]
10. Legal aid for the victims of abuses or their families should be made easily available enabling them to claim for compensation.
11. The legal machinery to combat torture should be strengthened and the prohibition of torture and other cruel, inhuman or degrading treatment or punishment should be incorporated in the Constitution.
12. The detailed guidelines should be formulated by the government in consultation with lawyers, bar associations, civil liberties groups and medical professional groups regarding interrogation of suspects; such guidelines should be published and also be continuously reviewed periodically in consultation with these groups to ensure that they continue to remain an effective mechanism for prevention of torture.
13. Keeping in view the flagrant violation of the fundamental rights of the accused and the de-humanizing aspect of the crime of custodial violence and also the growing rise in the crimes of this type, where only a few come to light and others do not, the recommendations of the Law Commission to bring

about appropriate changes in the system not only to curb the custodial crime but also to see that the custodial crime does not go unpunished, should be given serious consideration by the government and the legislature .[88]

14. The courts should also exhibit more sensitivity and adopt a realistic approach rather than a narrow technical approach, while dealing with the cases of custodial crime so that as far as possible within their powers, the guilty should not escape so that the victim of the crime has the satisfaction that ultimately the law has prevailed.[89]
15. Witnesses should be protected from intimidation and harassment and those accused of inflicting torture should be suspended from duty during such inquiries.
16. Legal provisions in Section 6 of the Armed Forces (Special Powers) Act, 1958 granting the security forces immunity from prosecution and provisions inhibiting prosecutions of police officer - such as exist under Section 197 of the *Cr. P.C., 1973,* — should be deleted.
17. The duty to disobey superior orders to inflict torture – as has been provided in Article 5 of the *U.N. Code of Conduct for Law Enforcement Officials* — should be incorporated in the *Indian Police Act, 1861.*
18. Suitable legal provisions should be made recognizing the right of detained accused - to have access to a medical examination, to request a judge or other independent body to order a second medical examination, and for victims of torture and their legal representatives the right to have access to the results of any medical examination.
19. Recommendations of the National Human Rights Commission for all post-mortem examinations in respect of deaths in police or jail custody to be video-filmed and the cassettes sent to the commission such as those proposed, should be implemented.[90] Families of those who die in police custody should have the right to insist that a medical or other qualified person nominated by the family be permitted to be present during the post-mortem examination.

20. In order to establish liability of the police in cases of custodial death the presumption of guilt should be raised against them.[91]
21. A Police Complaints Board consisting of a retired District and Sessions Judge (as Chairman) and a retired police officer of the rank of Superintendent of Police and a prominent citizen with administrative background (as members) may be constituted to look into and verify the complaints of custodial deaths by visiting the scene for ascertaining the facts. If in the opinion of the Board, a *prime facie* case exists, a direction should be issued to the local chief of police to register a criminal case against the police personnel concerned and also hand over the case to the Crime Branch, CID, for further investigation. Wherever a death occurs in police custody, a judicial inquiry by the District and Session Judge should be made mandatory.[92]
22. A Judicial Magistrate, vested with all powers to grant bail, record confessions, issue judicial process etc., should be made available round the clock at a designated place in the city or town to attend to the judicial needs of the arrestees. His presence and availability will automatically reduce the need for the police to hold the arrests overnight or when the courts are closed [93]
23. It has been found that the publicity provided by the media has led to several successful Public Interest Litigation, state intervention or community-action in the cases of violation of Human Rights of accused in general and in the cases of custodial deaths or fake encounters, in particular. It is desirable that the media must also promote popular recognition of all the rights enunciated by the declaration, through regular discussion and debate. It is undisputed that the role of media in safeguarding human rights is cardinal.[94]
24. In order to minimize the risk of being tortured at the hands of an unscrupulous investigating officer and also the violations of Human Rights, during the police

custody, the Magistrate should be empowered to permit the investing officer to further examine the accused in jail custody instead of the present practice of remanding him to police custody; this would greatly minimize the scope for practicing third degree methods by the police personnel.

25. It should be the duty of the officers-in-charge of police stations to formally notify all detainees of their rights; a list of the rights of all detainees in the local language should be displayed in all police-cells and prominent places in police stations.

2. Specific Recommendations and Suggestions Regarding an Accused during Detention

In addition to the above recommendations, the following specific suggestions may be put forward for the protection of human rights of an accused during detention:

1. Subject to search, identity and other security criteria, the right to meet the fellow men, parents and other family members cannot be denied to an accused in the light of Article 19 of the Constitution and its sweep.[95]
2. Facilities for interviews, visits and confidential communication with prisoners subject to discipline and security considerations should be given to lawyers nominated by the District and Sessions Judge.
3. District Magistrates and Session Judges shall personally or through surrogates, visit prisons in their jurisdiction and afford effective opportunities for ventilating legal grievances; shall make expeditious inquiries there into and take suitable remedial action. In approach cases reports shall be made to the High Court for the latter to initiate, if found necessary, *habeas corpus* action.
4. Necessary steps should be taken by States to implement effectively the Standard Minimum Rules for Treatment of Prisoners recommended by the United Nations especially those relating to work and wages, treatment with dignity, community contact and correctional strategies.

5. The Indian Prison Act, 1894 needs modification and the Prison Manual total overhaul.[96]
6. The rights of the detained accused should be protected by the court by its writ jurisdiction plus contempt power. To make this jurisdiction viable, free legal services to the detained accused (prisoner) should be promoted through recognized legal aid societies.
7. Many of the prison vices are related to sexual urge, which remains unsatisfied because of snapping of marital life of the prisoners. Therefore, the young inmates should be lodged separately and freed from exploitation by sexually starved adult prisoners.[97]
8. Over-crowding in jails often create serious problems related to better management and availability of the facilities. Therefore, all the must be decided all criminals trials should be decided by the subordinate courts on the basis of a time bound programme, as has been announced by the Supreme Court.[98]
9. The system of complaint box introduced in Tihar jail during some period needs to be adopted in other jails also and efforts should be made to ensure that the complaint so received are fairly inquire into and appropriate actions against the delinquent are taken expeditiously. Further, a full assurance should be given to all the detained accused that whoever lodge a complaint would not suffer any evil consequence for lodging the same.[99]
10. While in jail, communication with outside world gets snapped with a result that the inmate does not know what is happening even to his near and dear and, thus, additional trauma is caused. A liberal view should be adopted by the jail administration and other concerned authorities relating to communication with kith and kin.[100]
11. In order to ensure that an inmate of a jail comes out, not as a hardened criminal but as a reformed person, more and more open air prisons should be opened.[101]
12. At present the legal position is that a person detained

in jail as an under trial accused cannot vote but he can be a M.P., M.L.A., or Minister. This legal position should be changed and all under trial accused should be permitted to vote irrespective of their crime unless and until they are specifically barred from tendering their vote.[102]

13. Pre-trial detention should be used only where non-custodial measures such as bail cannot serve the interest of justice.
14. Special correctional-cum-orientation courses should be started for the prison staff inculcating the Constitutional values, therapeutic approaches and tension-free management.

3. Specific Recommendations and Suggestions with Regard to Juvenile Accused (Delinquent Juvenile/Juvenile in Conflict with Law)

With regard to the juvenile accused, it is submitted that although India had enacted separate legislation, i.e., *Juvenile Justice Act, 1986* which had been repealed and replaced by the *Juvenile Justice (Care and Protection of Children) Act, 2000,* by and large conforming to the standards laid down by the international human rights instruments, especially the *Beijing Rules, 1985,* it has been found that the State Governments had done very little in the past towards the implementation of the *J.J. Act, 1986,* and had again done nothing so far, although three years had passed, towards the implementation of the *JJ(C&P of C) Act, 2000,* by which new approach has been given to juvenile justice administration. The *JJ(C&P of C) Act, 2000* even after notification and implementation legally, is not in actual operation and, therefore, it is not possible to offer suggestions with regard to the *JJ(C&P of C) Act, 2000* in particular. However, as the underlying objectives of the *JJ (C&P of C) Act, 2000* and the *J.J. Act, 1986* are more or less same, some suggestions are put forward on the basis of the implementation of the *J.J. Act, 1986,* so that the objectives of the *JJ (C&P of C) Act, 2000,* be achieved and the human rights of juvenile accused may be protected in reality:

1. The necessary Rules should be made by the respective

State Governments for the implementation of the *JJ(C&P of C) Act, 2000.*

2. Special Juvenile Police Unit, as being contemplated under the *JJ(C&P of C)Act, 2000*, should be immediately set up.
3. The Magistrates manning the 'Juvenile Justice Board' should be appointed on the basis of their special knowledge in child psychology and child welfare and for this purpose special provision for their training should be made; a child friendly approach is required from them which is totally lacking at present.
4. There must be quick disposal of cases within the earliest possible period from the date of the arrest of the juvenile.
5. Police personnel should be instructed not to apply the methods in dealing with children which they apply in case of adult accused. Further, methods like handcuffing, collecting photographs or finger prints should be totally avoided because these methods are used in case of adult offenders and they would adversely affect the innocent minds of the juvenile accused.
6. The different Homes and Institutions established under the *J.J.Act, 1986*, are often referred to in common parlance as ***bachcha jails*** and not as Homes; in fact, such institutions are in reality similar to jails in their organization and conception. This concept requires change and the personnel managing such institutions should be properly trained and should also be directed to apply child-friendly approach in their behaviour.
7. Necessary medical facilities should be provided in the Homes and the doctors appointed therein should also be given proper training with special knowledge of child psychology.
8. Juvenile Justice System in India had in the past suffered due to lack of effective inter and intra-system coordination. Three main and inter independent power centres – The police, The Magistracy and the Personnel involved in managing Institutions, in effect pool their

resources in an ad hoc system of cooperation. They are governed by different agencies and instead of working in cooperation to achieve a common goal - justice to juvenile – work at cross purposes. An effective coordination must be established amongst these agencies meant for achieving the ultimate goal of justice to juvenile accused.

9. While adult accused in prisons are entitled to a set of clearly spelt out amenities, privileges and rights and receive the same to some extent, the inmates of corrective institutions are yet to receive benefits and facilities recognized under the Juvenile Justice legislations and rules: Accordingly steps should be taken to secure the same guarantees of fair process for protection for the juveniles as are available to adult accused.
10. Probation and remedial services are important and integral components of the juvenile justice system but a sufficient number of probation officers well trained and having knowledge of child psychology, science of human behaviour and child care are not available. Necessary steps are required to be taken.
11. There is very little awareness among the people about the juvenile justice system. The system, as it has operated till today, lacks public cooperation and support. Therefore, a mass awareness campaign should be carried out for seeking public cooperation and support.
12. The newly enacted *JJ(C&P of C) Act, 2000* lays down much emphasis upon the involvement of non-governmental organisations in the administration of juvenile justice; in order to implement the provisions of the Act, the active support of voluntary organizations, public spirited social activists and lawyers, media and non-governmental organizations are necessary. Necessary steps are required to be taken for soliciting such support.
13. Lastly, adequate budgetary provisions should be made

so that the Boards, Committees and the Homes established under the Act have necessary infrastructural facilities leading to proper functioning; further adequate arrangements for training of various personnel and agencies involved in the administration of juvenile justice system may be made. At the moment, the conditions in juvenile homes are appalling making reformation and rehabilitation of the juveniles a distant dream and the woes and miseries of the juveniles are further compounded by the apathy and indifference of the persons manning these institutions who deal with the cases of juveniles in a routine and mechanical manner and their commitment to the overall philosophy of juvenile justice is minimal.

To conclude, it may be submitted that the protection of Human Rights of an accused in pre-trial and administrative detention - under police custody or judicial custody – is a critical element in the humanization of the criminal justice system. Although granting certain human rights to an accused may raise a number of problems, but they are not insurmountable. Since human rights by definition are meant for all persons irrespective of their status, and moreover, a suspect or accused is presumed to be innocent until he is finally adjudged guilty by the court, respect for and promotion of his rights is all the more necessary in view of the hardships caused to him due to detention. Although as has been pointed out in the preceding chapters, number of rights have been recognized and granted to an accused by the Constitution and the general criminal laws in tune with the declarations made at international level, in majority of cases an accused is either unaware of his rights, or is unable to assert his rights, or the existing justice delivery system is inaccessible to him — It is more true in the cases of poor and downtrodden accused, female accused and delinquent juveniles. Therefore, there is an urgent need for creating legal awareness about the rights by spreading legal literacy not only amongst accused but also amongst the persons involved with the machinery of administration of criminal justice. In addition to this, proper orientation and training is required to be given to the persons involved in the administration of criminal justice like police, magistrates and jail authorities. Law is considered as an instrument of justice and administration of Criminal Justice System rests on three pillars —(a) Criminal Laws - Penal Code, Procedure Code, Evidence Act, etc; (b) The Structures and Institutions — Police, Prosecution, Courts, Prisons, Homes, etc. (c) The Personnel— Policemen, lawyers prosecutors, probation officers, judges etc. — each of which contributes to the strength and performance of the system as a whole. Weakness in any one pillar reflects on the productivity of the whole system. However, even if the laws are outdated and the institution archaic, if the personnel are well motivated and trained, the system will be able to perform at a reasonable level. Therefore, recruitment of appropriate personnel and their adequate training are most essential. Further, public awareness and social consciousness is to be generated particularly in relation to the female and juvenile accused. It is to be kept in mind that to deny the protective umbrella of human rights to an accused is not only repugnant to the rule of law and fundamental freedoms and basic rights to life, liberty and security, it would also be morally reprehensible and counter productive from the standpoint of crime control. It is hoped that the findings of the present study and the suggestions and recommendation made herein would be helpful in bringing fruitful results of the constitutional mandates and efforts made by the Supreme Court in connection with the human rights of an accused (including a juvenile) granted to him for the purposes of protecting his life, dignity and personal liberty of which he is deprived of as soon as he is alleged to be an accused.

REFERENCES

1. Constitution of India, Article 22(1) and Cr. P.C.,1973, S. 50.
2. Cr. P.C.,1973 , S. 55.
3. *Ibid.*, Ss. 436 and 439.
4. *Ibid.*, S. 303 and Constitution of India, Article. 22(1).
5. *Ibid.*, Ss. 41 and 51 and *Ibid.*, Article 22.
6. *Ibid.*, Ss. 93, 94, 97, 100(4) and 165.
7. Based on judicial decisions.
8. *Ibid.*
9. Cr. P.C., 1973, Ss. 56 and 57 and Constitution of India, Article 22(2).

10. *Ibid.*, Ss. 436, 437 and 439.
11. *Ibid.*, Ss. 303 and 304 and Constitution of India, Article 39-A and Article 22(1).
12. Cr.P.C., 1973, S. 169.
13. *Ibid.*, S. 49.
14. *Ibid.*, Ss. 51(1) and 51 (2).
15. *Ibid.*, S. 54 .
16. Based on judicial decisions.
17. Cr. P.C., 1973, Ss. 167(5) and (6) and 173.
18. *Ibid.*, S. 303 and Constitution of India, Articles 2(1) and 39-A.
19. *Ibid.*, Ss. 167(2) (1), 436, 437 and 439.
20. Based on Supreme Court's decisions.
21. Cr. P.C., 1973, Ss. 207 and 208.
22. *Ibid.*, Ss. 468-473.
23. *Ibid.*, Ss. 218, 228, and 240(2).
24. Evidence Act, 1872, Ss. 101-104.
25. Cr. P.C., 1973, S. 327 .
26. *Ibid.*, Ss. 167, 209 and 309 and Constitution of India, Article 21 as well as Supreme Court's decisions.
27. *Ibid.*, S. 300 and Constitution of India, Article 20(3).
28. *Ibid.*, S. 273.
29. *Ibid.*, S. 231(2), 242, 246 and Evidence Act, 1872, Ss. 137, 138, 139 and 145.
30. *Ibid.*, S. 300 and Constitution of India, Article 20(2).
31. *Ibid.*, S. 235(2).
32. *Ibid.*, S. 304 and Constitution of India, Article 39-A.
33. *Ibid.*, Ss. 436 and 437.
34. *Ibid.*, Ss. 233, 243 and 247.
35. Based on Supreme Court's decisions.
36. Cr. P.C., 1973, S. 363 (1).
37. Constitution of India, Article 20 (1).
38. Cr. P.C., 1973, S. 313 read with Section 315 to call co-accused u/s 319 of Cr. P.C., 1973.
39. Cr. P.C., 1973, S. 314.
40. Constitution of India, Article 21.
41. The scheme of separation of judiciary as envisaged in Cr.P.C., 1973 and also Sections 493, 327 and 121 of Cr. P.C., 1973.
42. Cr. P.C., 1973, Ss. 250 and 358.
43. *Ibid.*, S. 380.
44. U.P. Jail Manual, Section 412.
45. *Ibid.*, Section 412.
46. *Ibid.*, Section 417.

47. *Ibid.*, Section 422.
48. *Ibid.*, Section 424.
49. *Ibid.*, Sections 427 and 429.
50. *Ibid.*, Section 431.
51. *Ibid.*, Section 432.
52. *Ibid.*, Section 435.
53. *Ibid.*, Section 435.
54. *Ibid.*, Section 436.
55. *Ibid.*, Section 435.
56. *Ibid.*, Section 436.
57. *Ibid.*, Section 439.
58. *Ibid.*, Section 447.
59. *Ibid.*, Section 457-B.
60. *Ibid.*, Section 458.
61. *Ibid.*, Section 451.
62. *Ibid.*, Sections 457-A, 457-E and 457-F.
63. *Ibid.*, Section 341(a).
64. *Ibid.*
65. *Ibid.*
66. *Ibid.*, Section 343.
67. *Ibid.*, Section 349.
68. *Ibid.*, Section 350.
69. *Ibid.*
70. *Ibid.*, Section 354.
71. *Ibid.*, Section 359.
72. *Ibid.*, Section 362.
73. *Ibid.*, Section 363.
74. *Ibid.*, Sections 324 and 325.
75. *Ibid.*, Section 332.
76. *Ibid.*, Section 332.
77. *Ibid.*, Section 330(2).
78. *Ibid.*, Sections 330(3) and (4).
79. *Ibid.*, Section 323.
80. *Ibid.*, Section 422.
81. See, *supra*.
82. For details see, Sen, Shanker, "U.N. Convention against Torture", *The Hindustan Times* (New Delhi), 17 Nov. 1995; Singh, Prakash, "Police Accountability to the People", *Hindustan Times* (New Delhi), 28 Nov. 1995; Karan, Vijay, "Human Rights: Breaking the Torture Habit", *India Today*, March 15,1993; Mahajan Krishna, "SC Should Monitor Custodial Death", *The Indian Express* (New Delhi) 12 April, 1992; Sammaiah, M., "Role of the Police vis-a-vis Universal

Declaration of Human Rights", S.C.J., Vol. 3 (1996), 21-27; Upadhyay, C.M., "Human Rights in Pre-trial Detention", A.P.H. Publications, New Delhi, 1999.

83. The National Human Rights Commission also suggested, through a letter dated 9 Dec. 1994, addressed to the Prime Minister to acceding to the Convention against Torture and Other Forms of Cruel, Inhuman and Degrading Treatment or Punishment, Annual Report, (1994-95) p. 17, Para 4.27. The Commission had again urged the Government of India, Human Rights New Letter, Jan. 1997, p. 2.
84. The National Human Rights Commission has lent to an unique campaign first time launched by the Kerala Police Officers Association for the promotion of human rights awareness at Thiruvananthapuram, Human Rights Newsletter, Feb. 1995, p. 4; The Commission has again reiterated its view to all States Governments on 16 Nov. 1995, Human Rights Newsletter, Dec. 1995, p. 3.
85. National Human Rights Commission, Annual Report (1995-96) 16. para 3.24; Sec also, Abhinandan Jha v. Dinesh Mishra, A I R 1968 SC 117.
86. See also, A. Nallasivan V. State of Tamil Nadu, 1995 Cri. L.J. 2754.
87. National Human Rights Commission, Annual Report (1995-96) 15, para 3.21.
88. Tandon, M.P., "Custodial Death: Torture in Police Custody", Legal Education Newsletter, Jan. 1996, 6-7.
89. *Ibid.*, at 7; see also. Chandabai v. State of M.P., 1997 Cri. L.J. 3844.
90. *Supra*, note 87 at para 3.22. When examining reports on custodial death the N.H.R.C. was struck by the often unsatisfactory manner in which post-mortem examinations were conducted and reached the dismaying conclusion that, on occasion, the doctors concerned were bowing to police pressures when writing their reports. There was often a substantial time gap between the post-mortem examination and the writing of the reports; facilities in many mortuaries were abysmal; there was a lack of trained and qualified personnel. A system of further examination of post-mortem report would greatly minimize to this kind of negligence.
91. See, State of M.P. v. Shyamsunder Trivedi, (1995) 4 SCC 262; D.K. Basu v. State of W.B., (1997) 1 SCC 416 at 432-433. See also, 113th Report of the Law Commission of India.
92. Subramanian, S., "Human Rights: International Challenges," Vol. I. 240 (1997).
93. *Ibid.*, at 239.

94. 'Role of media in safeguarding human rights is cardinal,' *The Times of India* Newspaper (New Delhi) 25 Jan. 1999.
95. Dharambir v. State of Uttar Pradesh, (1979) 3 S CC 645.
96. National Human Rights Commission, Annual Report (1994-95) p. 14, para 4.21; see also Human Rights Newsletter, Sept. 1995, p. 1; *infra*, note 97 at p. 402.
97. Rama Murthy v. State of Karnatak, 1997 SCC (Cri) 386 at 400.
98. *Ibid.*, at 395. see also Common Cause v. Union of India, (1996) 4 SCC 33; (1996) 6 SCC 775 (Clarified).
99. *Ibid.*, at 400.
100. *Ibid.*
101. *Ibid.*, at 401.
102. For details, see, Sharma, Gokulesh, "Voting Human Rights of Prisoners...", A I R (Journal) Vol. 85 (1998) p. 117.

Select Bibliography

(International Instruments, Reports, Books, Articles, Statutes, Journals, Magazines and Newspapers)

A. INTERNATIONAL INSTRUMENTS

African charter on Human and Peoples Rights (Nairobi, 26 June 1981) (entry into force, 21 Oct. 1986), OAU, document CAB/LEG/67/3Rev. *Compilation,* Vol. II.

American Convention on Human Rights (San Jose 22 Nov. 1969) (entry into force, 18 July 1978), United Nations, Treaty Series, Vol. 1144, p. 123; *Compilation,* Vol. II.

Basic Principles for the Treatment of Prisoners (1990), *Compilation,* Vol. I, p. 263.

Body of Principles for the Protection of All Persons under any From of Detention or Imprisonment (1988), *Compilation,* Vol. I, p. 265.

Charter of the United Nations (entry into force, 24 Oct. 1945), Government of India Publication, New Delhi.

Code of Conduct for Law Enforcement Officials (1979), *Compilation,* Vol. I, p. 312.

Convention against Torture and Other Cruel, Inhuman or Degrading Treatment or Punishment (entry into force, 26 June 1987), *Compilation,* Vol. I, p. 293.

Convention for the Protection of Human Rights and Fundamental Freedoms (Rome, 4 Nov. 1950) *Compilation,* Vol. II.

Convention the Rights of the child (entry into force, 2 Sept. 1990) *Compilation,* Vol. I, p. 174.

Declaration on the Protection of All Persons from Enforced Disappearance (1992) *Compilation,* Vol. I, p. 401.

Guidelines on the Role Prosecutors (1990), *Compilation,* Vol. I, p. 330.

International Covenant on Civil and Political Rights (New York, 16 Dec. 1966) (entry into force, 23 March 1966). *Compilation,* Vol. I, p. 20.

Principles on the Effective Prevention and Investigation of Extralegal, Arbitrary and summary Executions (1989), *Compilation,* Vol. I, p. 409.

Standard Minimum Rules for the Treatment of Prisoners (1955), *Compilation,* Vol. I, p. 243.

United Nations Guidelines for the Prevention of Juvenile Delinquency (The Riyadh Guidelines) (1990), *Compilation,* Vol. I, p. 346.

United Nations Rules for the Protection of Juveniles Deprived of their Liberty (1990), *Compilation,* Vol. I, p. 275.

United Nations Standard Minimum Rules for Non-custodial Measure (The Tokyo Rules (1990), *Compilation,* Vol. I, p. 226.

United Nations Standard Minimum Rules for the Administration of Juvenile Justice (The Beijing Rules) (1985), *Compilation,* Vol. 1, p. 356.

Universal Declaration of Human Rights (1948), *Compilation,* Vol. I, p. 1.

Yearbook of International Law Commission, Vol. II, Part-2, A.C N4/SER. A/1993/Add. 1, *United Nations* (1995).

Yearbook of the United Nations, Special Edition, U.N. Fiftieth Anniversary 1945-1995, United Nations Publication, New York, 1995, (Sales No. E. 95.1.50).

B. REPORTS

Amnesty International Report 1996, London.

Amnesty International, *Torture in the Eighties,* 1984, Londón.

Annual report of the National Human Rights Commission (2000-01) New Delhi.

Annual report of the National Human Rights Commission (2001-02) New Delhi.

First Report of the National Police Commission,1979.

First Report of Human Rights Working Group on Arbitrary Detention E/CN-4/ 1992/20, annex 1(1992).

Human Rights in India (The Update Amnesty International Report), Vistaar Publication, New Delhi (1993).

In Jail, 1978, A Report by the Kuldip Nayar.

Report of a Royal Commission on Criminal Procedure, *Command Papers*, 8092 (1981).

Report of the All-India Committee on Jail Reforms, 1980-83.

Report of the Expert Committee on Legal Aid.

Report of the Group of Officers on Prison Administration chaired by Shri R.V. Kapur (1987).

Report of the National Expert Committee on Women Prisoners, 1987.

Second Report of the National Police Commission, 1979.

Second Report on Human Rights Working Group on Arbitrary Detention, E.CN.4/1993/24 (1993).

Study of the Right of Everyone to be free from Arrest, Detention and Exile, 1964.

Third Report of the National Police Commission, 1980.

The Law Commission of India, 78th Report.

The Law Commission of India, 113th Report.

C. BOOKS

Diwan, Paras & Diwan, Peeyush; *Human Rights and the Law: Universal and India*, Deep Publication, New Delhi.

Gaur, K.D.; *Human Right of Detenues and Prisoners and Prison Reforms Directive Principles, Jurisprudence*, Seema Publications, Paris (1982).

Humphrey, John; *The International Law of Human Rights*, UNESCO Publishing Corporation, Delhi (1989).

Iyer, V.R. Krishna; *Human Rights and the Inhuman Wrongs*, B.R. Publishing Corporation, Delhi (1990).

Iyer, V.R. Krishna ; *Human Rights and the Law*, Vespal Law House Indore (1984).

Krishnamurty, S. ; *Human Rights and the India Police*, R.R. Publishers, Bangalore (1st ed.) (1994).

Mookerjee, Ashutosh ; *Juvenile Justice* S. C. Sarkar and Sons Pvt. Ltd. Calcutta (1989).

Rodley, Nigel S.; *The Treatment of Prisoners under International Law*, UNESCO : Cleredon Press (1987).

Sharma, S.S.; *Legal Aid to the Poor*, Deep & Deep Publications, New Delhi (1993).

Singh Sehgal, B.P. (ed.); *Human Rights in India*, Deep & Deep Publications, New Delhi, (1995).

Subramaniam, S.; *Human Rights : International Challenges*, Manas Publications, New Delhi, Vol. I, (1997).

Upadhyaya, C.M.; *Human Rights in Pre-trial Detention*, A.P.H. Publishing Corporation, 5 New Delhi (1999).

D. ARTICLES

Bal Krishna; "Criminal Justice System Questioned", *The Hindustan Times* (New Delhi) 17 March, 1997.

Banerjee Nandini G.; "In Custody of Death", *The Hindustan Times* (New Delhi), 29 March, 1995.

Baweja, Harinder; "Tihar Jail; Picture of Neglect", *India Today*, (New Delhi) July 15, 1995.

Gaur, K.D.; "Poor Victim of Uses Abuses of Criminal Law and Process in India", *J.I.L.I.*, Vol. 35 (1993), 183-232.

Hydervali, B.; "Compensation to Victims of Lock-up of Deaths - A Judicial Study", 1994 *Cr LJ (Journal)* 135-140.

Jaswal, P.S. and Jaswal, Nishtha; "Right to Personal Liberty and Handcuffing : Some Observations", *U.I.L.I.*, Vol. 33 (1991) 246.

John, Wildon; "Behind Bars, in Custody of Apathy", *The Hindustan Times* (New Delhi) 5 Feb. 1995.

Kagzi, M.C.J.; "Judicial Control of Administrative Discretion under Preventive Dentention Laws; An Indian Experience", *Public Law* (1965), 49.

Kamboj, N.S.; "Police Custodial Death : A Growing Abuse to Human Rights in India", *J.I.L.I.*, Vol. 36 (1994), 372-377.

Kumar, Vijay; "Individual Liberty and the Abuse of Police Power of Arrest and Detention : A Broader Perspective", 1995 *Cri LJ (Journal)* 97-101.

Manohar, Sujata V.; "Judiciary and Human Rights", *I.J.L.I.*, Vol. 36, (1996) 39-54.

Muhammad, Haji, N.A. Noor; "Guarantees for Accused Persons under the U.N. Human Rights Convenants", *I.J.Li.I.*, Vol. 20 (1980), 177-196.

Nath, S., "Legal Aid to the Poor and Downtrodden as the Backbone of Human Right to Fair Trial – The Indian Approach" –

Proceedings of International Conference of International Congress on Legal Sciences, Belgium, 1986.

Razdan, Usha; "Apex Court Towards Humanizing the Administration of Juvenile Jutice", *J.I.L.I.*, Vol. 33 (1991) 366-387.

Saini, R.S.; "Custodial Torture in Law and Practice wit h Reference to India", *J.I.L.I.*, Vol. 36 (1994), 21-27.

Sen, Shankar; "U.N. Convention against Torture", *The Hindustan Times* (New Delhi) 17 Nov. 1995.

Srivastava B.P.; "Right against Arbitrary Arrest and Detention under Article 9 of the Covenant as Recognized and Protected under the India Law", *I.J.I.L.* Education Newsletter, Jan. 1996, 6-7.

United Nations; "Juvenile Justice and the Implementation of the United Nations Standard Minimum rules for the Administration of Juvenile Justice", International Review of Criminal Policy, No. 43-44 (1994) United Nations Publications (Sales No. E. 94.IV.5.).

Vibhute, K.I.; "Compensating Victims of Crime in India : An Appraisal", *J.I.L.I.*, Vol. 32 (1990) 68-81.

E. STATUTES

The Armed Forces (Special Powers) Act, 1958.

The Children Act, 1960.

The Code of Criminal Procedure, 1898.

The Code of Criminal Procedure, 1973 (Act No. 02 of 1974).

The Constitution of India.

The Indian Evidence Act, 1872 (Act No. 01 of 1872).

The Indian Penal Code, 1860 (Act No. 45 of 1860).

The Indian Prison Act, 1894 (Act No. 09 of 1894).

The Juvenile Justice Act, 1986 (Act No. 53 of 1986).

The Juvenile Justice (Care and Protection of Children) Act, 2000.

The Legal Services Authorities Act, 1987 (Act No. 39 of 1987).

The Legal Services Authorities (Amendment) Act, 1994 (Act No. 59 of 1994).

The Police Act, 1861 (Act No. 05 of 1861).

The Protection of Human Rights Act, 1993 (Act No. 10 of 1994).

F. JOURNALS

All India Reporter (Journal).
Criminal Law Journal (Journal)
Human Rights Newsletter.
Indian Journal of International Law.
Journal of Indian Law Institute.
Journal of International Commission of Jurists.
Legal Education Newsletter.
Supreme Court Journal

G. MAGAZINES AND NEWSPAPERS

India Today, New Delhi.
The Hindustan Times, New Delhi.
The Hindustan Times, Lucknow.
The Indian Express, New Delhi.
The Statesman, New Delhi.
The Times of India, New Delhi.

Index